HYDRA CONQUERED THE UNITED STATES, FOLLOWING A LEADER WITH STEVE ROGERS' FACE. CAPTAIN AMERICA RETURNED, AND HYDRA FELL. SO THE WAR IS OVER...RIGHT?

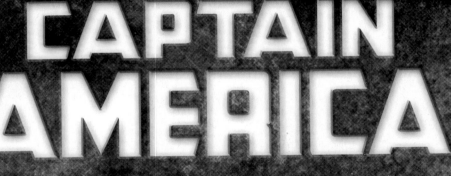

CAPTAIN AMERICA

WINTER IN AMERICA

Ta-Nehisi Coates
WRITER

Leinil Francis Yu
PENCILER

Gerry Alanguilan with **Leinil Francis Yu** [#3 & #5]
INKERS

VC's Joe Caramagna [#1-6] & **Cory Petit** [Free Comic Book Day]
LETTERERS

Alex Ross [#1-6] and
Leinil Francis Yu & **Sunny Gho** [Free Comic Book Day]
COVER ART

Alanna Smith
ASSOCIATE EDITOR

Tom Brevoort
EDITOR

CAPTAIN AMERICA CREATED BY JOE SIMON & JACK KIRBY

COLLECTION EDITOR **JENNIFER GRÜNWALD**
ASSISTANT EDITOR **DANIEL KIRCHHOFFER**
ASSISTANT MANAGING EDITOR **MAIA LOY**
ASSISTANT MANAGING EDITOR **LISA MONTALBANO**

VP PRODUCTION & SPECIAL PROJECTS **JEFF YOUNGQUIST**
SVP PRINT, SALES & MARKETING **DAVID GABRIEL**
BOOK DESIGNER **ADAM DEL RE**
EDITOR IN CHIEF **C.B. CEBULSKI**

CAPTAIN AMERICA BY TA-NEHISI COATES VOL. 1: WINTER IN AMERICA. Contains material originally published in magazine form as CAPTAIN AMERICA (2018) #1-6 and FREE COMIC BOOK DAY 2018 (AVENGERS/CAPTAIN AMERICA) #1. Fourth printing 2021. ISBN 978-1-302-91194-2. Published by MARVEL WORLDWIDE, INC., a subsidiary of MARVEL ENTERTAINMENT, LLC. OFFICE OF PUBLICATION: 1290 Avenue of the Americas, New York, NY 10104. **Printed in Canada.** KEVIN FEIGE, Chief Creative Officer; DAN BUCKLEY, President, Marvel Entertainment; JOE QUESADA, EVP & Creative Director; DAVID BOGART, Associate Publisher & SVP of Talent Affairs; TOM BREVOORT, VP, Executive Editor; NICK LOWE, Executive Editor, VP of Content, Digital Publishing; DAVID GABRIEL, VP of Print & Digital Publishing; JEFF YOUNGQUIST, VP of Production & Special Projects; ALEX MORALES, Director of Publishing Operations; DAN EDINGTON, Managing Editor; RICKEY PURDIN, Director of Talent Relations; JENNIFER GRÜNWALD, Senior Editor, Special Projects; SUSAN CRESPI, Production Manager; STAN LEE, Chairman Emeritus. For information regarding advertising in Marvel Comics or on Marvel.com, please contact Vit DeBellis, Custom Solutions & Integrated Advertising Manager, at vdebellis@marvel.com. For Marvel subscription inquiries, please call 888-511-5480. **Manufactured between 11/12/2021 and 12/14/2021 by SOLISCO PRINTERS, SCOTT, QC, CANADA.**

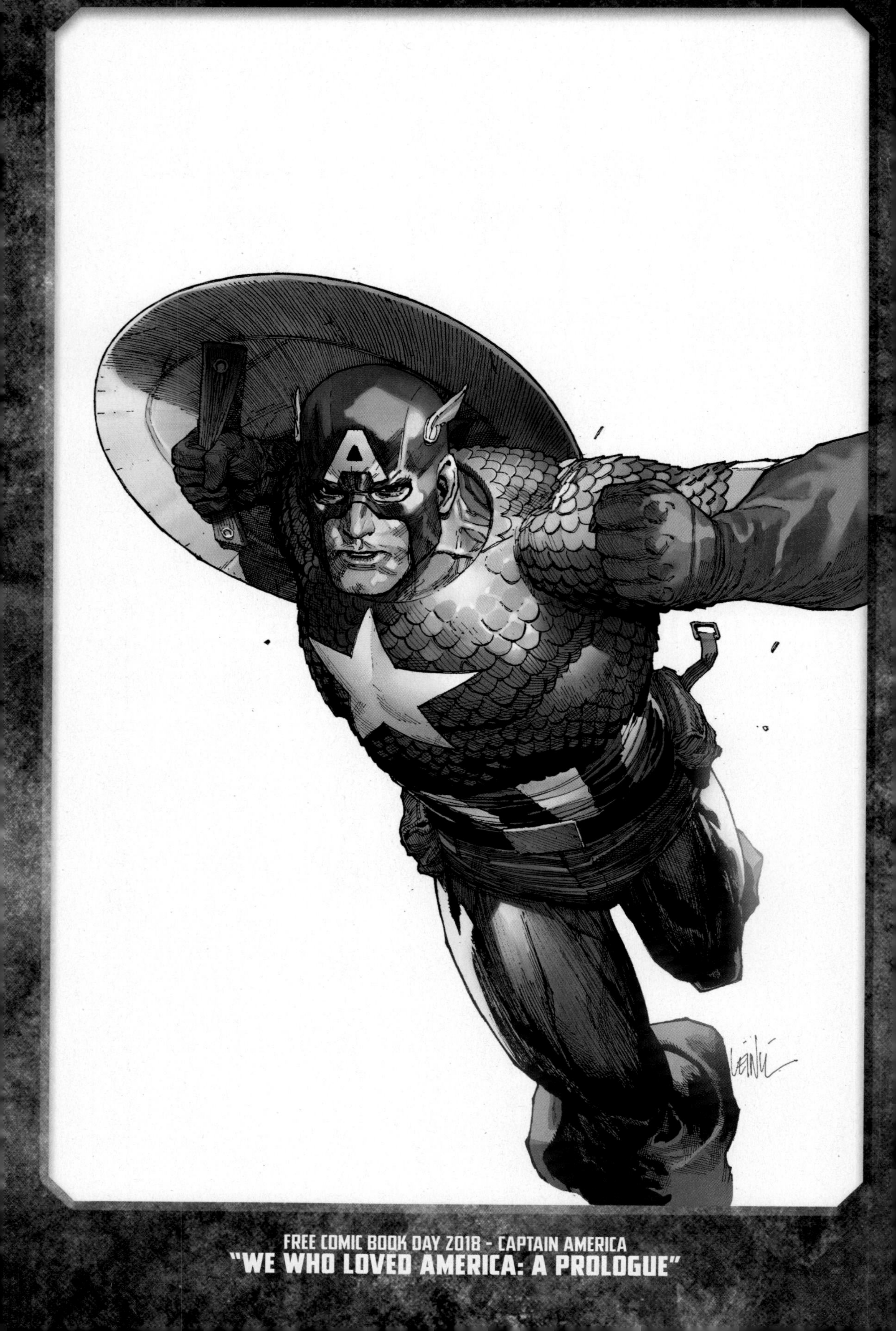

FREE COMIC BOOK DAY 2018 - CAPTAIN AMERICA
"WE WHO LOVED AMERICA: A PROLOGUE"

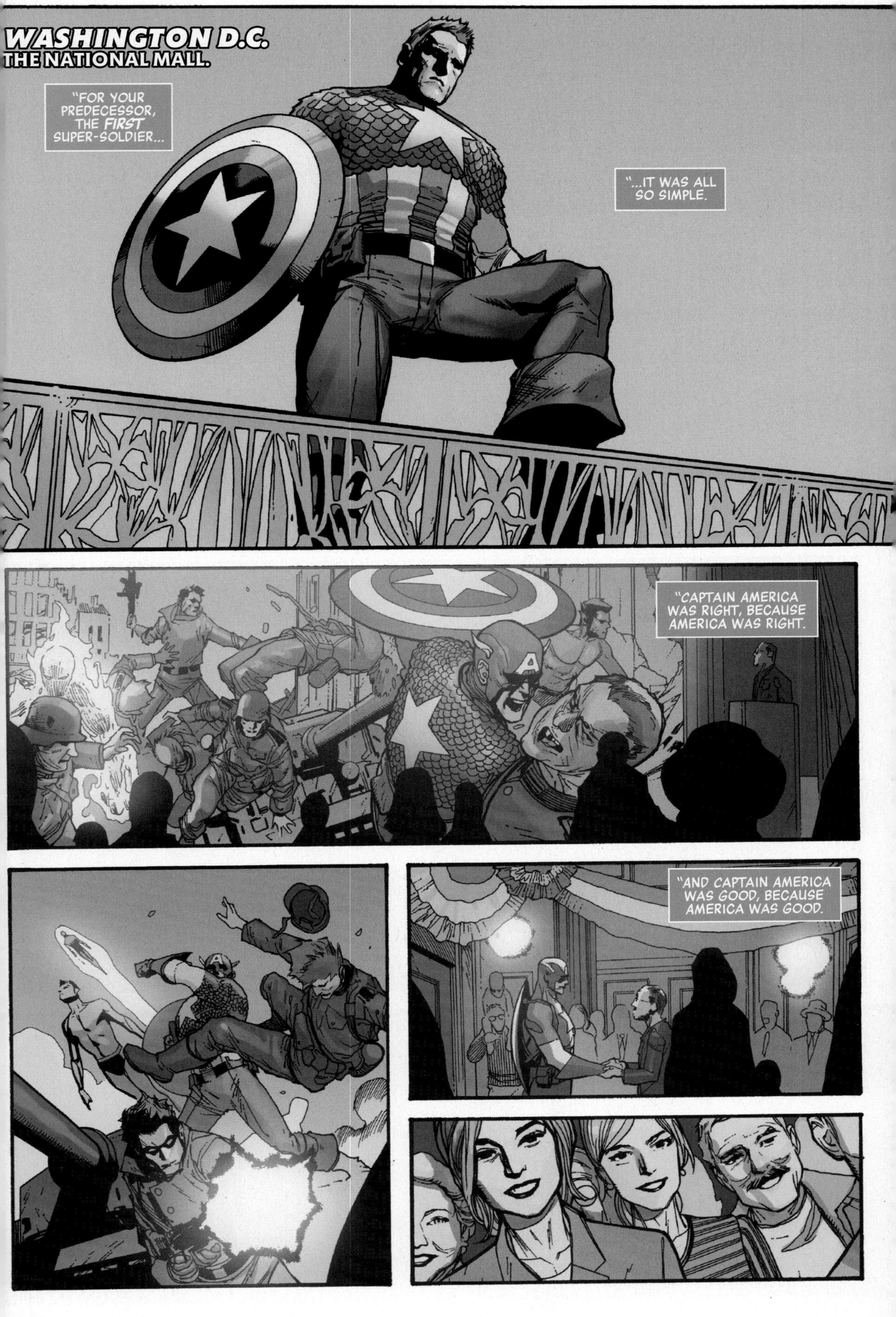
WASHINGTON D.C.
THE NATIONAL MALL.
"FOR YOUR PREDECESSOR, THE *FIRST* SUPER-SOLDIER...
"...IT WAS ALL SO SIMPLE.
"CAPTAIN AMERICA WAS RIGHT, BECAUSE AMERICA WAS RIGHT.
"AND CAPTAIN AMERICA WAS GOOD, BECAUSE AMERICA WAS GOOD.

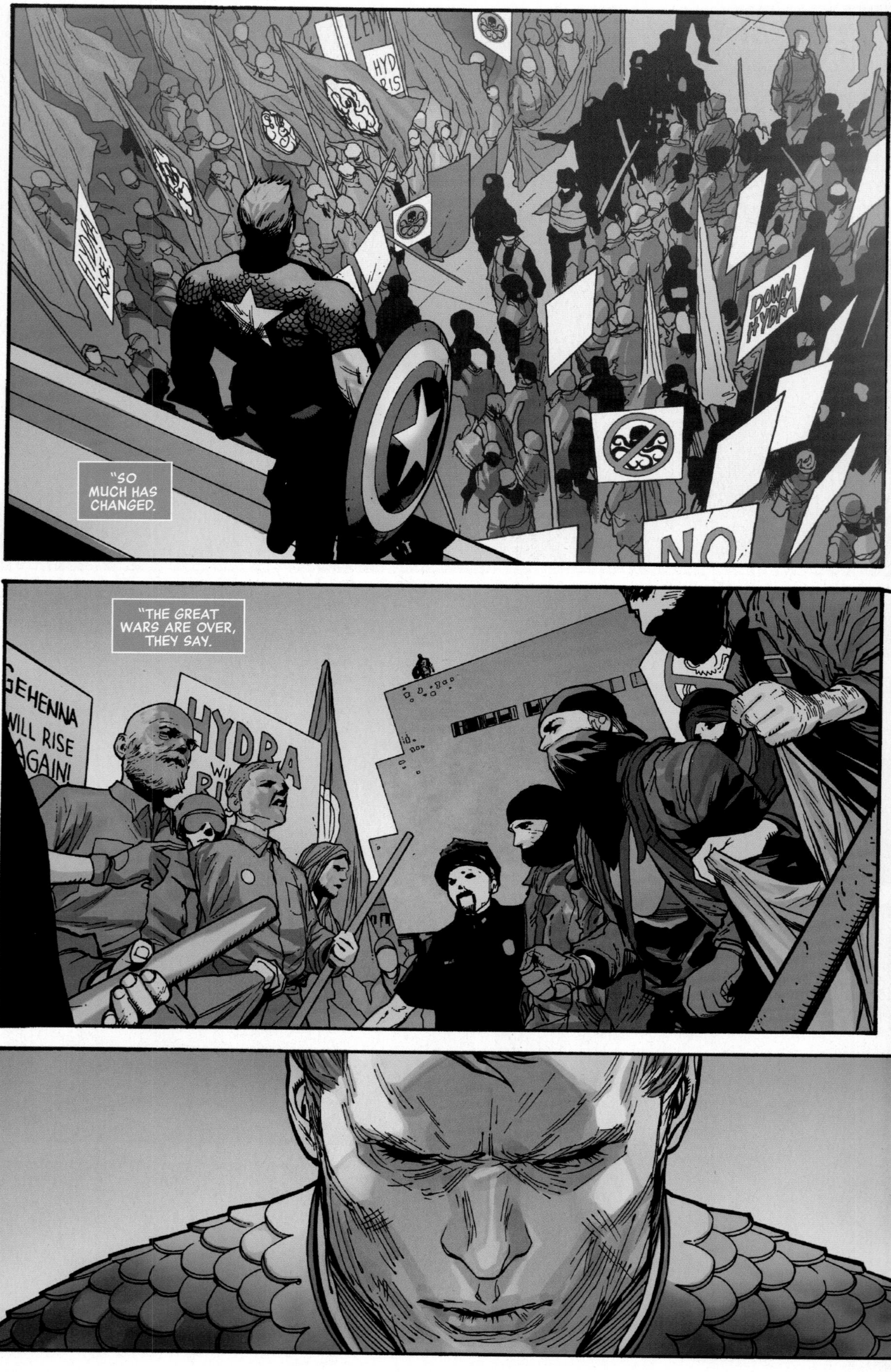
"SO MUCH HAS CHANGED.
DOWN HYDRA
NO
"THE GREAT WARS ARE OVER, THEY SAY.
GEHENNA WILL RISE AGAIN!
HYDRA

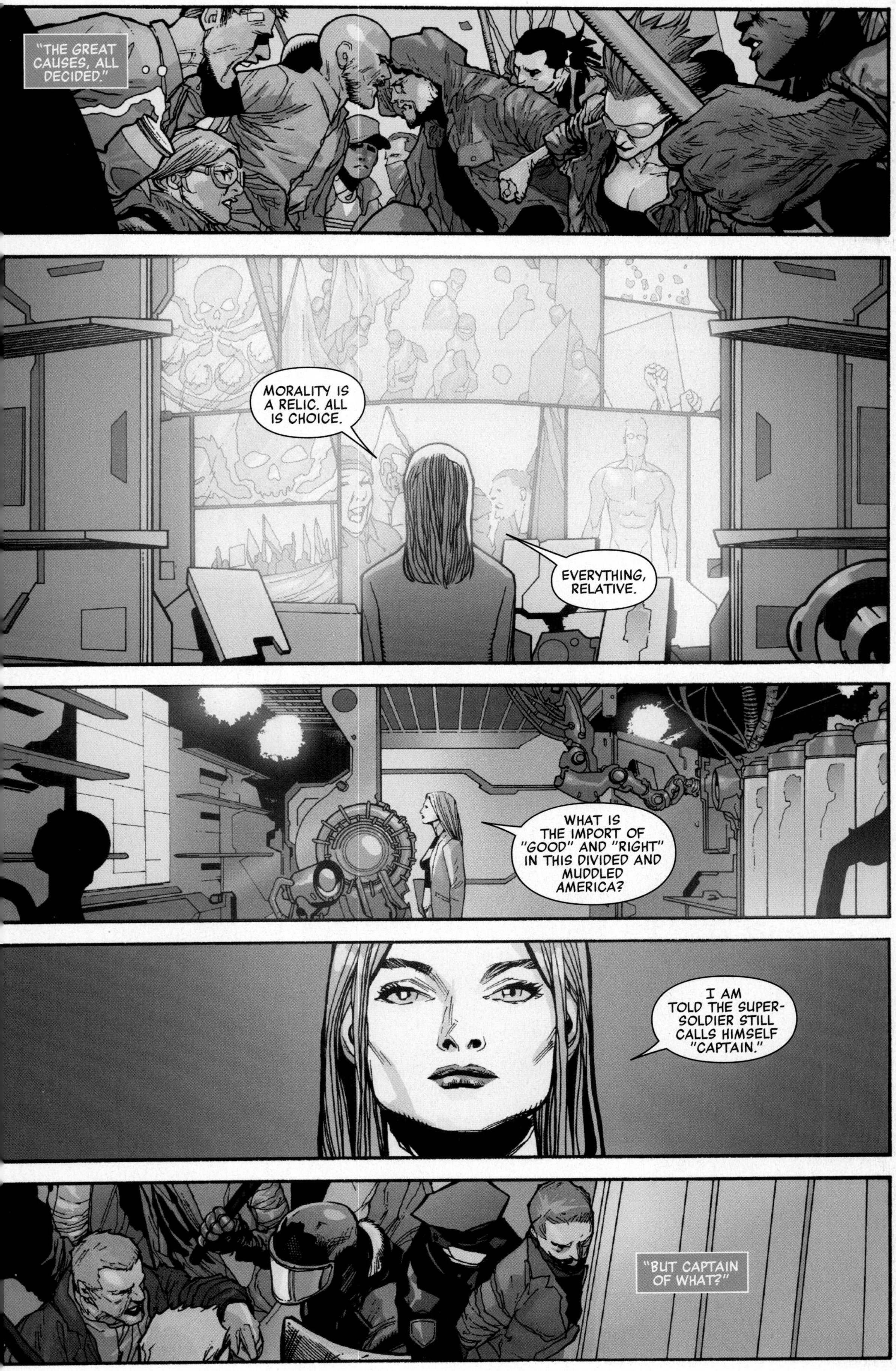
"THE GREAT CAUSES, ALL DECIDED."
MORALITY IS A RELIC. ALL IS CHOICE.
EVERYTHING, RELATIVE.
WHAT IS THE IMPORT OF "GOOD" AND "RIGHT" IN THIS DIVIDED AND MUDDLED AMERICA?
I AM TOLD THE SUPER-SOLDIER STILL CALLS HIMSELF "CAPTAIN."
"BUT CAPTAIN OF WHAT?"

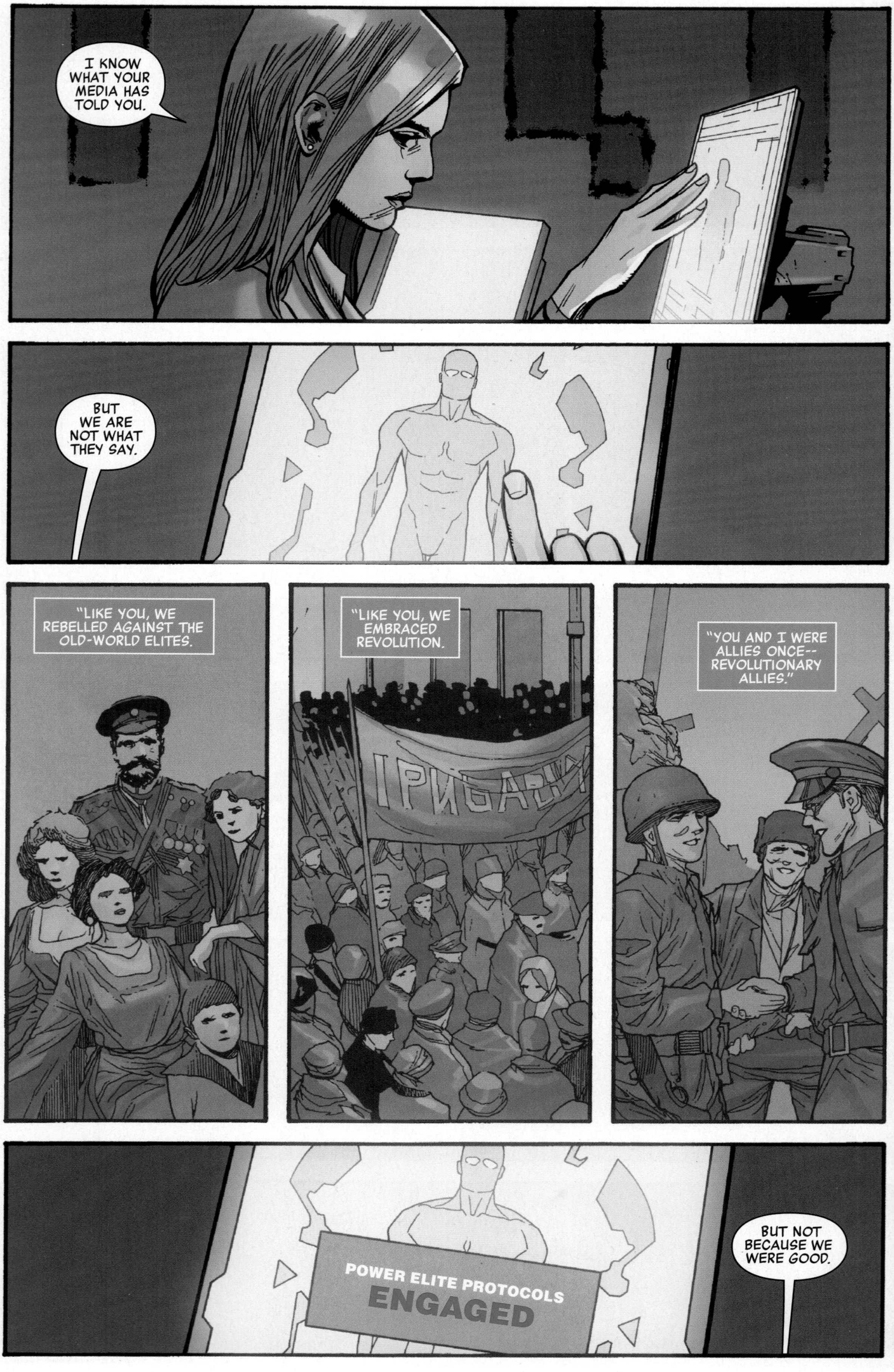
I KNOW WHAT YOUR MEDIA HAS TOLD YOU.
BUT WE ARE NOT WHAT THEY SAY.
"LIKE YOU, WE REBELLED AGAINST THE OLD-WORLD ELITES.
"LIKE YOU, WE EMBRACED REVOLUTION.
"YOU AND I WERE ALLIES ONCE-- REVOLUTIONARY ALLIES."
POWER ELITE PROTOCOLS
ENGAGED
BUT NOT BECAUSE WE WERE GOOD.

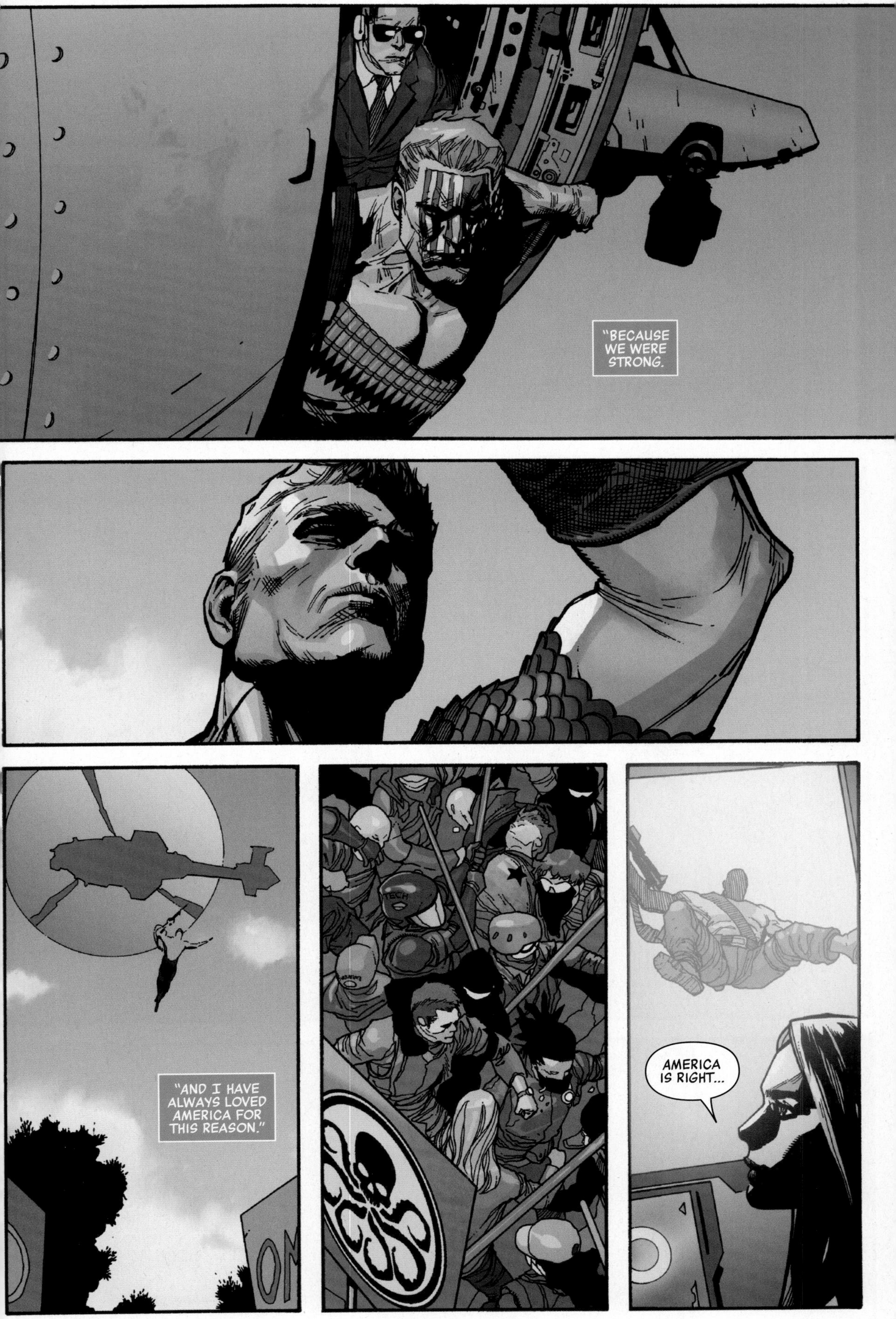
"BECAUSE WE WERE STRONG.
"AND I HAVE ALWAYS LOVED AMERICA FOR THIS REASON."
AMERICA IS RIGHT...

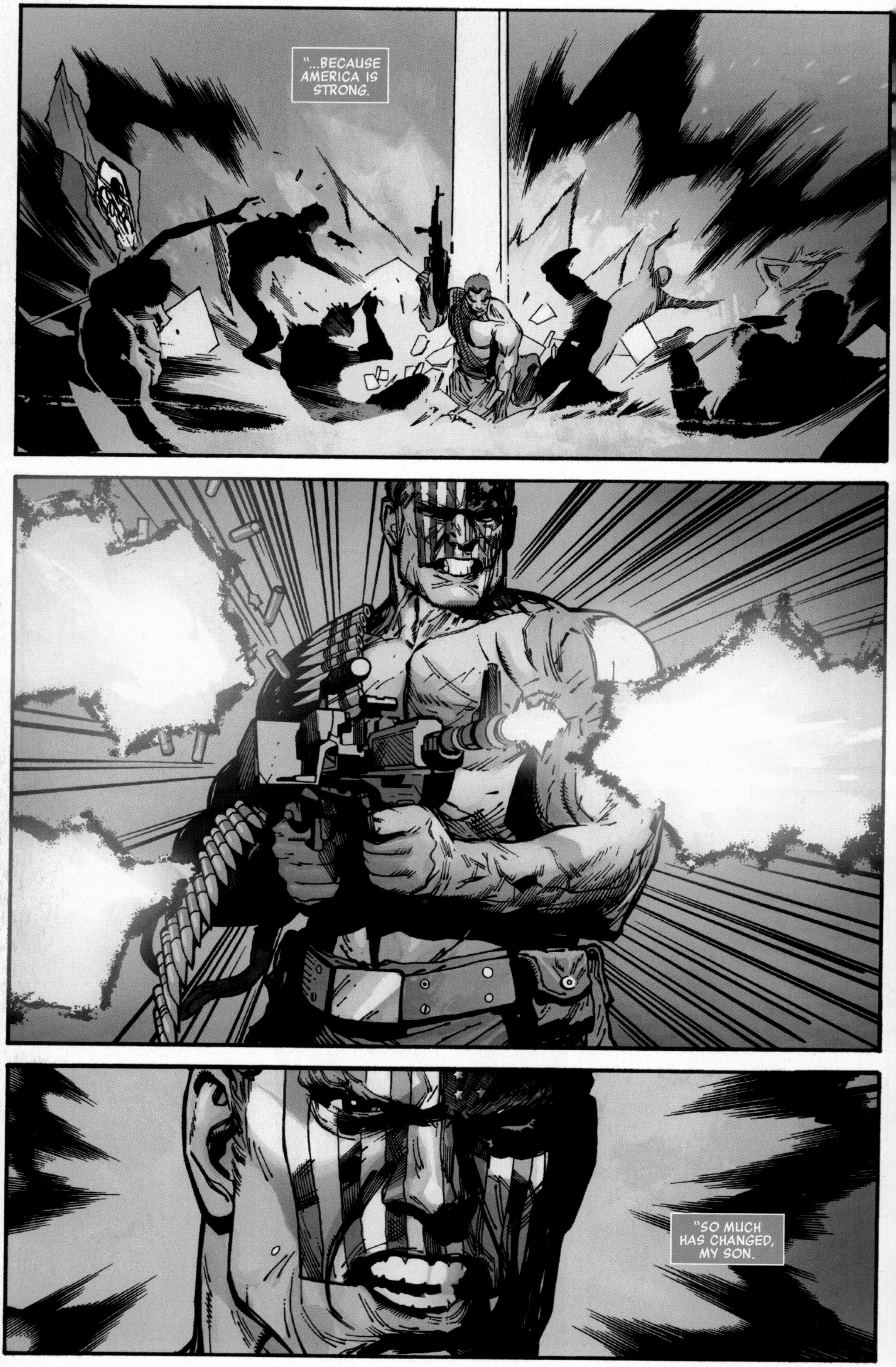
"...BECAUSE AMERICA IS STRONG.
"SO MUCH HAS CHANGED, MY SON.

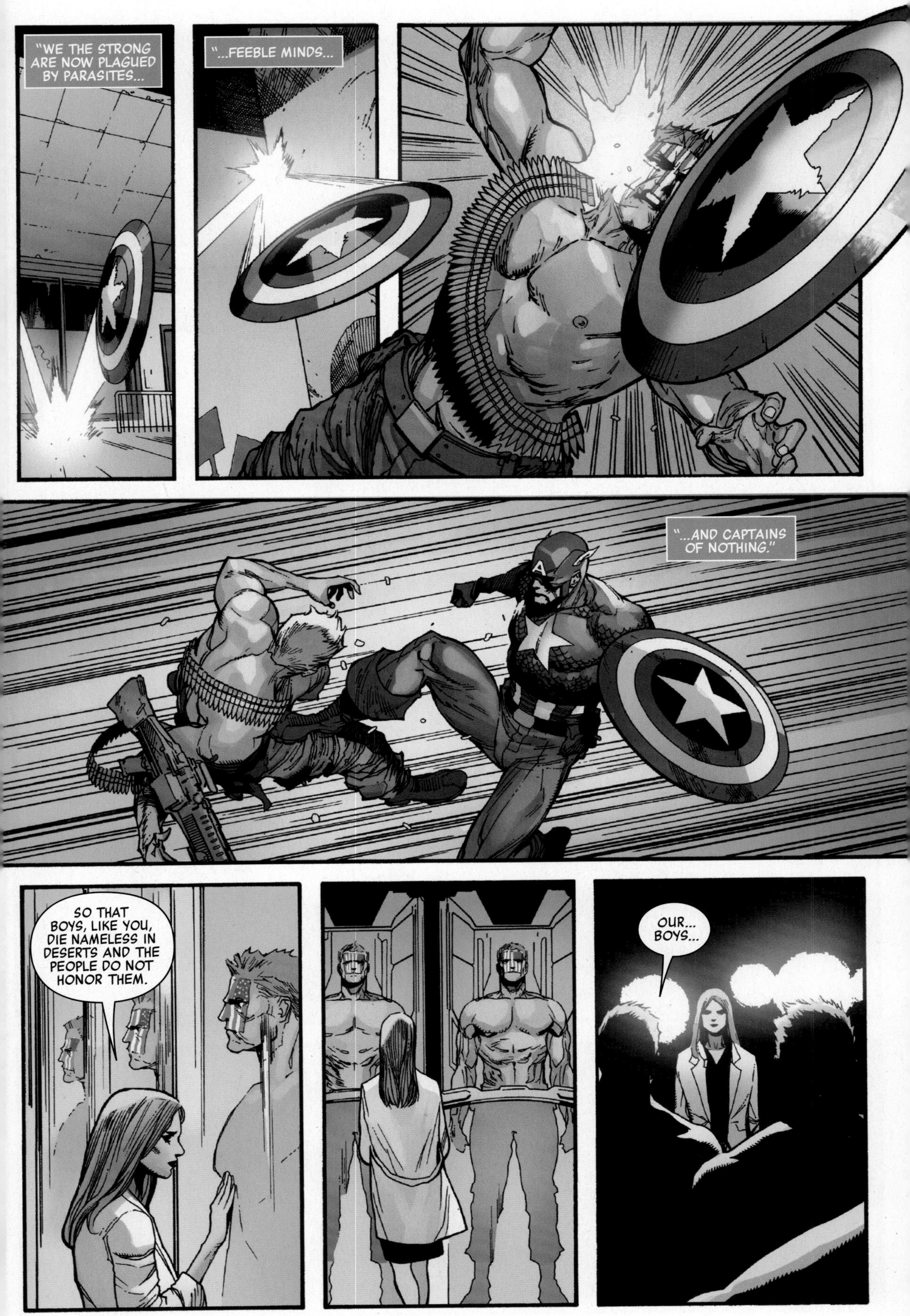
"WE THE STRONG ARE NOW PLAGUED BY PARASITES...
"...FEEBLE MINDS...
"...AND CAPTAINS OF NOTHING."
SO THAT BOYS, LIKE YOU, DIE NAMELESS IN DESERTS AND THE PEOPLE DO NOT HONOR THEM.
OUR... BOYS...

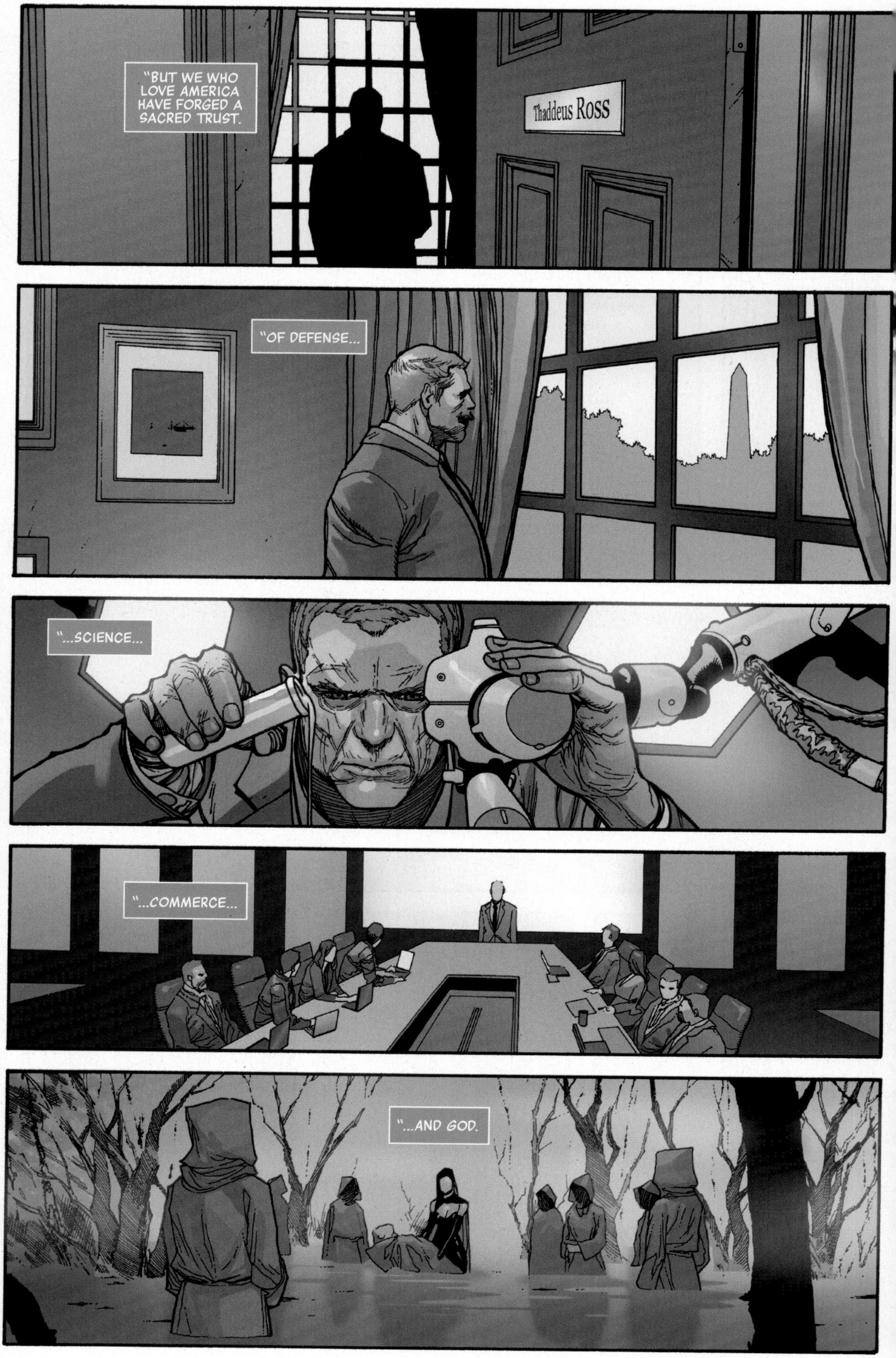
"BUT WE WHO LOVE AMERICA HAVE FORGED A SACRED TRUST.
Thaddeus Ross
"OF DEFENSE...
"...SCIENCE...
"...COMMERCE...
"...AND GOD.

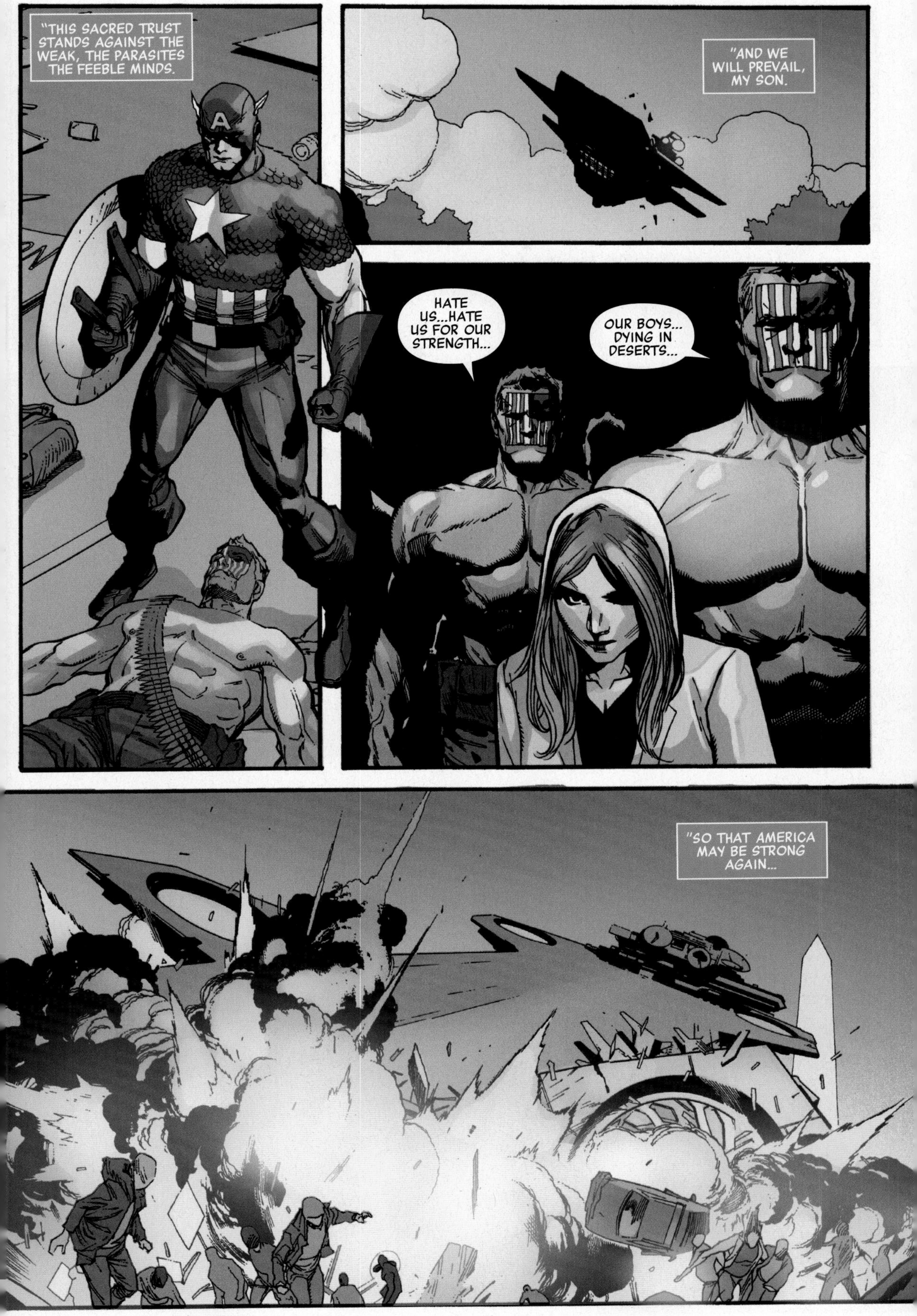
"THIS SACRED TRUST STANDS AGAINST THE WEAK, THE PARASITES THE FEEBLE MINDS.
"AND WE WILL PREVAIL, MY SON.
HATE US...HATE US FOR OUR STRENGTH...
OUR BOYS... DYING IN DESERTS...
"SO THAT AMERICA MAY BE STRONG AGAIN...

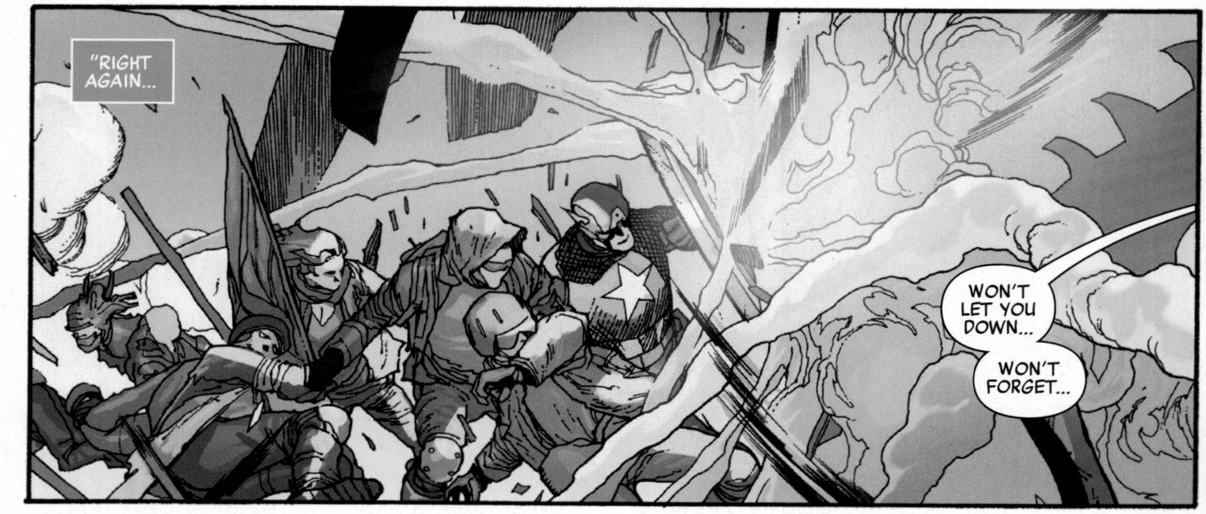
"RIGHT AGAIN...
WON'T LET YOU DOWN...
WON'T FORGET...

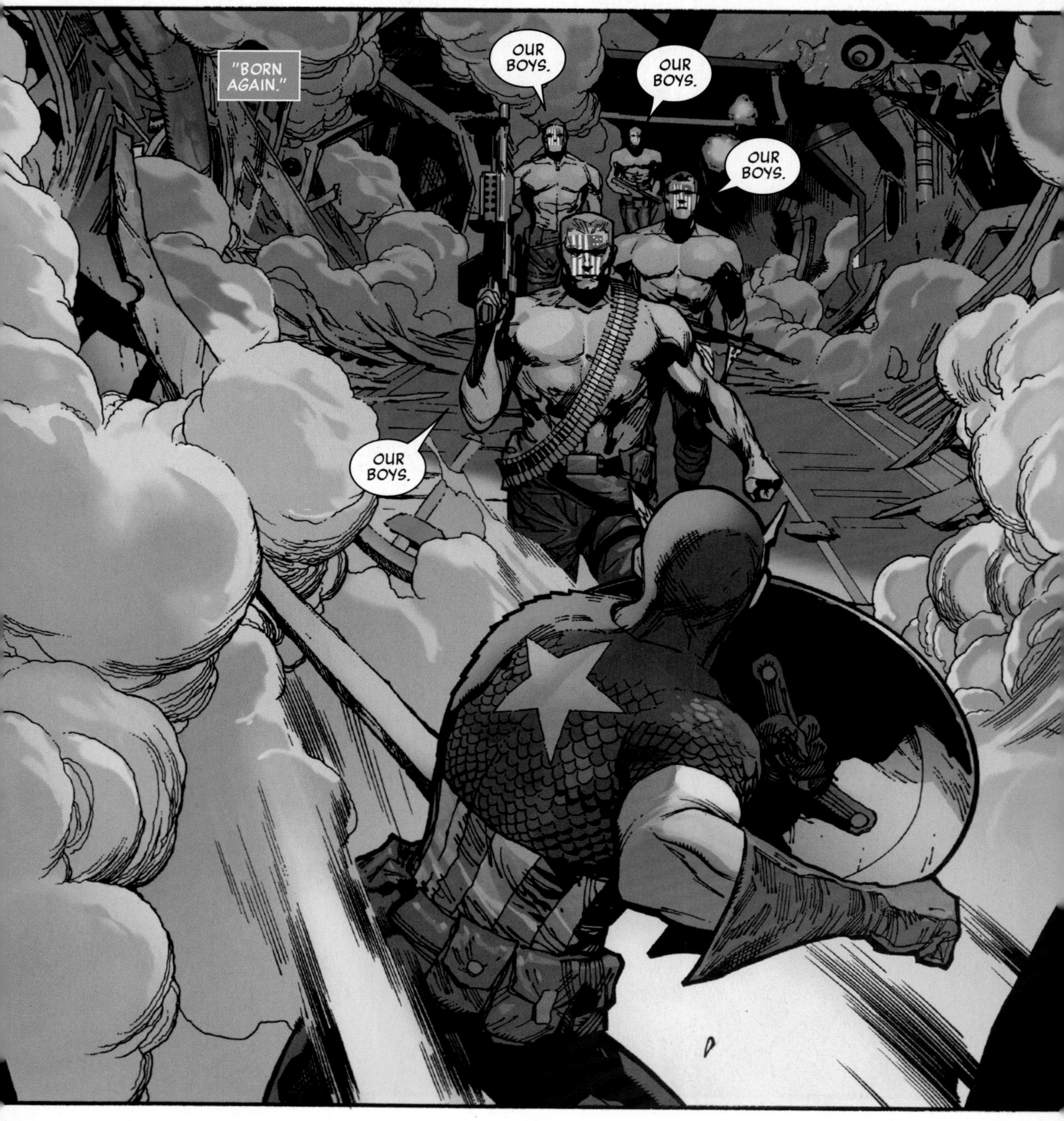
"BORN AGAIN."
OUR BOYS.
OUR BOYS.
OUR BOYS.
OUR BOYS.

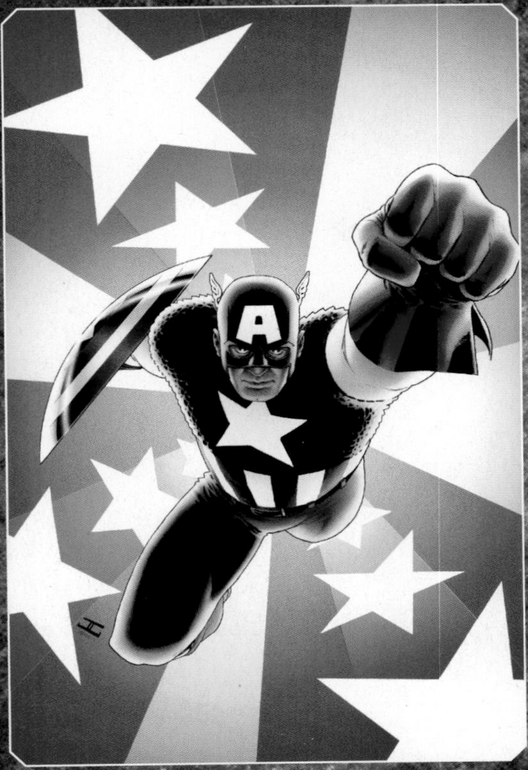

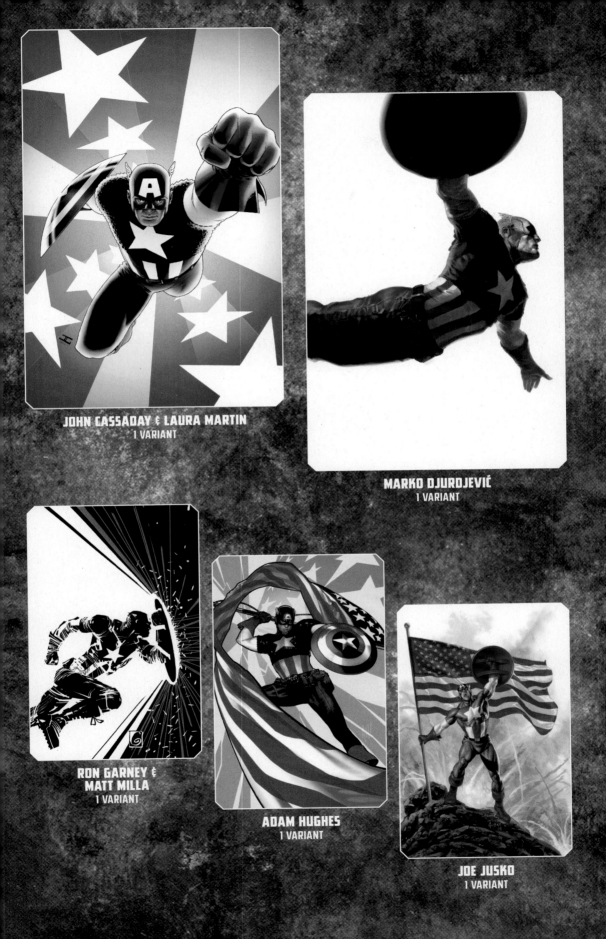

JOHN CASSADAY & LAURA MARTIN
1 VARIANT

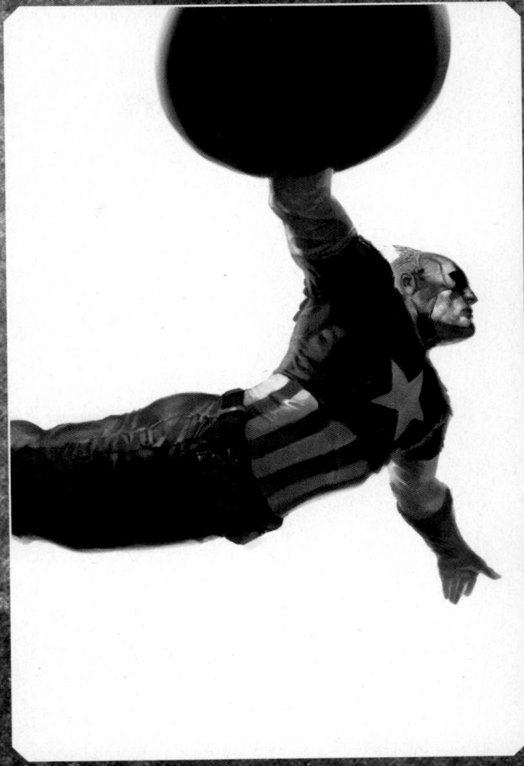

MARKO DJURDJEVIĆ
1 VARIANT

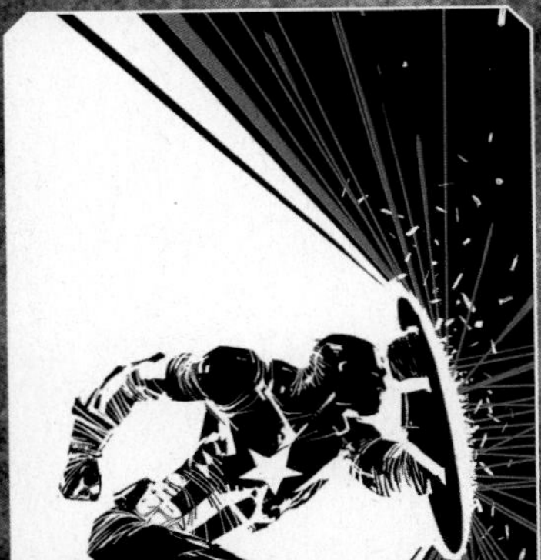

RON GARNEY & MATT MILLA
1 VARIANT

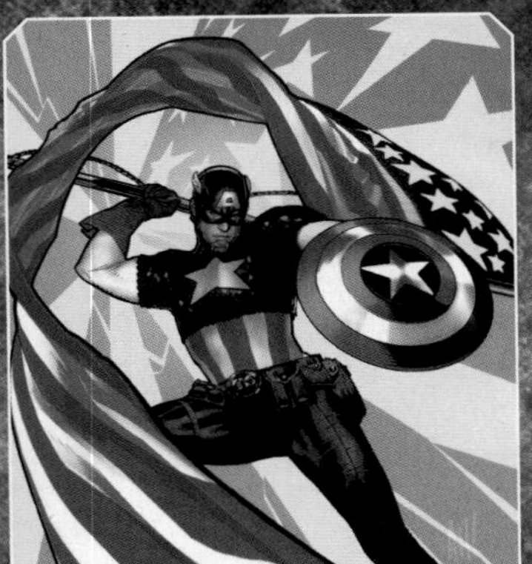

ADAM HUGHES
1 VARIANT

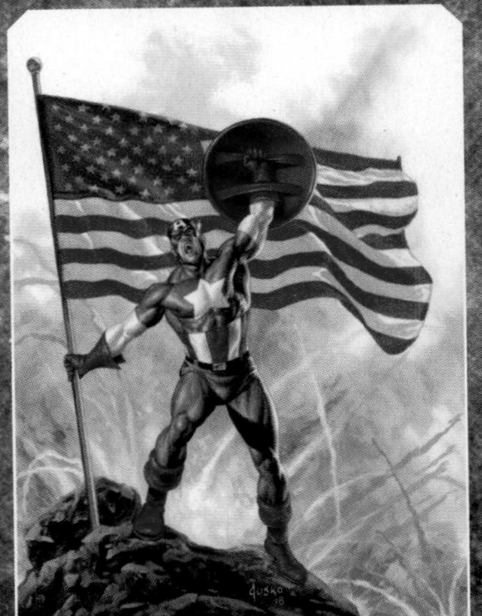

JOE JUSKO
1 VARIANT

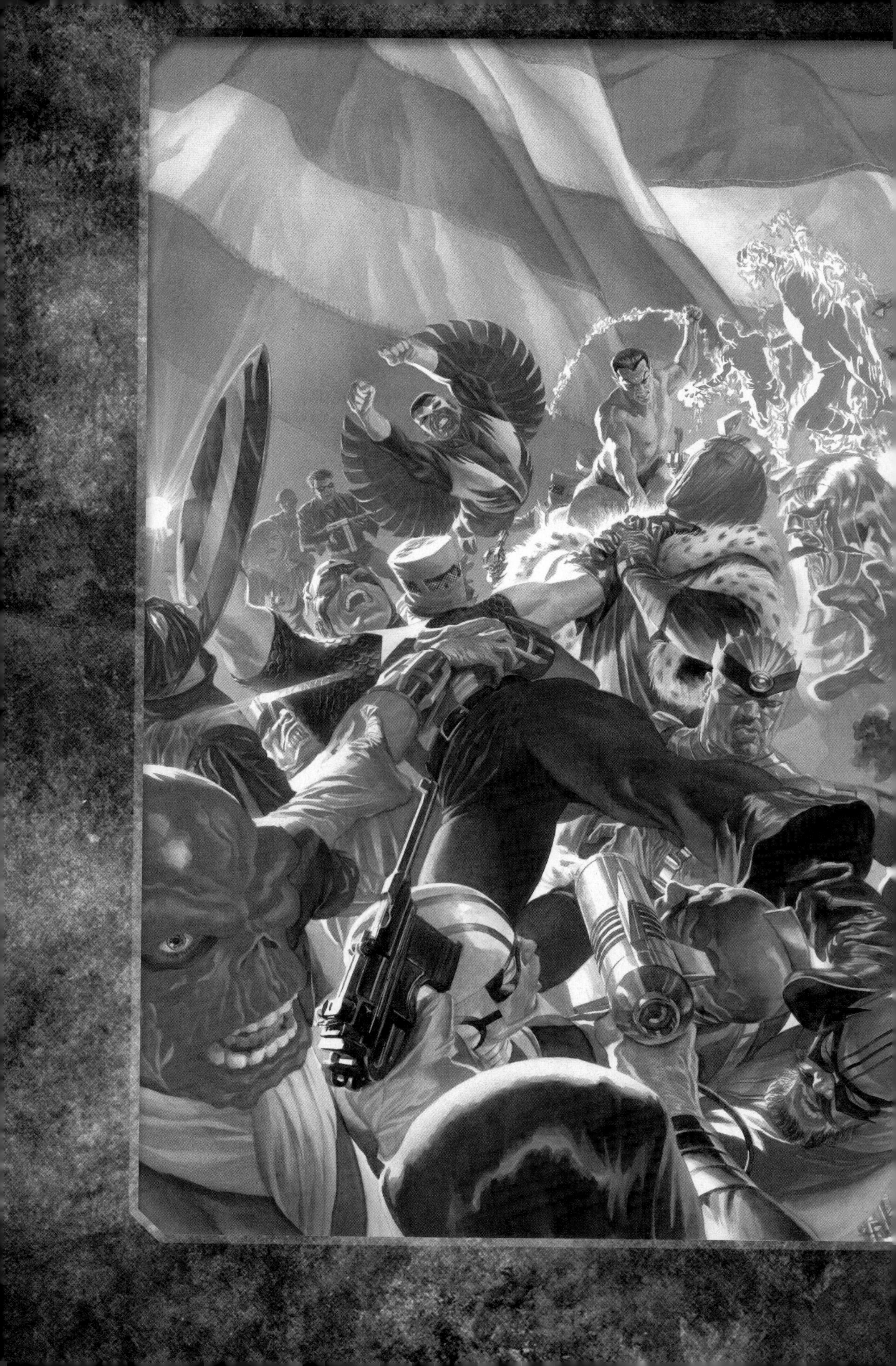

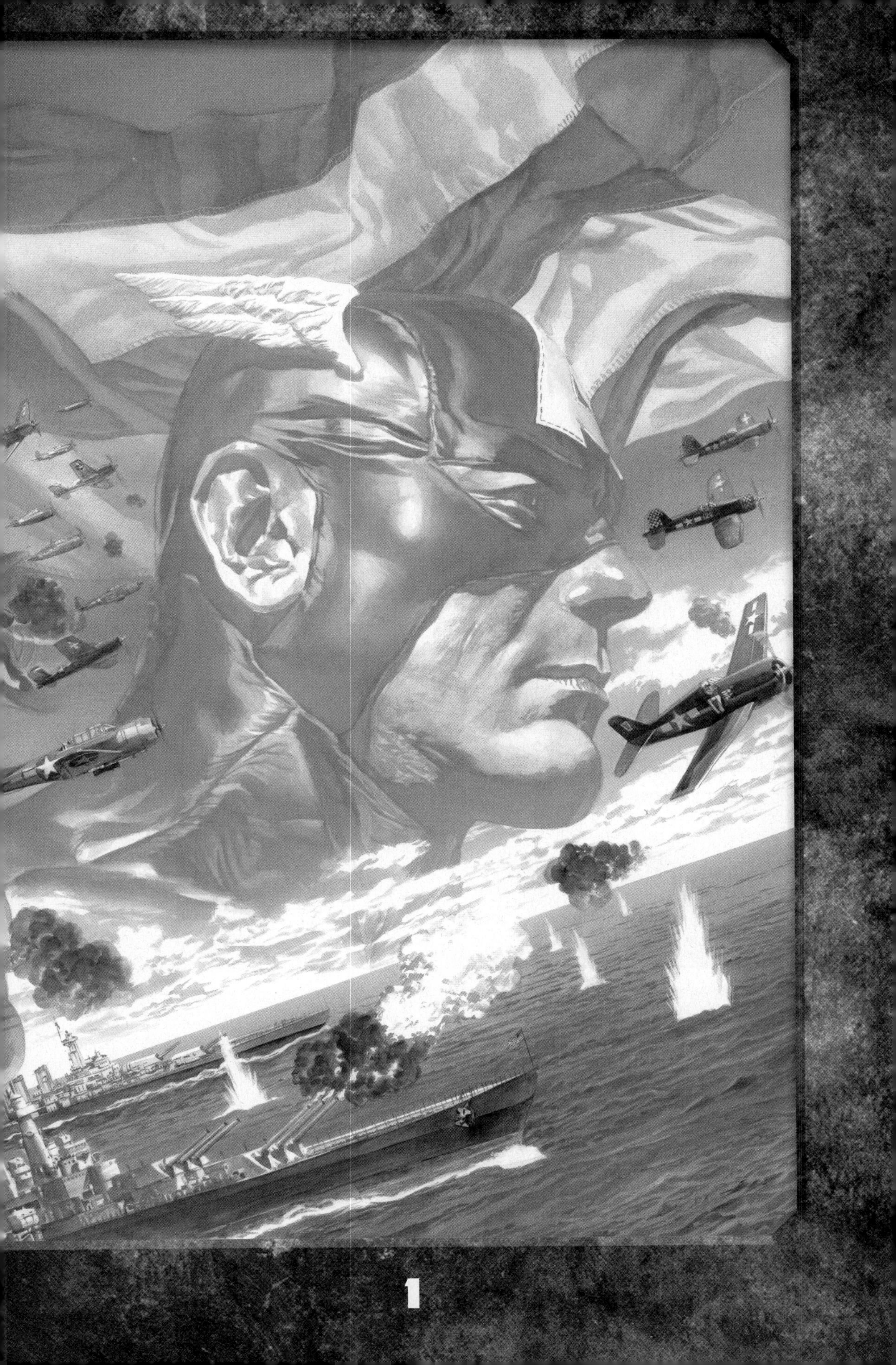

1

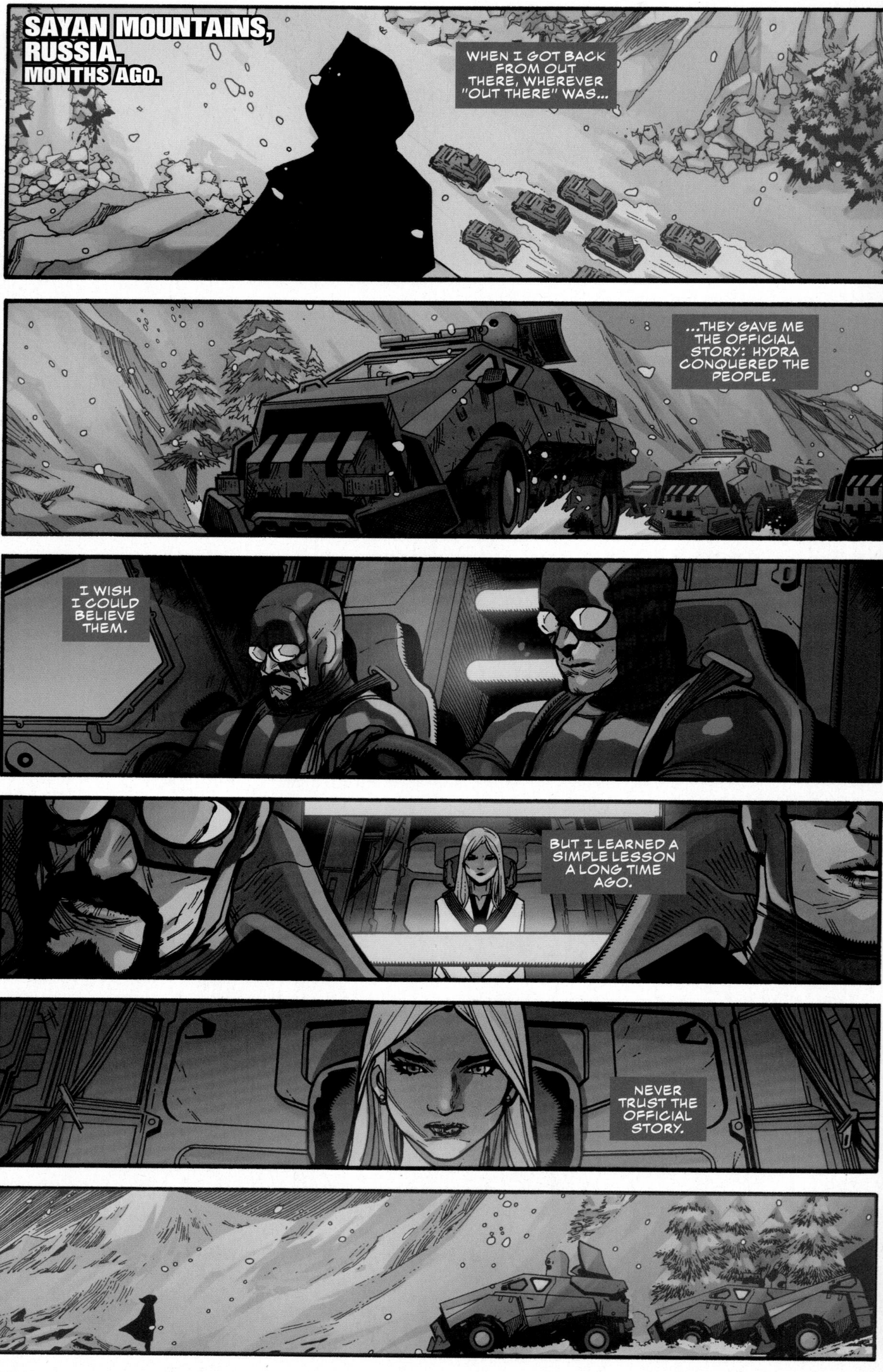
SAYAN MOUNTAINS, RUSSIA.
MONTHS AGO.
WHEN I GOT BACK FROM OUT THERE, WHEREVER "OUT THERE" WAS...
...THEY GAVE ME THE OFFICIAL STORY: HYDRA CONQUERED THE PEOPLE.
I WISH I COULD BELIEVE THEM.
BUT I LEARNED A SIMPLE LESSON A LONG TIME AGO.
NEVER TRUST THE OFFICIAL STORY.

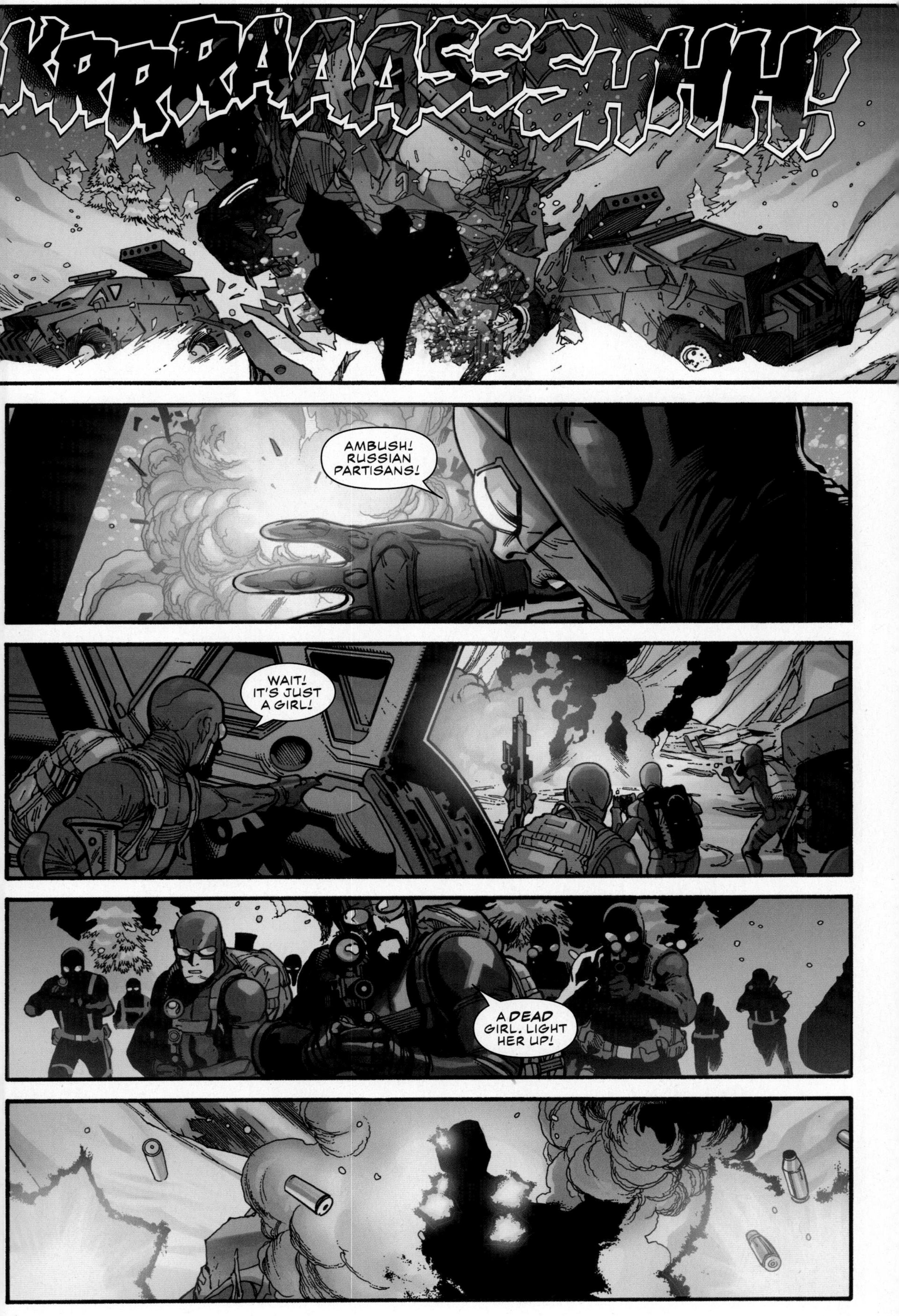
KRRRAAASSSHHH!
AMBUSH! RUSSIAN PARTISANS!
WAIT! IT'S JUST A GIRL!
A DEAD GIRL. LIGHT HER UP!

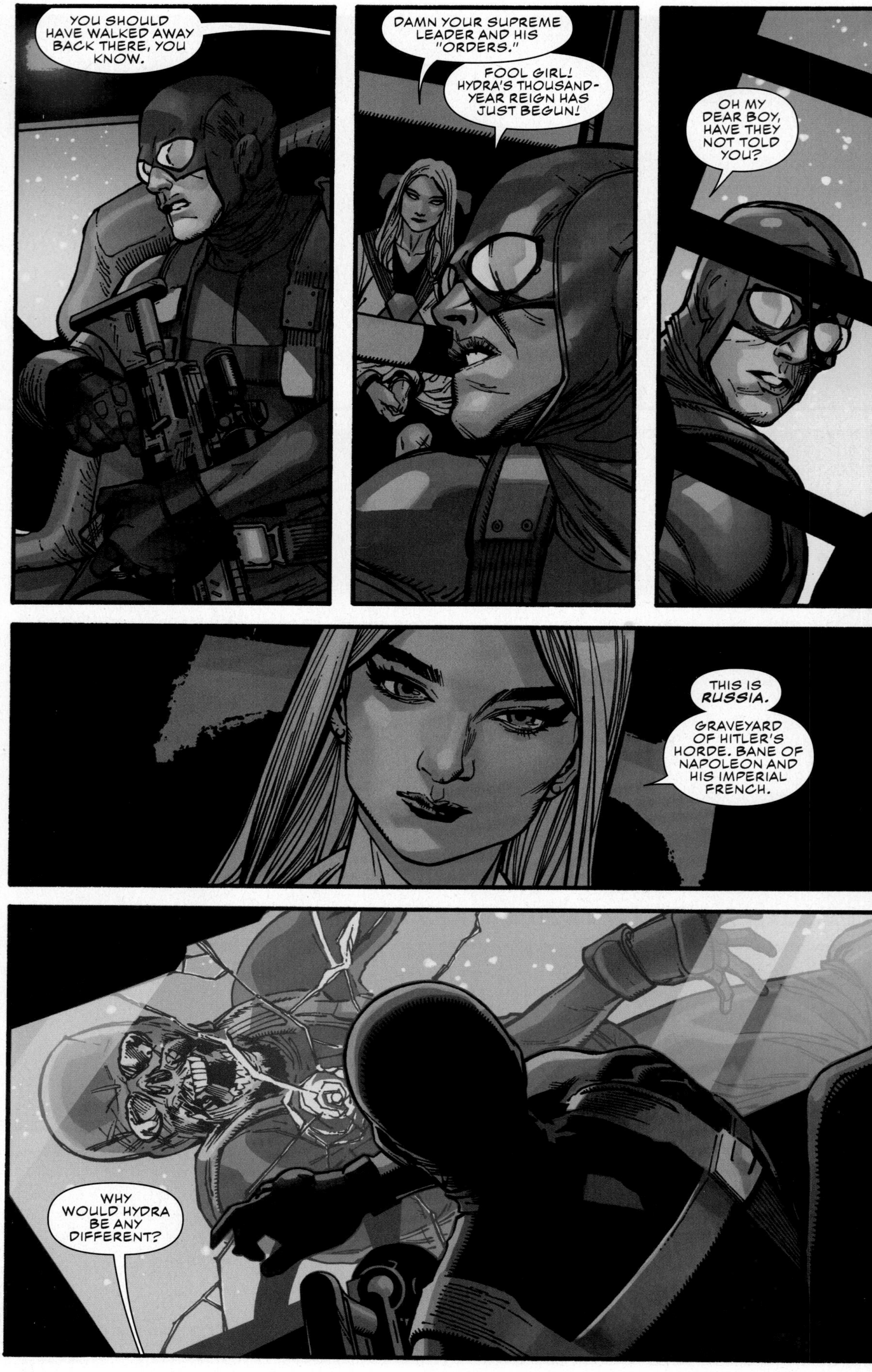
YOU SHOULD HAVE WALKED AWAY BACK THERE, YOU KNOW.
DAMN YOUR SUPREME LEADER AND HIS "ORDERS."
FOOL GIRL! HYDRA'S THOUSAND-YEAR REIGN HAS JUST BEGUN!
OH MY DEAR BOY, HAVE THEY NOT TOLD YOU?
THIS IS RUSSIA.
GRAVEYARD OF HITLER'S HORDE. BANE OF NAPOLEON AND HIS IMPERIAL FRENCH.
WHY WOULD HYDRA BE ANY DIFFERENT?

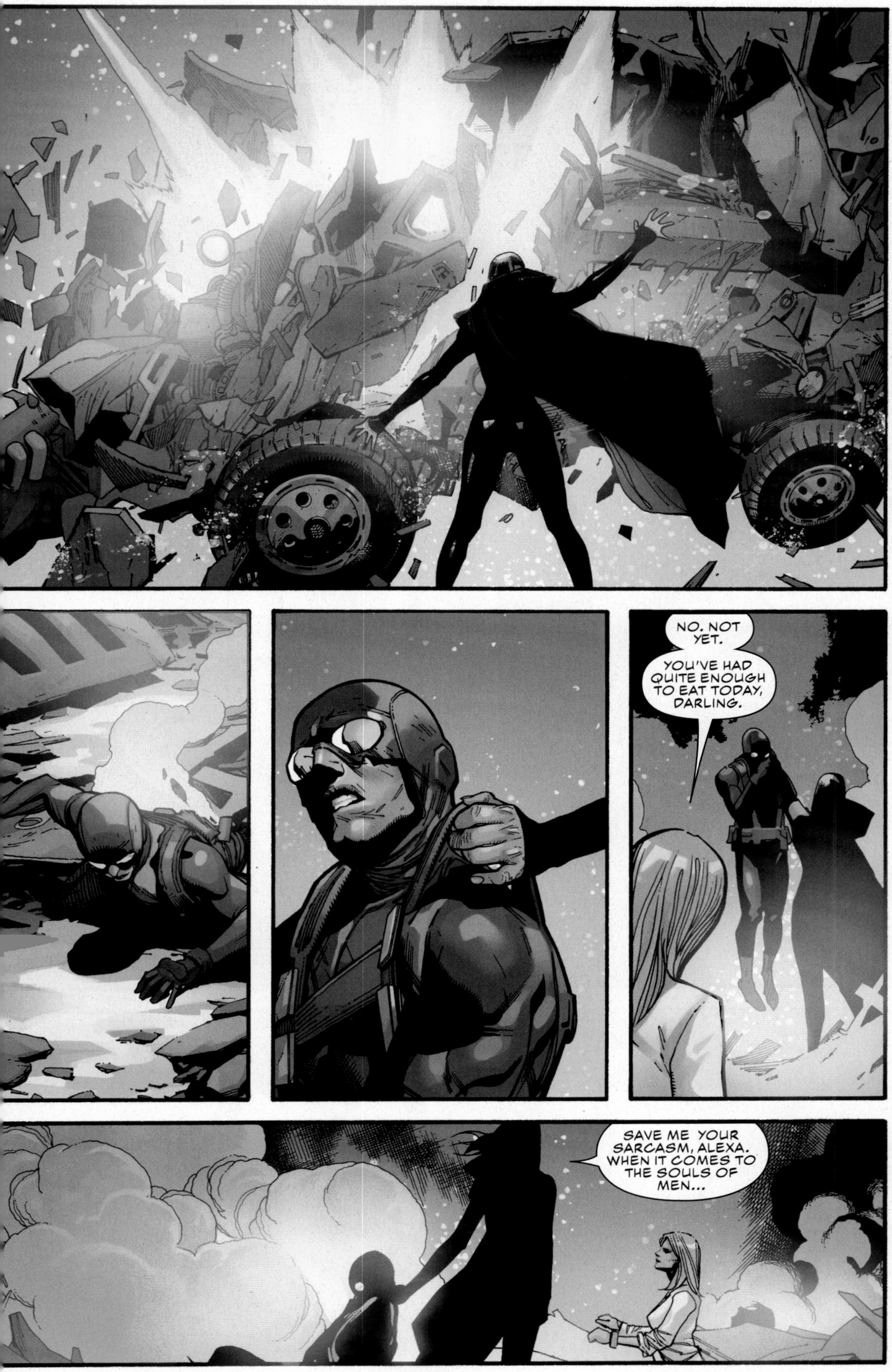
NO. NOT YET.
YOU'VE HAD QUITE ENOUGH TO EAT TODAY, DARLING.
SAVE ME YOUR SARCASM, ALEXA. WHEN IT COMES TO THE SOULS OF MEN...

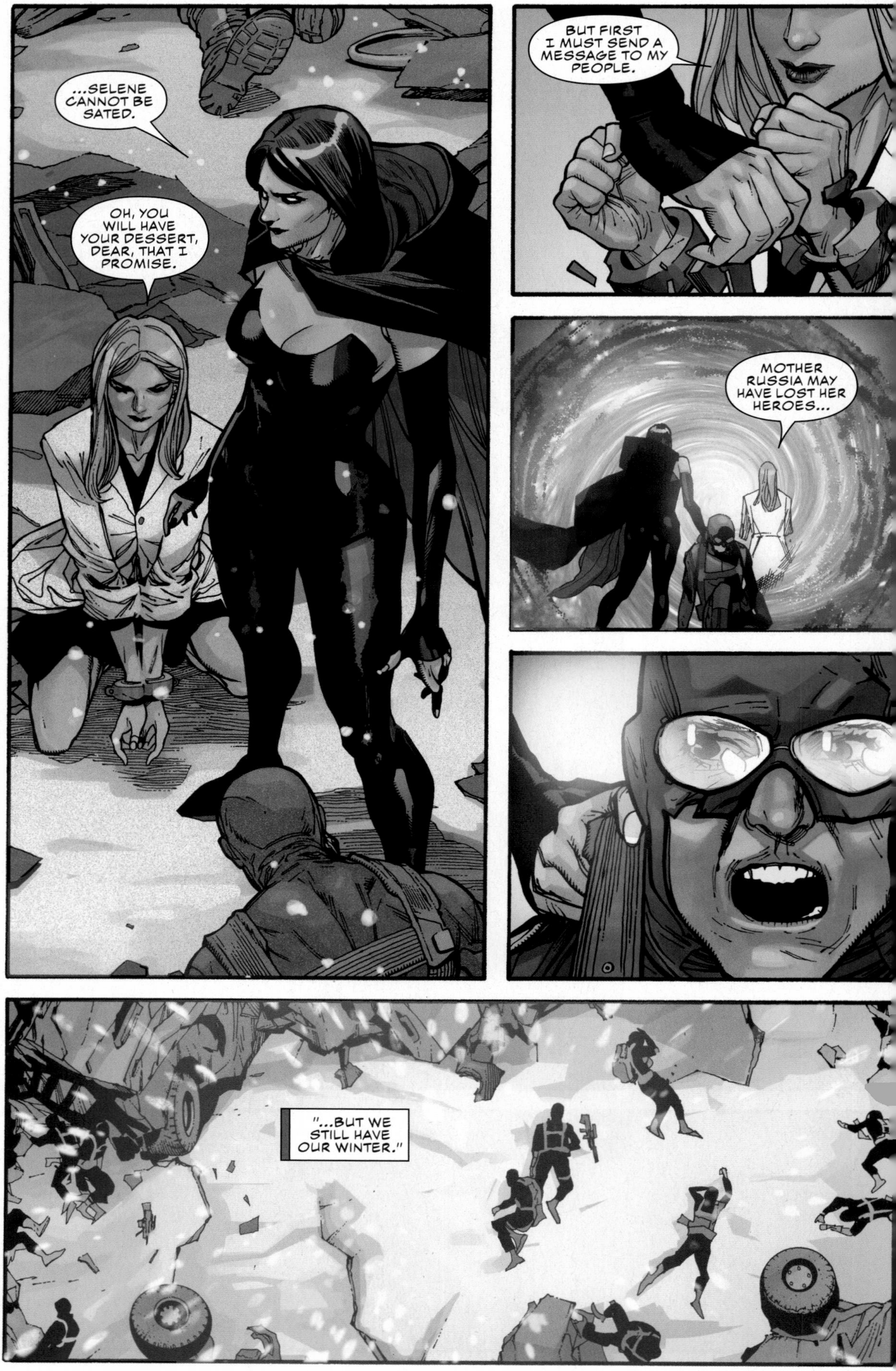
...SELENE CANNOT BE SATED.
OH, YOU WILL HAVE YOUR DESSERT, DEAR, THAT I PROMISE.
BUT FIRST I MUST SEND A MESSAGE TO MY PEOPLE.
MOTHER RUSSIA MAY HAVE LOST HER HEROES...
"...BUT WE STILL HAVE OUR WINTER."

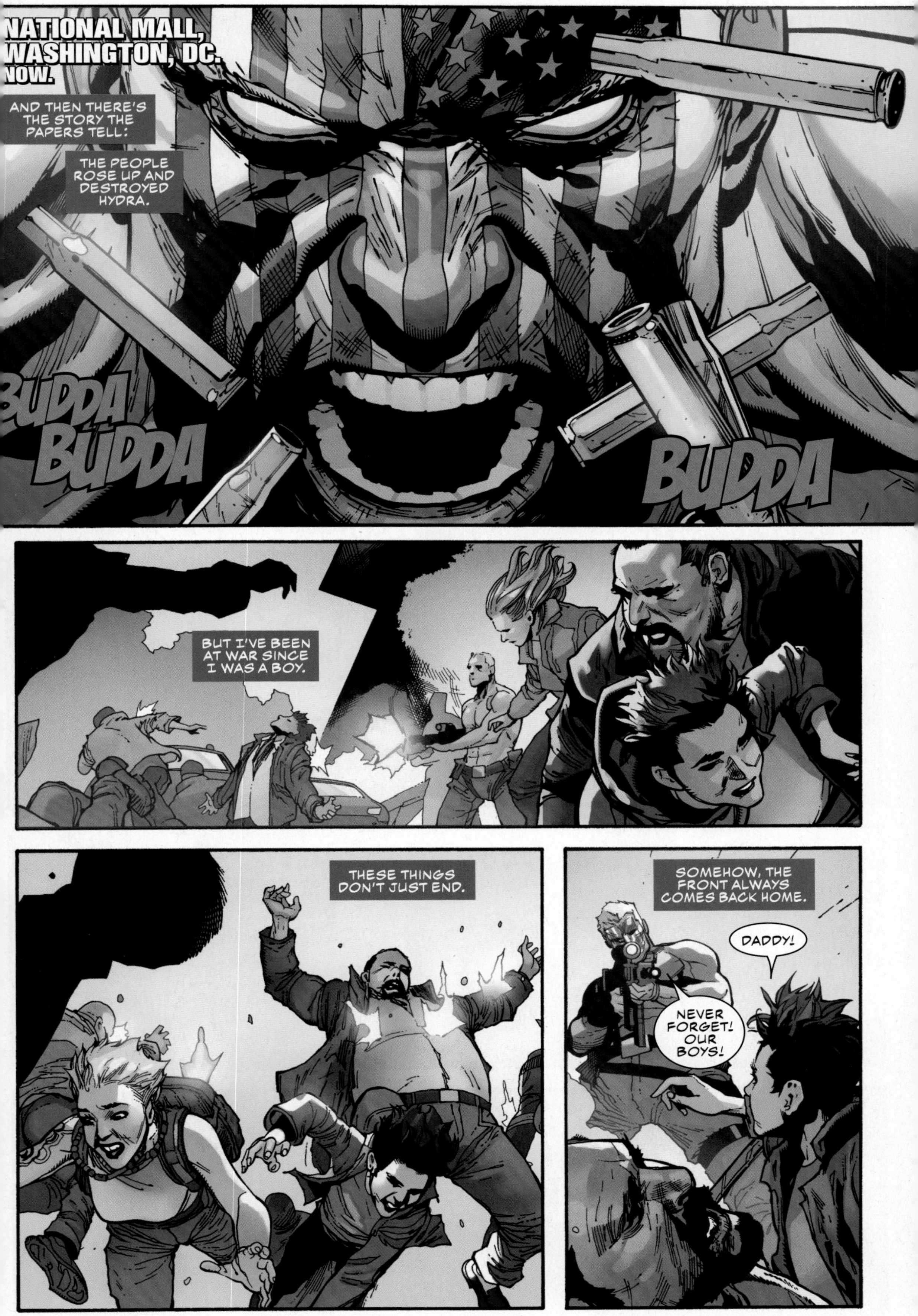
NATIONAL MALL, WASHINGTON, DC. NOW.
AND THEN THERE'S THE STORY THE PAPERS TELL:
THE PEOPLE ROSE UP AND DESTROYED HYDRA.
BUDDA BUDDA
BUDDA
BUT I'VE BEEN AT WAR SINCE I WAS A BOY.
THESE THINGS DON'T JUST END.
SOMEHOW, THE FRONT ALWAYS COMES BACK HOME.
DADDY!
NEVER FORGET! OUR BOYS!

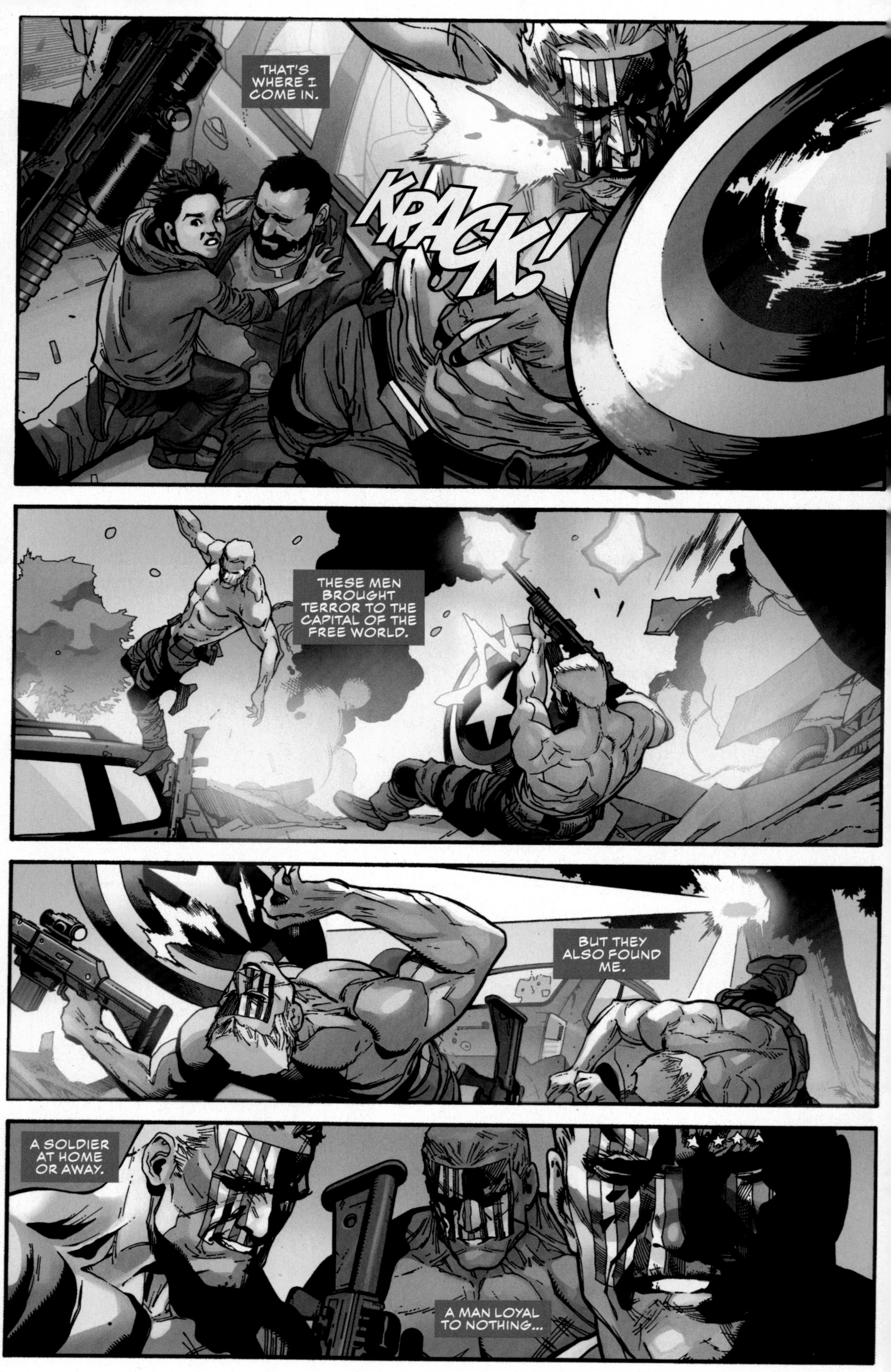
THAT'S WHERE I COME IN.
KRACK!
THESE MEN BROUGHT TERROR TO THE CAPITAL OF THE FREE WORLD.
BUT THEY ALSO FOUND ME.
A SOLDIER AT HOME OR AWAY.
A MAN LOYAL TO NOTHING...

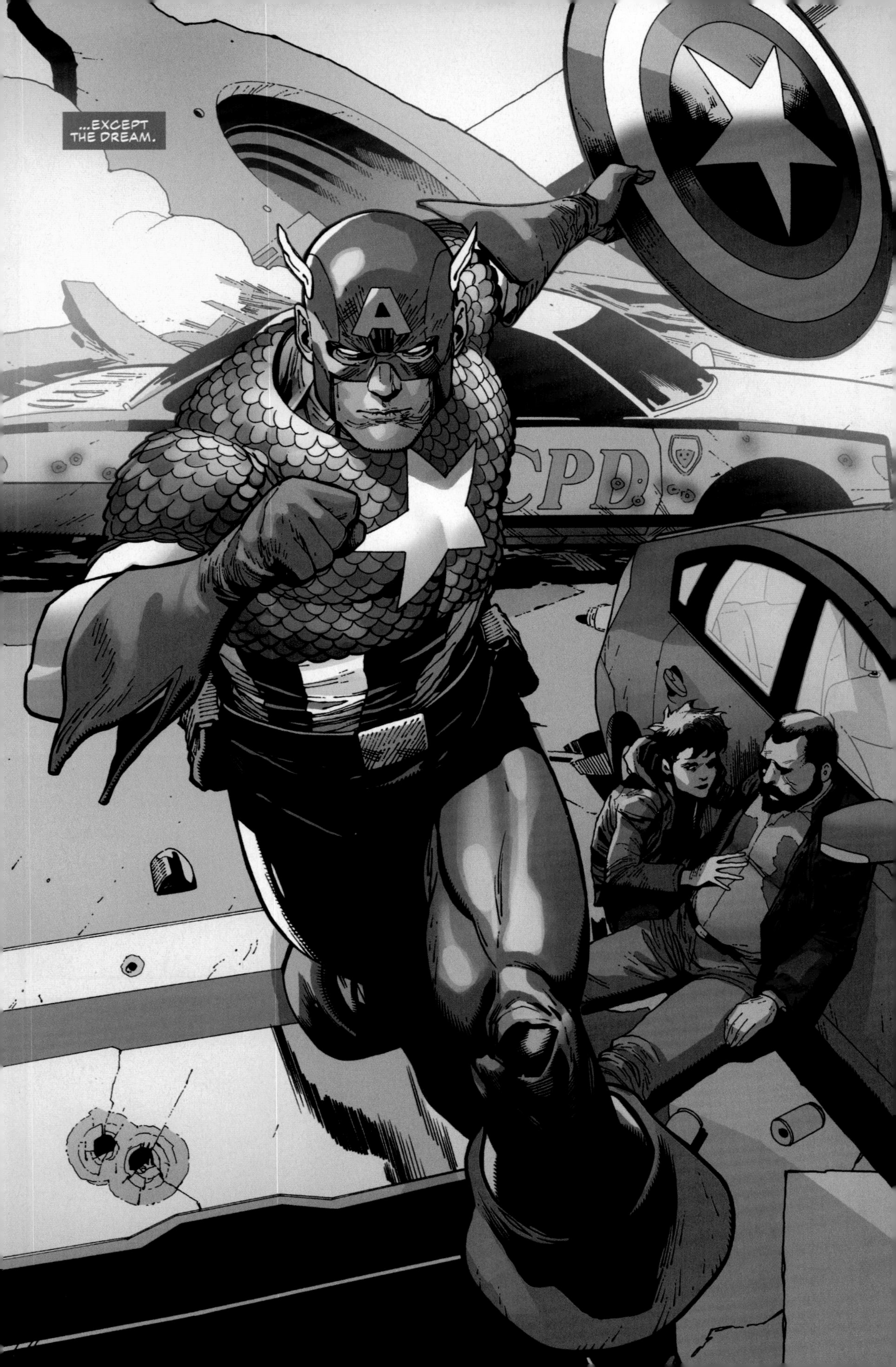
...EXCEPT THE DREAM.
CPD

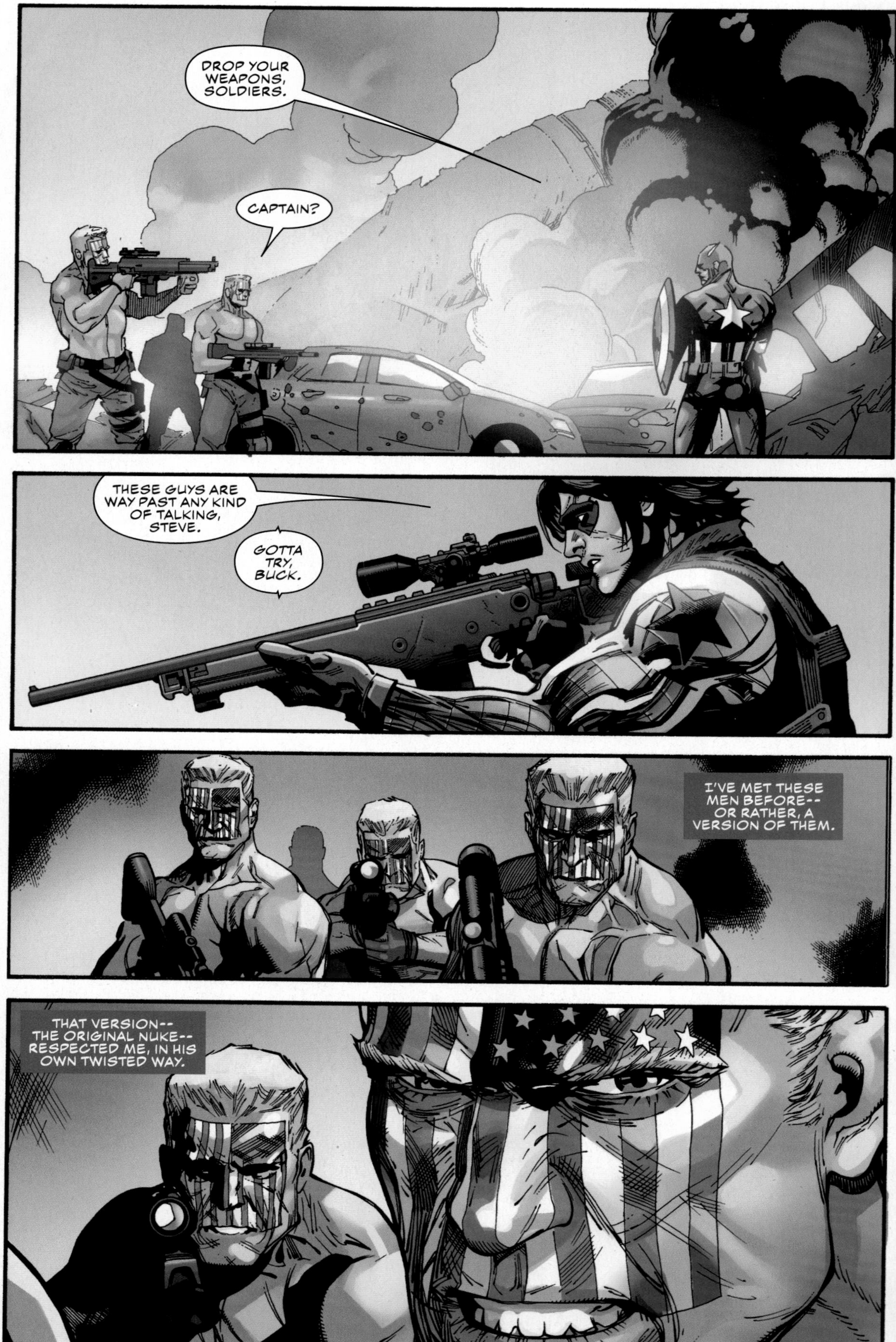
DROP YOUR WEAPONS, SOLDIERS.
CAPTAIN?
THESE GUYS ARE WAY PAST ANY KIND OF TALKING, STEVE.
GOTTA TRY, BUCK.
I'VE MET THESE MEN BEFORE-- OR RATHER, A VERSION OF THEM.
THAT VERSION-- THE ORIGINAL NUKE-- RESPECTED ME, IN HIS OWN TWISTED WAY.

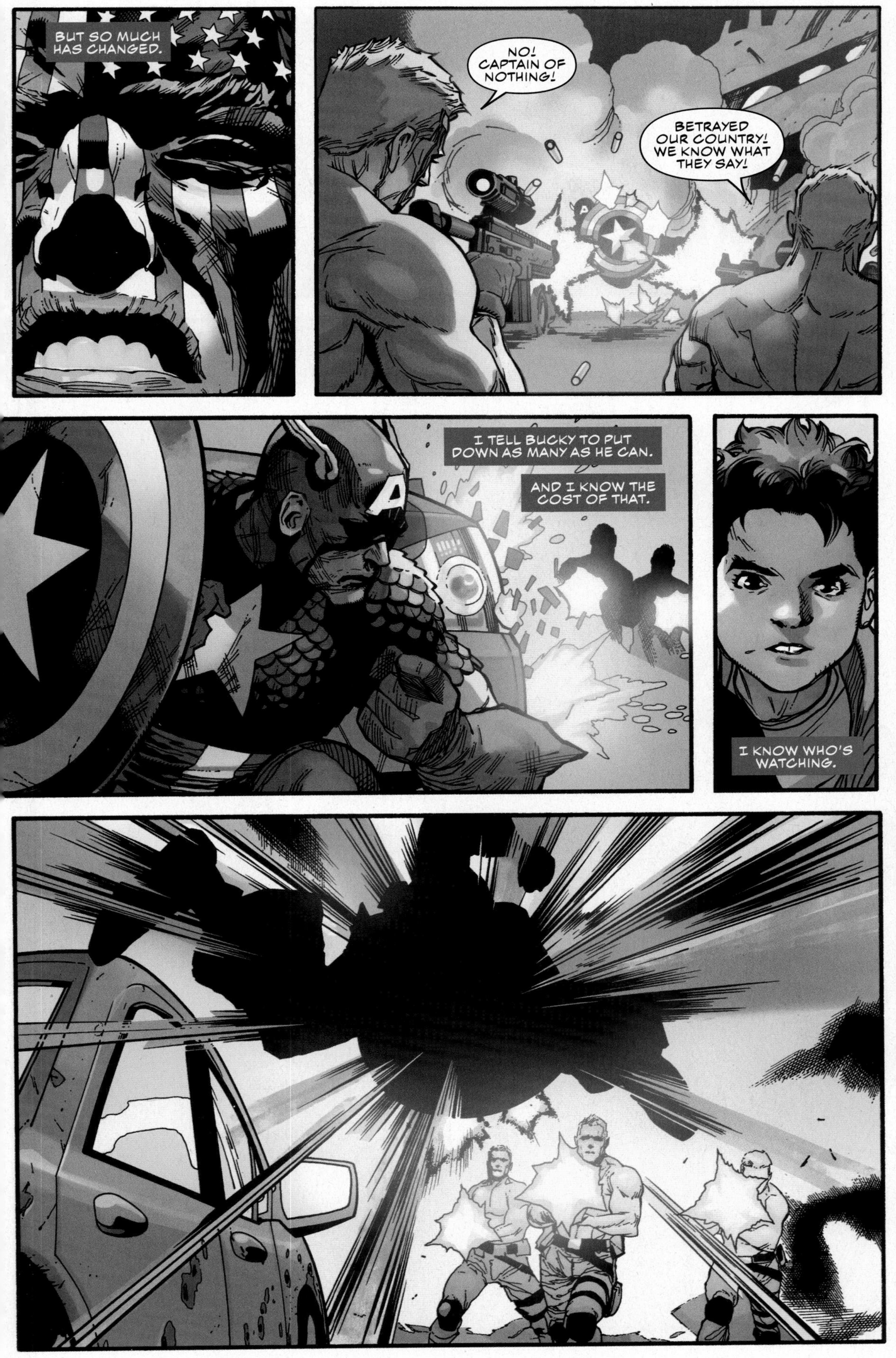

BUT SO MUCH HAS CHANGED.
NO! CAPTAIN OF NOTHING!
BETRAYED OUR COUNTRY! WE KNOW WHAT THEY SAY!
I TELL BUCKY TO PUT DOWN AS MANY AS HE CAN.
AND I KNOW THE COST OF THAT.
I KNOW WHO'S WATCHING.

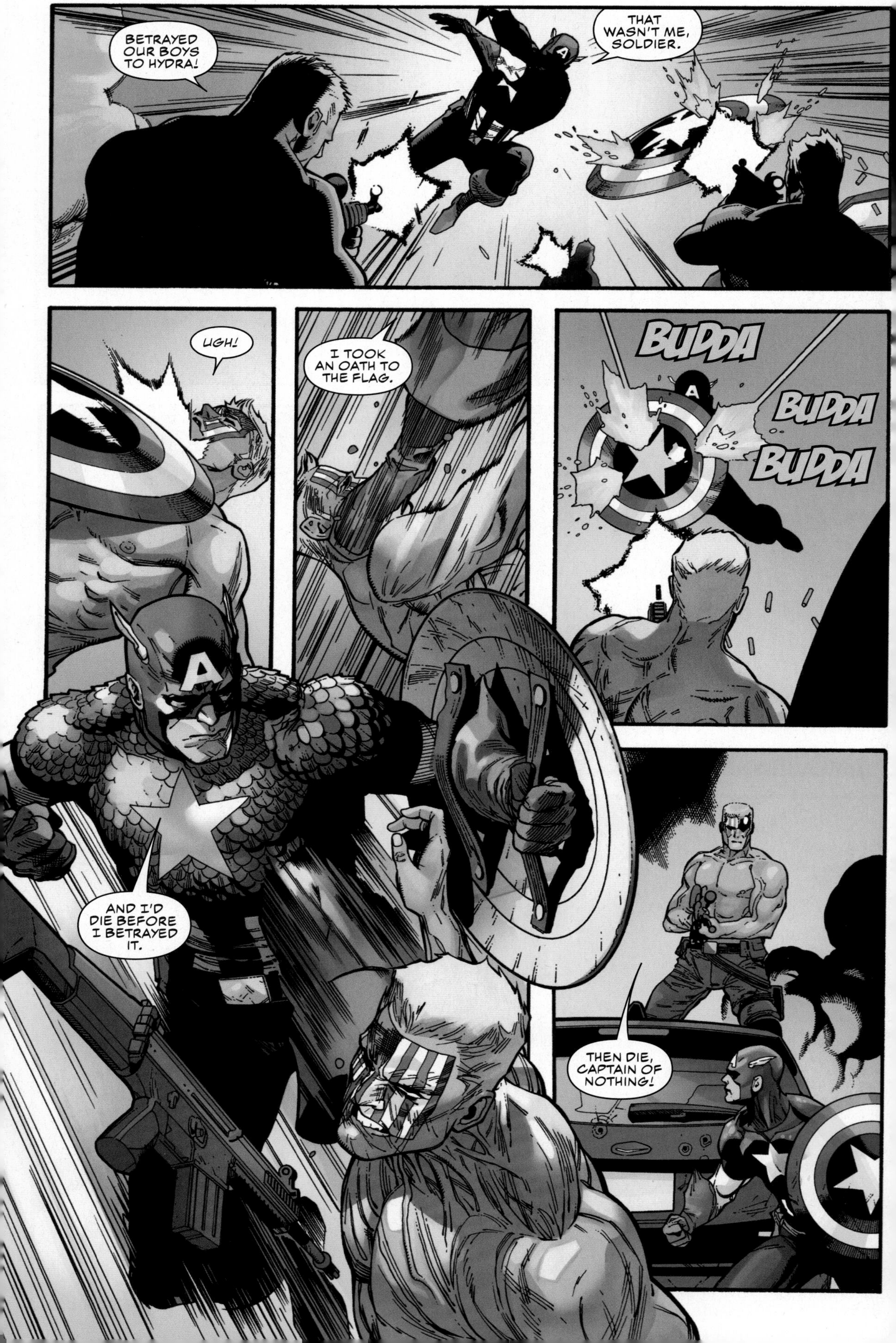
BETRAYED OUR BOYS TO HYDRA!
THAT WASN'T ME, SOLDIER.
UGH!
I TOOK AN OATH TO THE FLAG.
BUDDA
BUDDA
BUDDA
AND I'D DIE BEFORE I BETRAYED IT.
THEN DIE, CAPTAIN OF NOTHING!

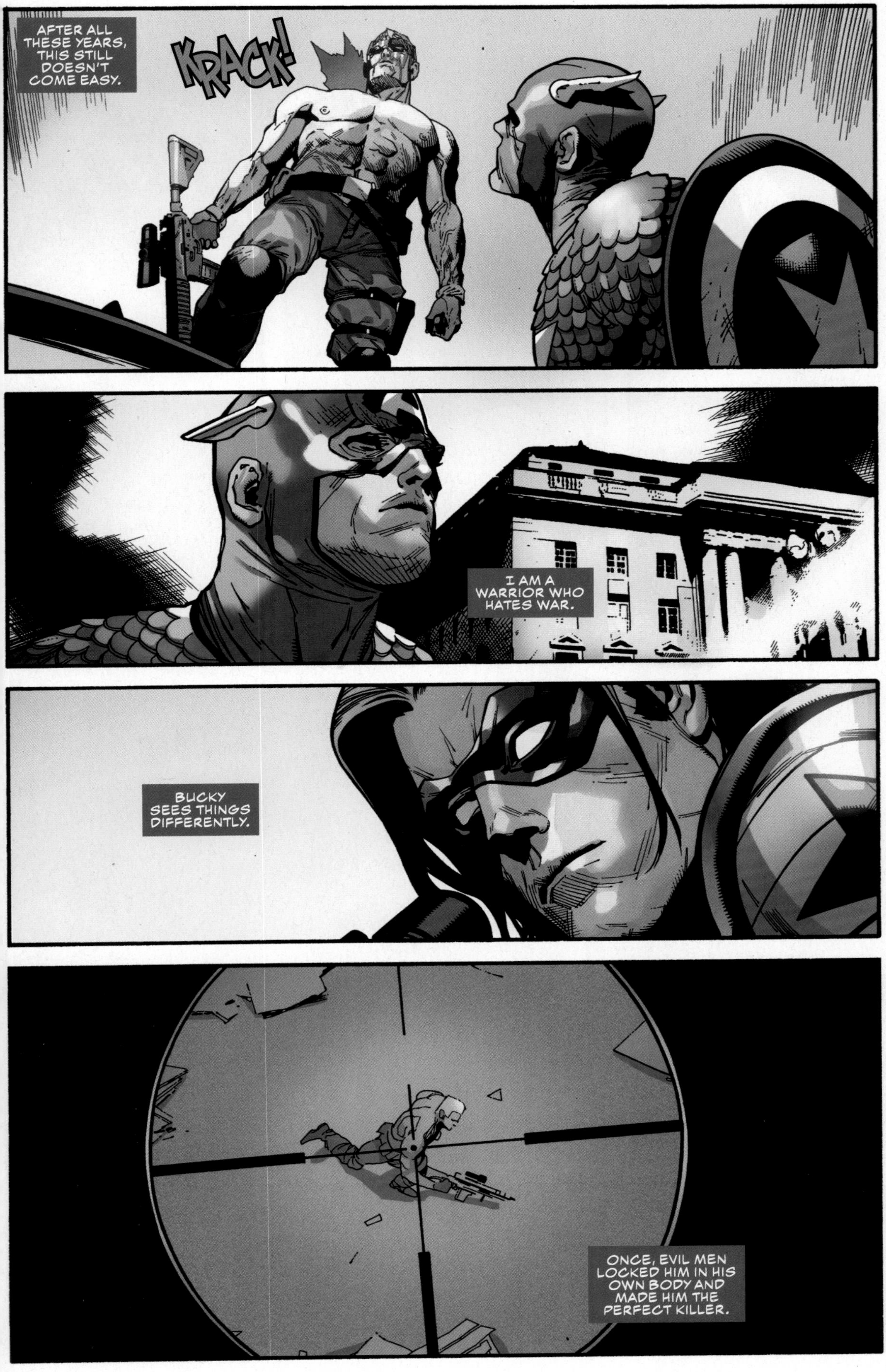
AFTER ALL THESE YEARS, THIS STILL DOESN'T COME EASY.
KRACK!
I AM A WARRIOR WHO HATES WAR.
BUCKY SEES THINGS DIFFERENTLY.
ONCE, EVIL MEN LOCKED HIM IN HIS OWN BODY AND MADE HIM THE PERFECT KILLER.

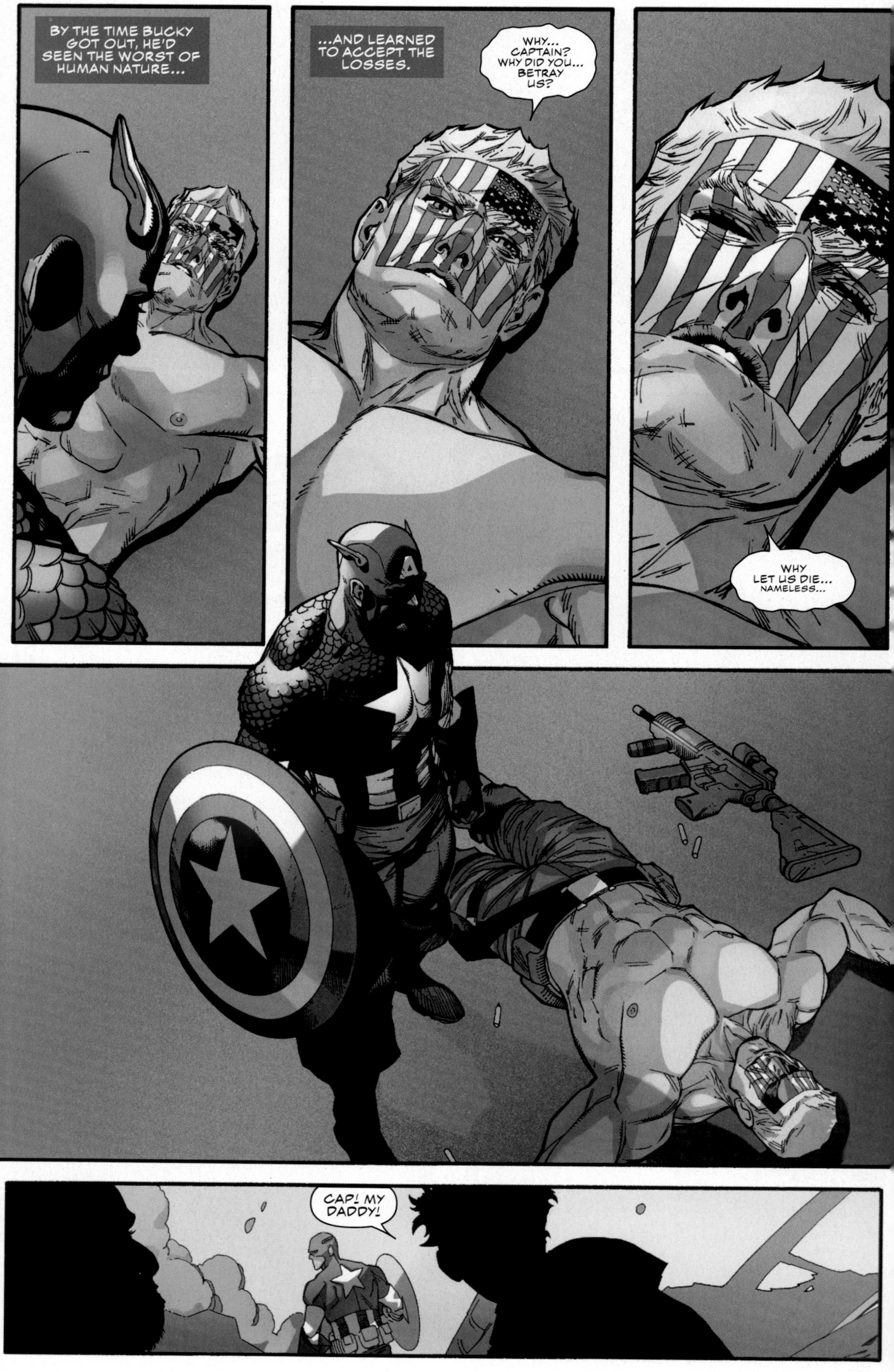
BY THE TIME BUCKY GOT OUT, HE'D SEEN THE WORST OF HUMAN NATURE...
...AND LEARNED TO ACCEPT THE LOSSES.
WHY... CAPTAIN? WHY DID YOU... BETRAY US?
WHY LET US DIE... NAMELESS...
CAP! MY DADDY!

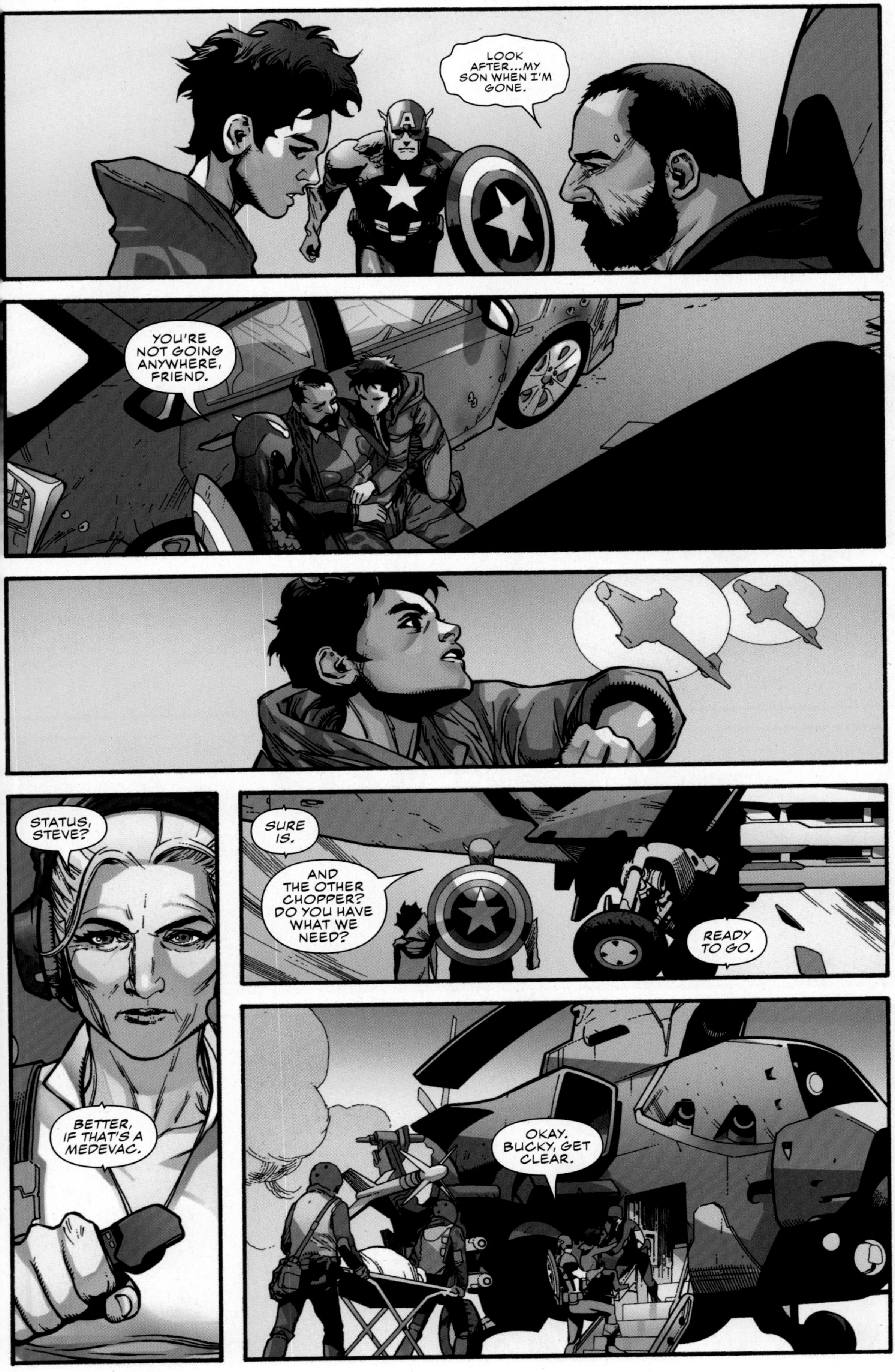
LOOK AFTER...MY SON WHEN I'M GONE.
YOU'RE NOT GOING ANYWHERE, FRIEND.
STATUS, STEVE?
SURE IS.
AND THE OTHER CHOPPER? DO YOU HAVE WHAT WE NEED?
READY TO GO.
BETTER, IF THAT'S A MEDEVAC.
OKAY. BUCKY, GET CLEAR.

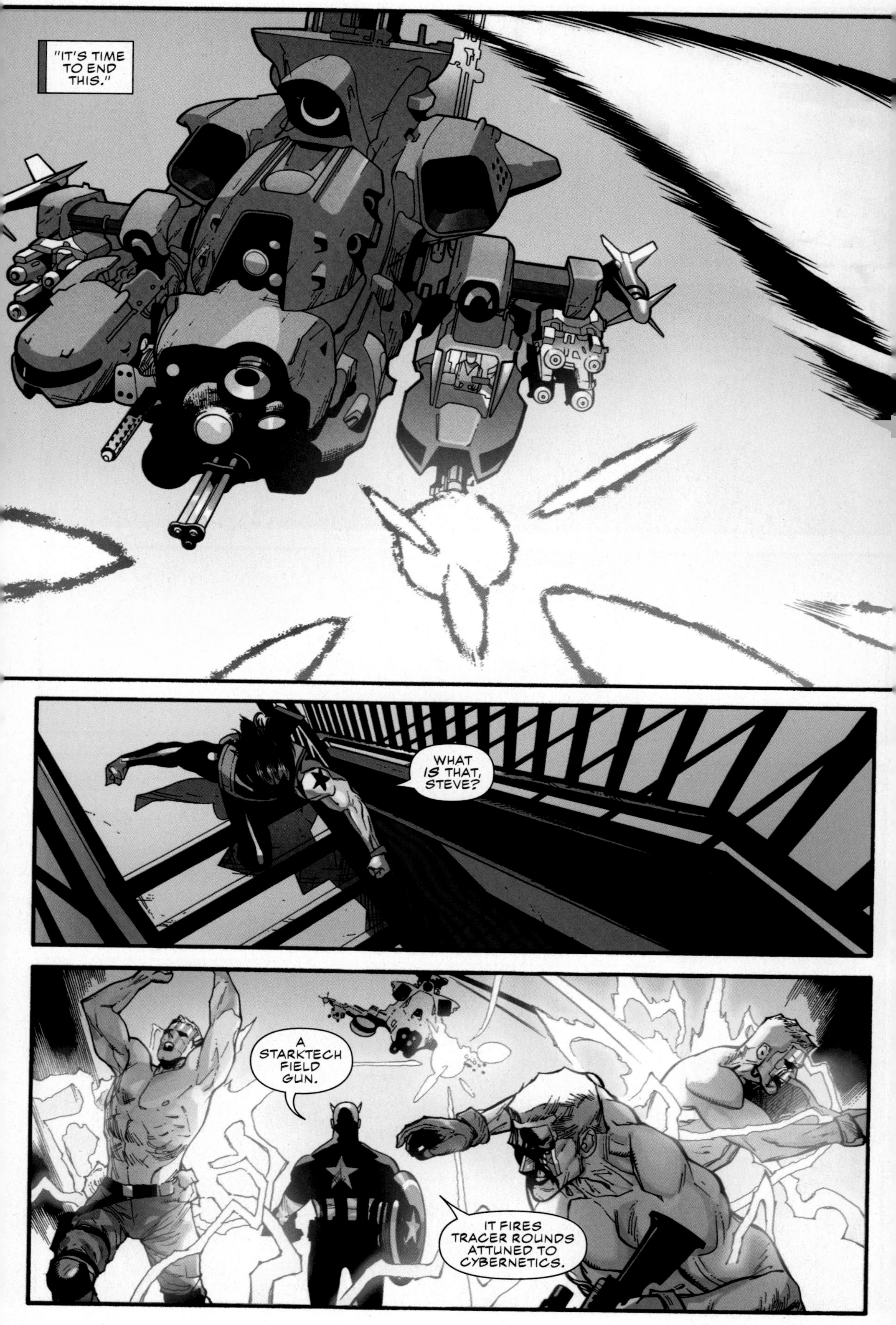
"IT'S TIME TO END THIS."
WHAT IS THAT, STEVE?
A STARKTECH FIELD GUN.
IT FIRES TRACER ROUNDS ATTUNED TO CYBERNETICS.

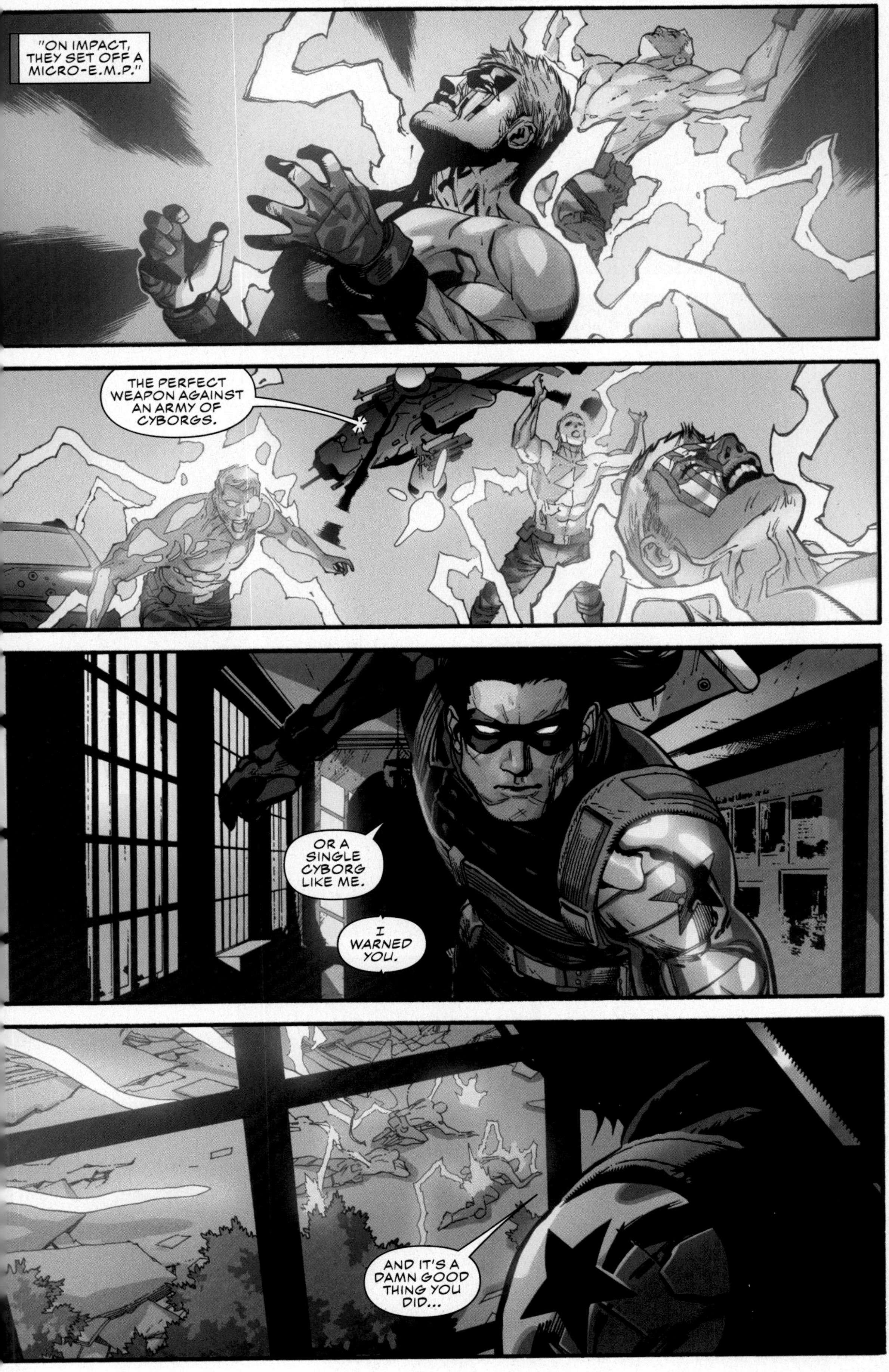
"ON IMPACT, THEY SET OFF A MICRO-E.M.P."
THE PERFECT WEAPON AGAINST AN ARMY OF CYBORGS.
OR A SINGLE CYBORG LIKE ME.
I WARNED YOU.
AND IT'S A DAMN GOOD THING YOU DID...

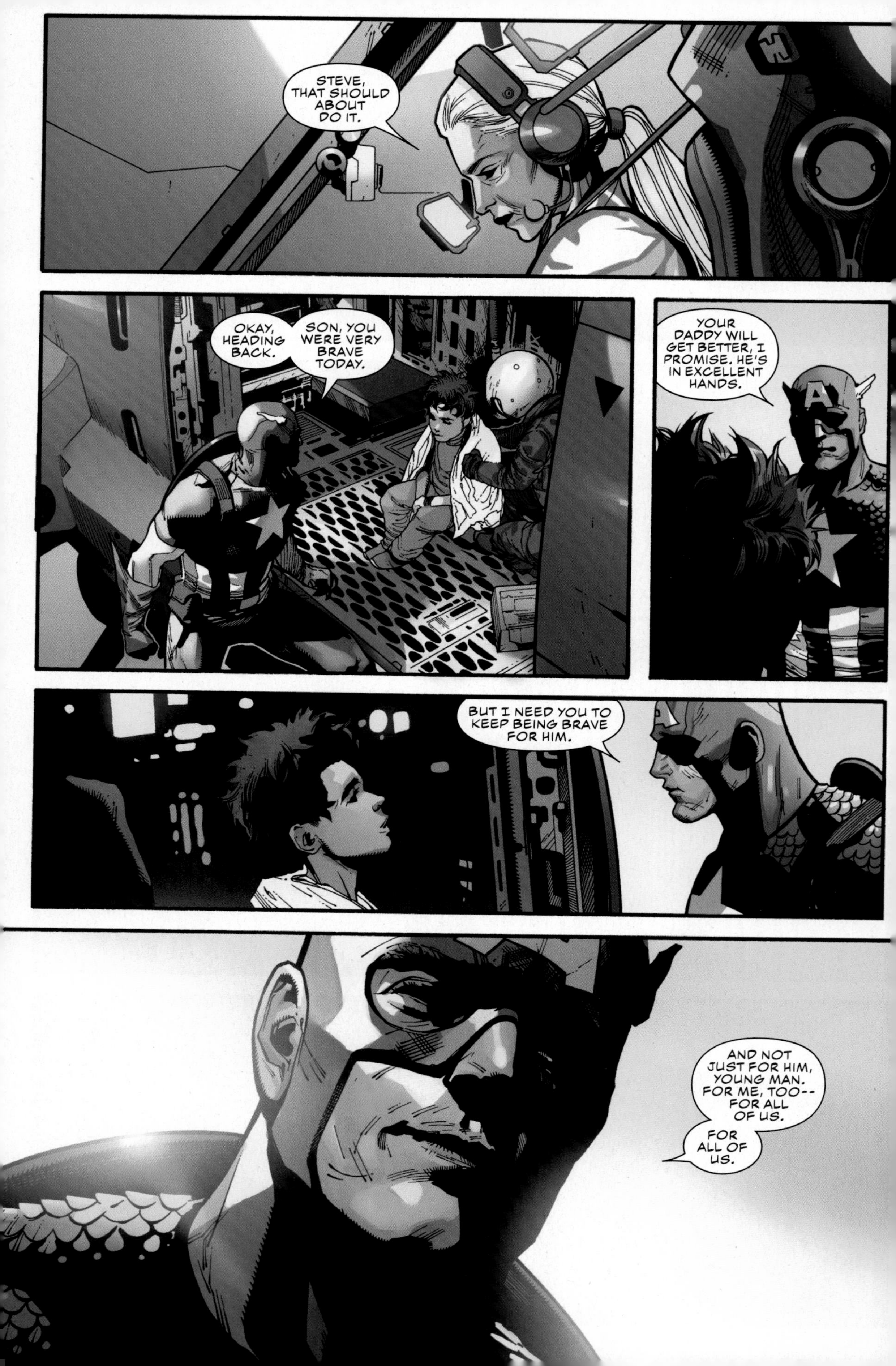
STEVE, THAT SHOULD ABOUT DO IT.
OKAY, HEADING BACK.
SON, YOU WERE VERY BRAVE TODAY.
YOUR DADDY WILL GET BETTER, I PROMISE. HE'S IN EXCELLENT HANDS.
BUT I NEED YOU TO KEEP BEING BRAVE FOR HIM.
AND NOT JUST FOR HIM, YOUNG MAN. FOR ME, TOO-- FOR ALL OF US.
FOR ALL OF US.

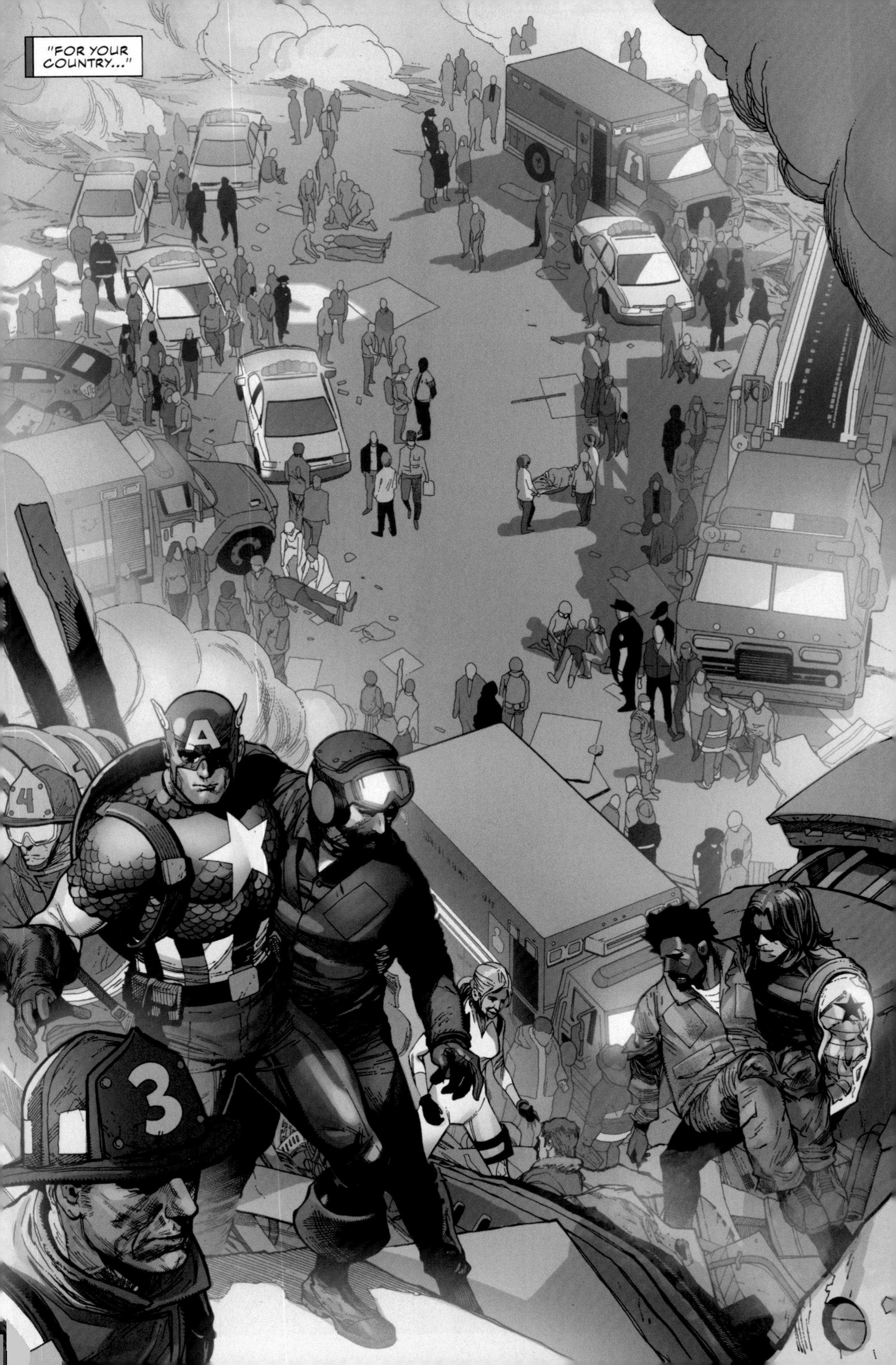
"FOR YOUR COUNTRY..."

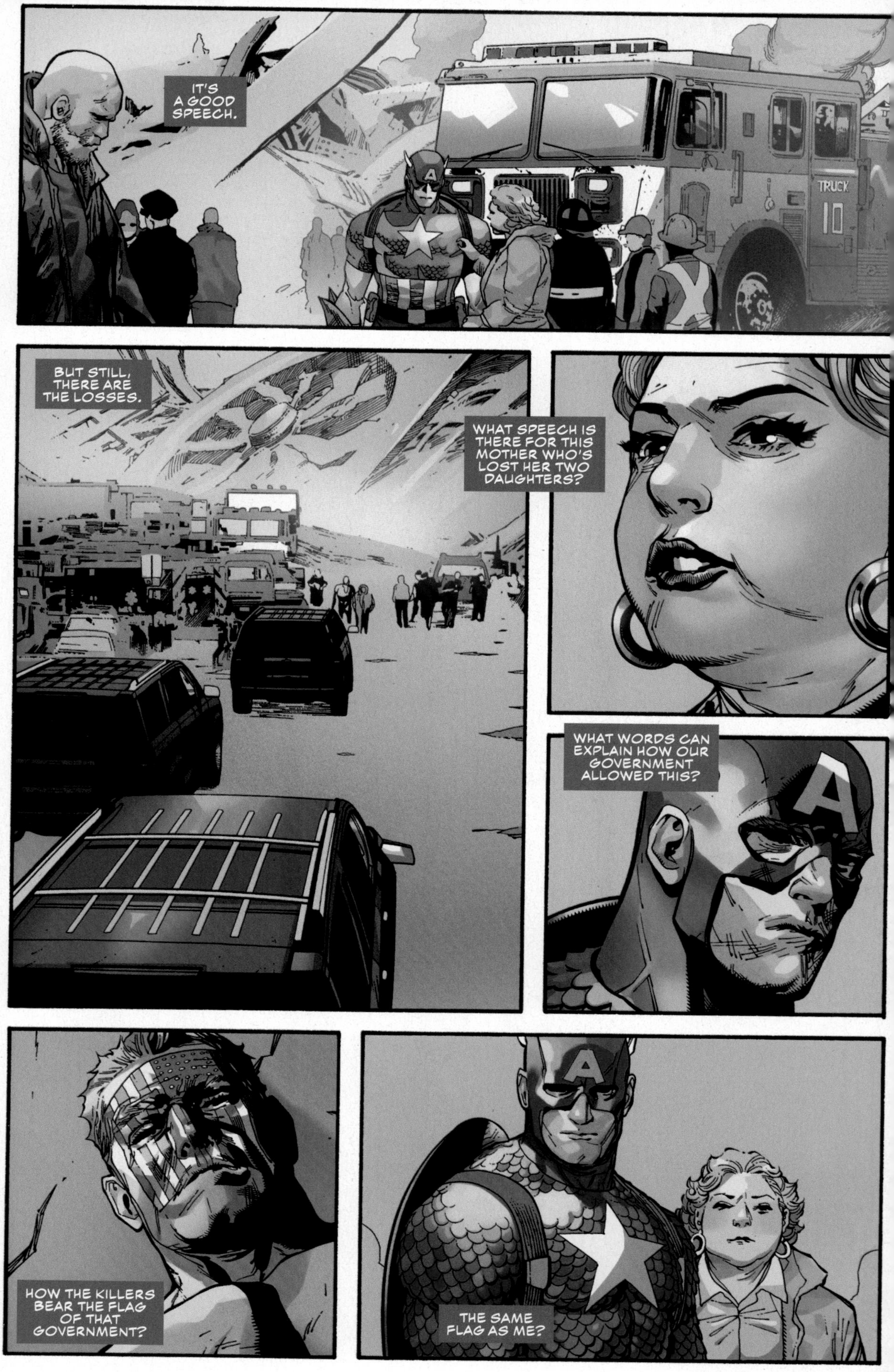
IT'S A GOOD SPEECH.
TRUCK 10
BUT STILL, THERE ARE THE LOSSES.
WHAT SPEECH IS THERE FOR THIS MOTHER WHO'S LOST HER TWO DAUGHTERS?
WHAT WORDS CAN EXPLAIN HOW OUR GOVERNMENT ALLOWED THIS?
HOW THE KILLERS BEAR THE FLAG OF THAT GOVERNMENT?
THE SAME FLAG AS ME?

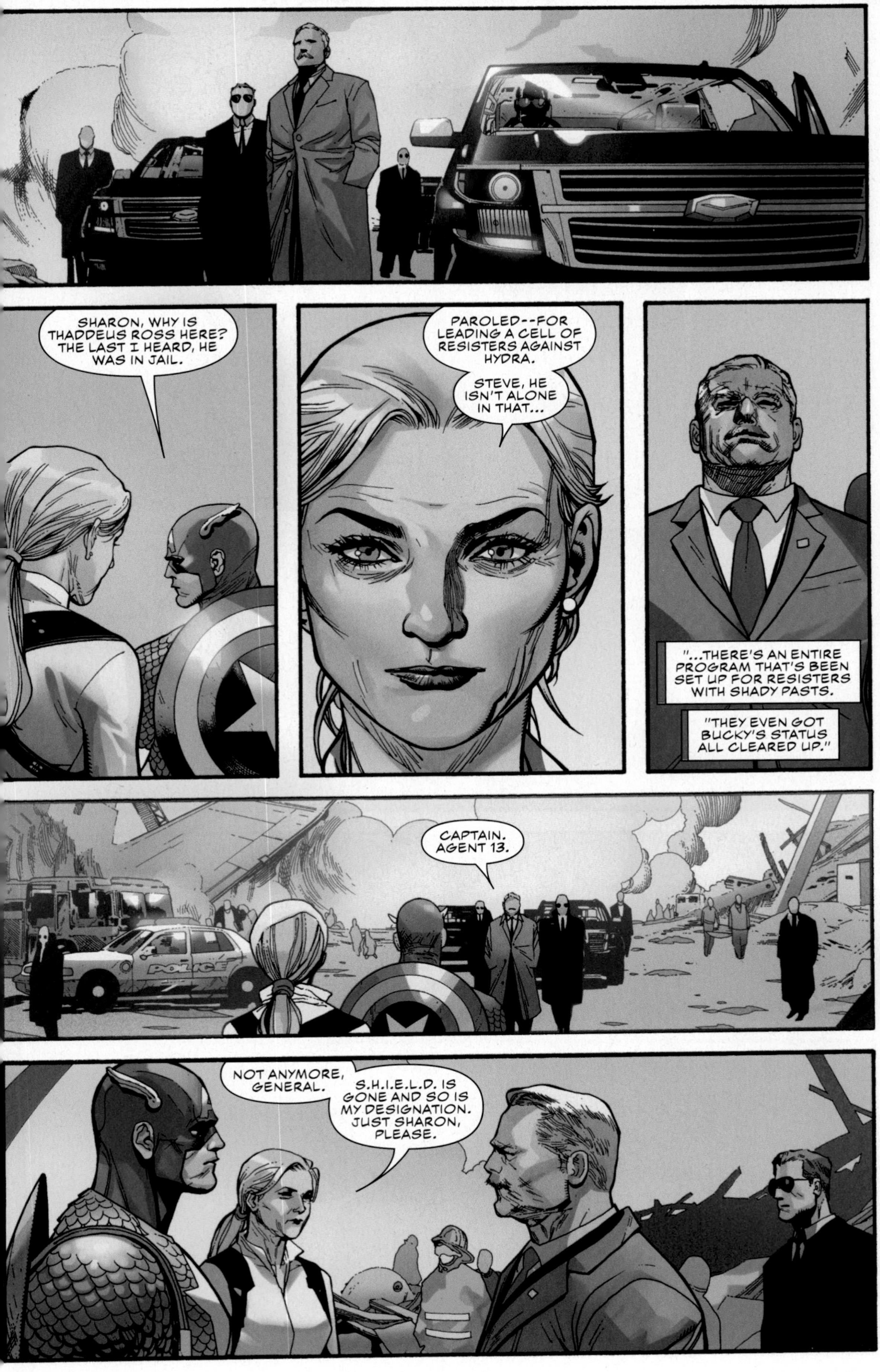
SHARON, WHY IS THADDEUS ROSS HERE? THE LAST I HEARD, HE WAS IN JAIL.
PAROLED--FOR LEADING A CELL OF RESISTERS AGAINST HYDRA.
STEVE, HE ISN'T ALONE IN THAT...
"...THERE'S AN ENTIRE PROGRAM THAT'S BEEN SET UP FOR RESISTERS WITH SHADY PASTS.
"THEY EVEN GOT BUCKY'S STATUS ALL CLEARED UP."
CAPTAIN. AGENT 13.
POLICE
NOT ANYMORE, GENERAL.
S.H.I.E.L.D. IS GONE AND SO IS MY DESIGNATION. JUST SHARON, PLEASE.

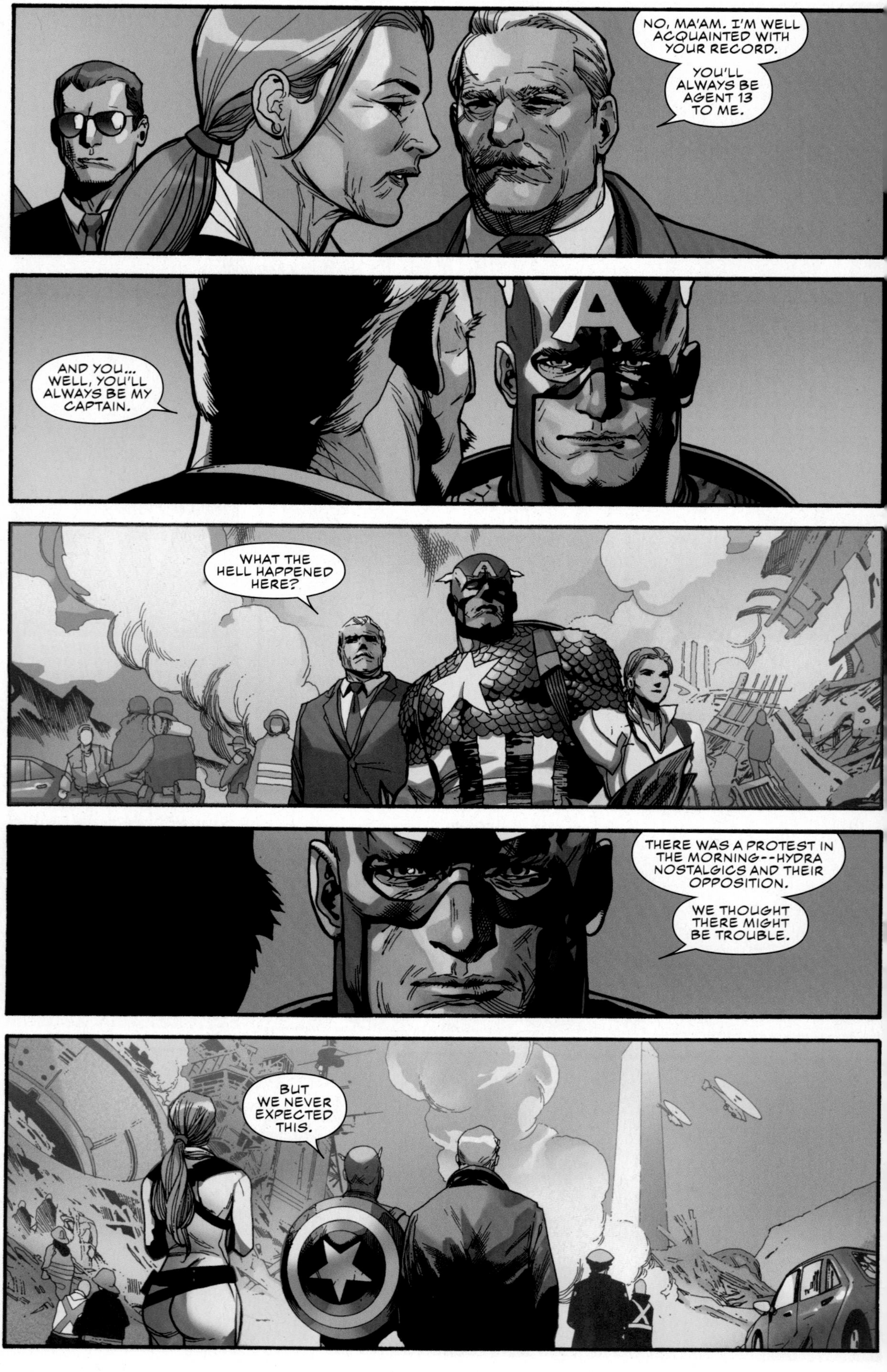
NO, MA'AM. I'M WELL ACQUAINTED WITH YOUR RECORD.
YOU'LL ALWAYS BE AGENT 13 TO ME.
AND YOU... WELL, YOU'LL ALWAYS BE MY CAPTAIN.
WHAT THE HELL HAPPENED HERE?
THERE WAS A PROTEST IN THE MORNING--HYDRA NOSTALGICS AND THEIR OPPOSITION.
WE THOUGHT THERE MIGHT BE TROUBLE.
BUT WE NEVER EXPECTED THIS.

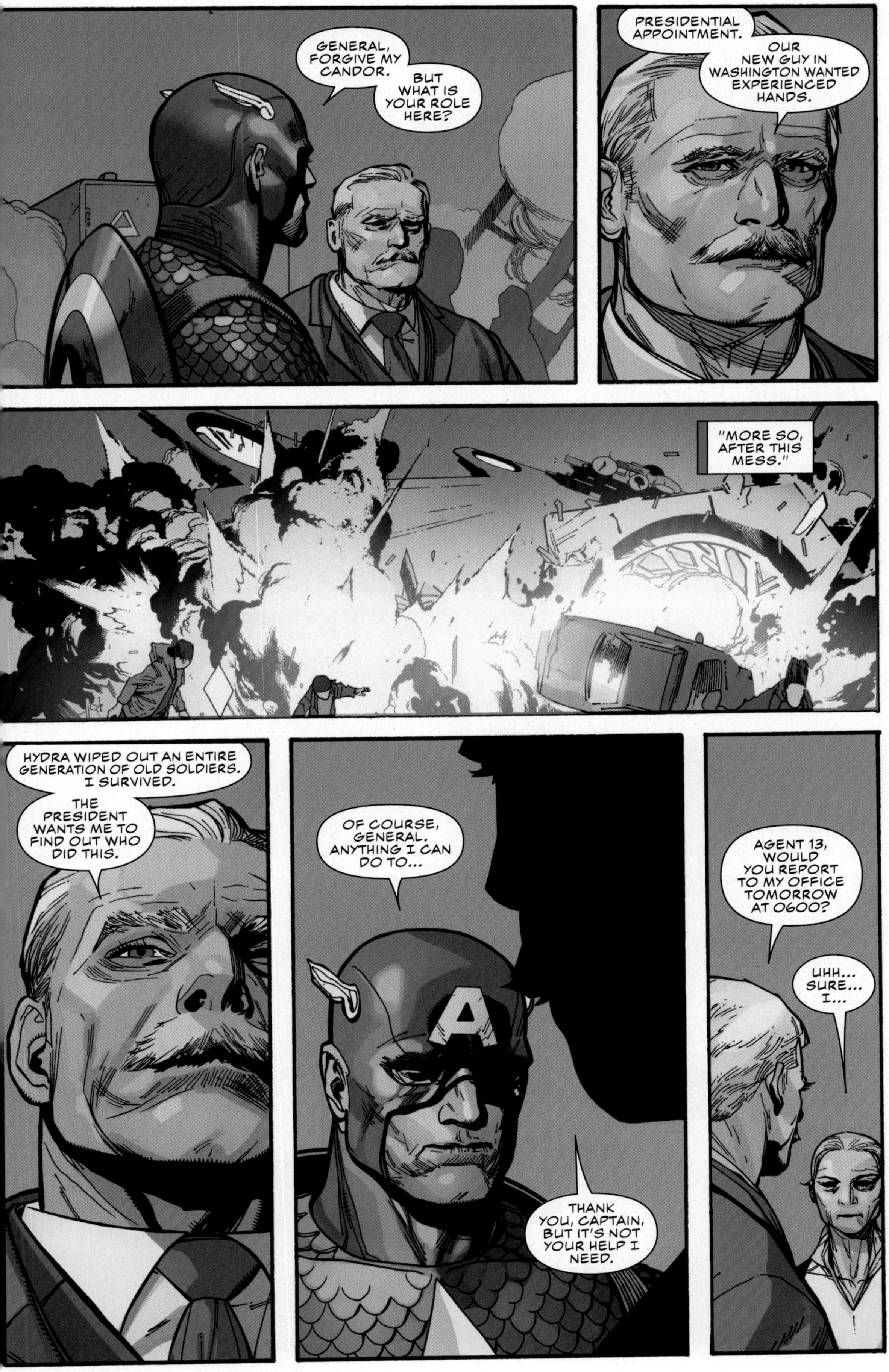
GENERAL, FORGIVE MY CANDOR.
BUT WHAT IS YOUR ROLE HERE?
PRESIDENTIAL APPOINTMENT.
OUR NEW GUY IN WASHINGTON WANTED EXPERIENCED HANDS.
"MORE SO, AFTER THIS MESS."
HYDRA WIPED OUT AN ENTIRE GENERATION OF OLD SOLDIERS. I SURVIVED.
THE PRESIDENT WANTS ME TO FIND OUT WHO DID THIS.
OF COURSE, GENERAL. ANYTHING I CAN DO TO...
THANK YOU, CAPTAIN, BUT IT'S NOT YOUR HELP I NEED.
AGENT 13, WOULD YOU REPORT TO MY OFFICE TOMORROW AT 0600?
UHH... SURE... I...

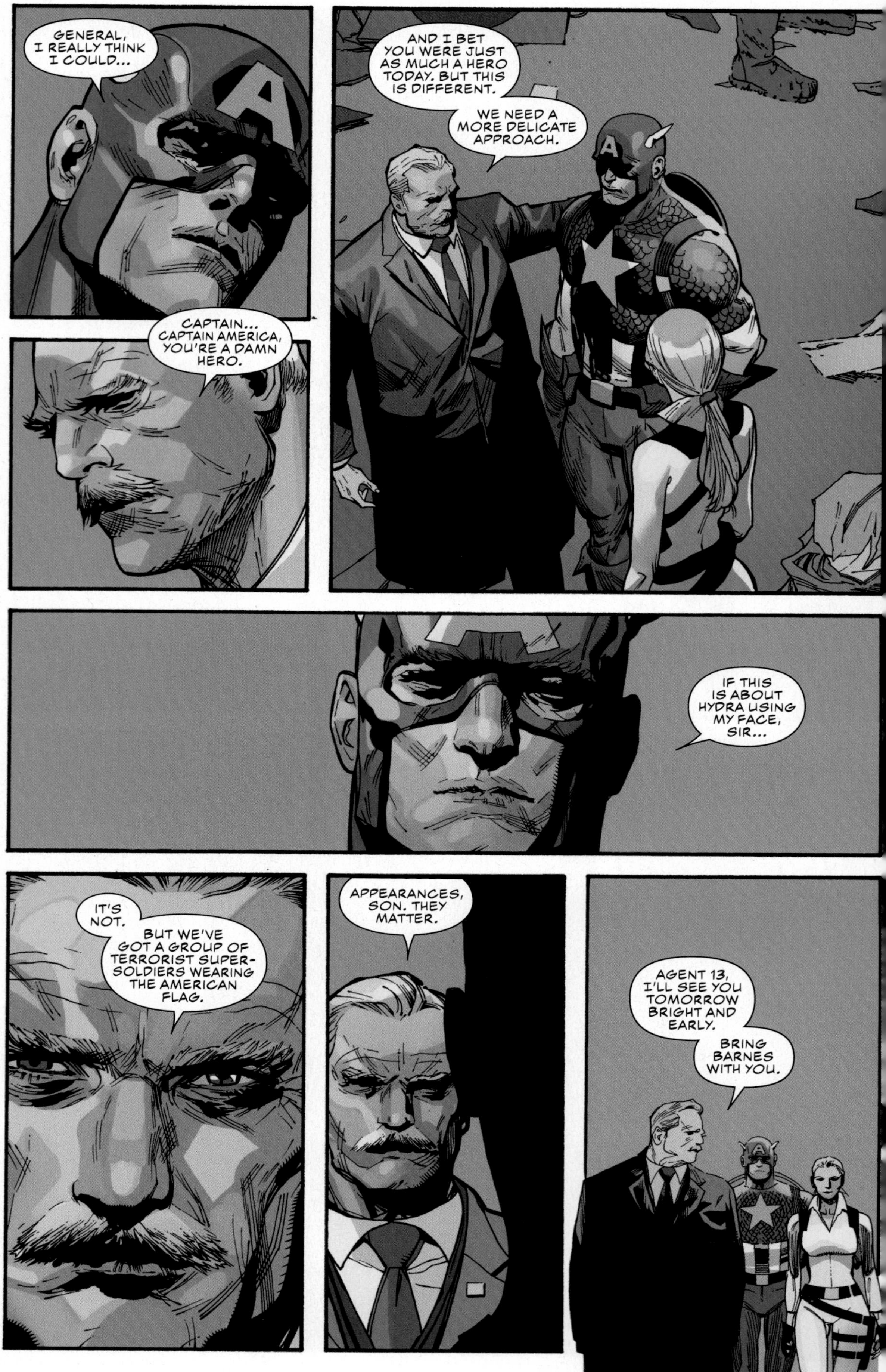
GENERAL, I REALLY THINK I COULD...
CAPTAIN... CAPTAIN AMERICA, YOU'RE A DAMN HERO.
AND I BET YOU WERE JUST AS MUCH A HERO TODAY. BUT THIS IS DIFFERENT.
WE NEED A MORE DELICATE APPROACH.
IF THIS IS ABOUT HYDRA USING MY FACE, SIR...
IT'S NOT.
BUT WE'VE GOT A GROUP OF TERRORIST SUPER-SOLDIERS WEARING THE AMERICAN FLAG.
APPEARANCES, SON. THEY MATTER.
AGENT 13, I'LL SEE YOU TOMORROW BRIGHT AND EARLY.
BRING BARNES WITH YOU.

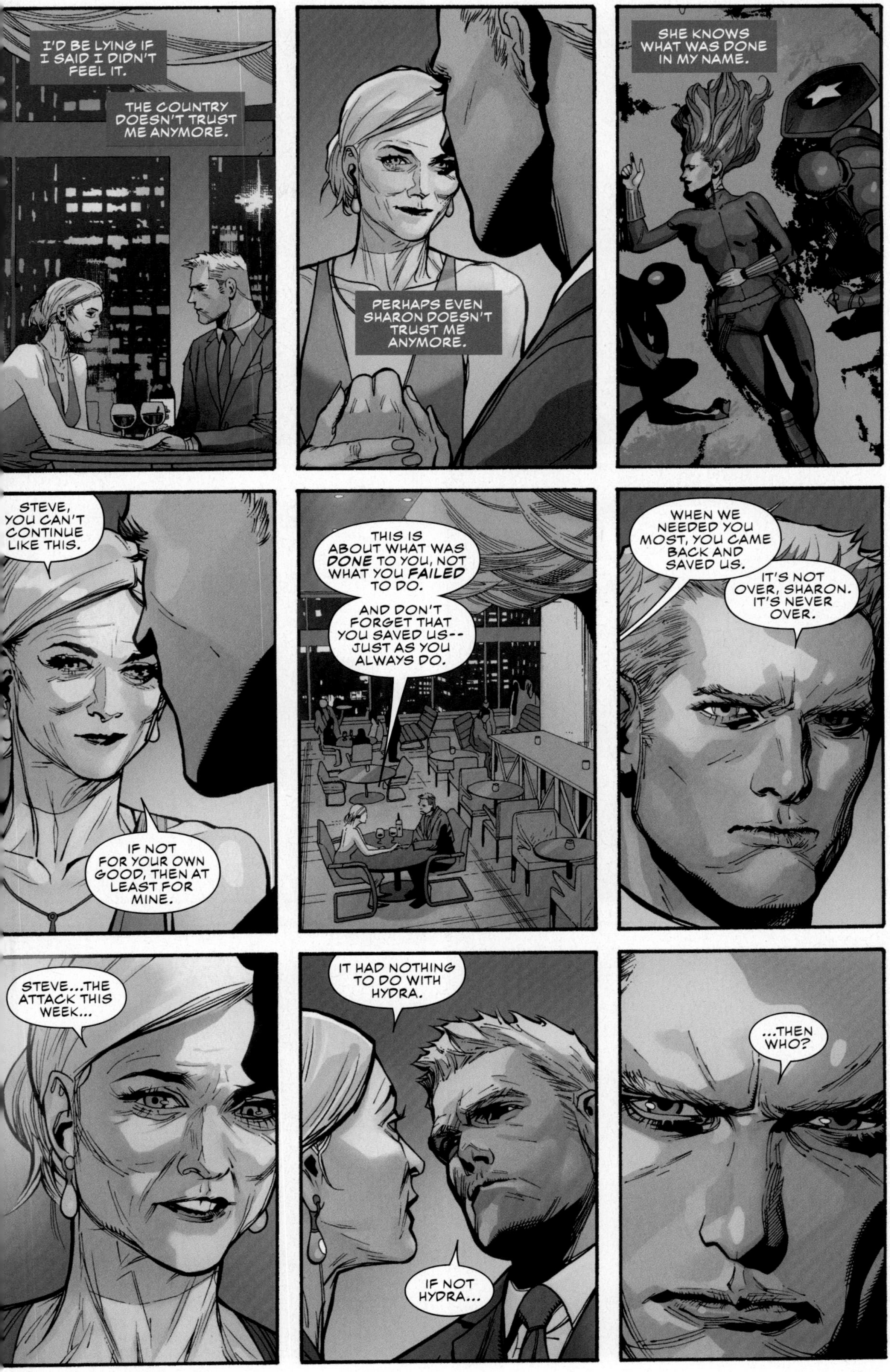
I'D BE LYING IF I SAID I DIDN'T FEEL IT.
THE COUNTRY DOESN'T TRUST ME ANYMORE.
PERHAPS EVEN SHARON DOESN'T TRUST ME ANYMORE.
SHE KNOWS WHAT WAS DONE IN MY NAME.
STEVE, YOU CAN'T CONTINUE LIKE THIS.
IF NOT FOR YOUR OWN GOOD, THEN AT LEAST FOR MINE.
THIS IS ABOUT WHAT WAS DONE TO YOU, NOT WHAT YOU FAILED TO DO.
AND DON'T FORGET THAT YOU SAVED US--JUST AS YOU ALWAYS DO.
WHEN WE NEEDED YOU MOST, YOU CAME BACK AND SAVED US.
IT'S NOT OVER, SHARON. IT'S NEVER OVER.
STEVE...THE ATTACK THIS WEEK...
IT HAD NOTHING TO DO WITH HYDRA.
IF NOT HYDRA...
...THEN WHO?

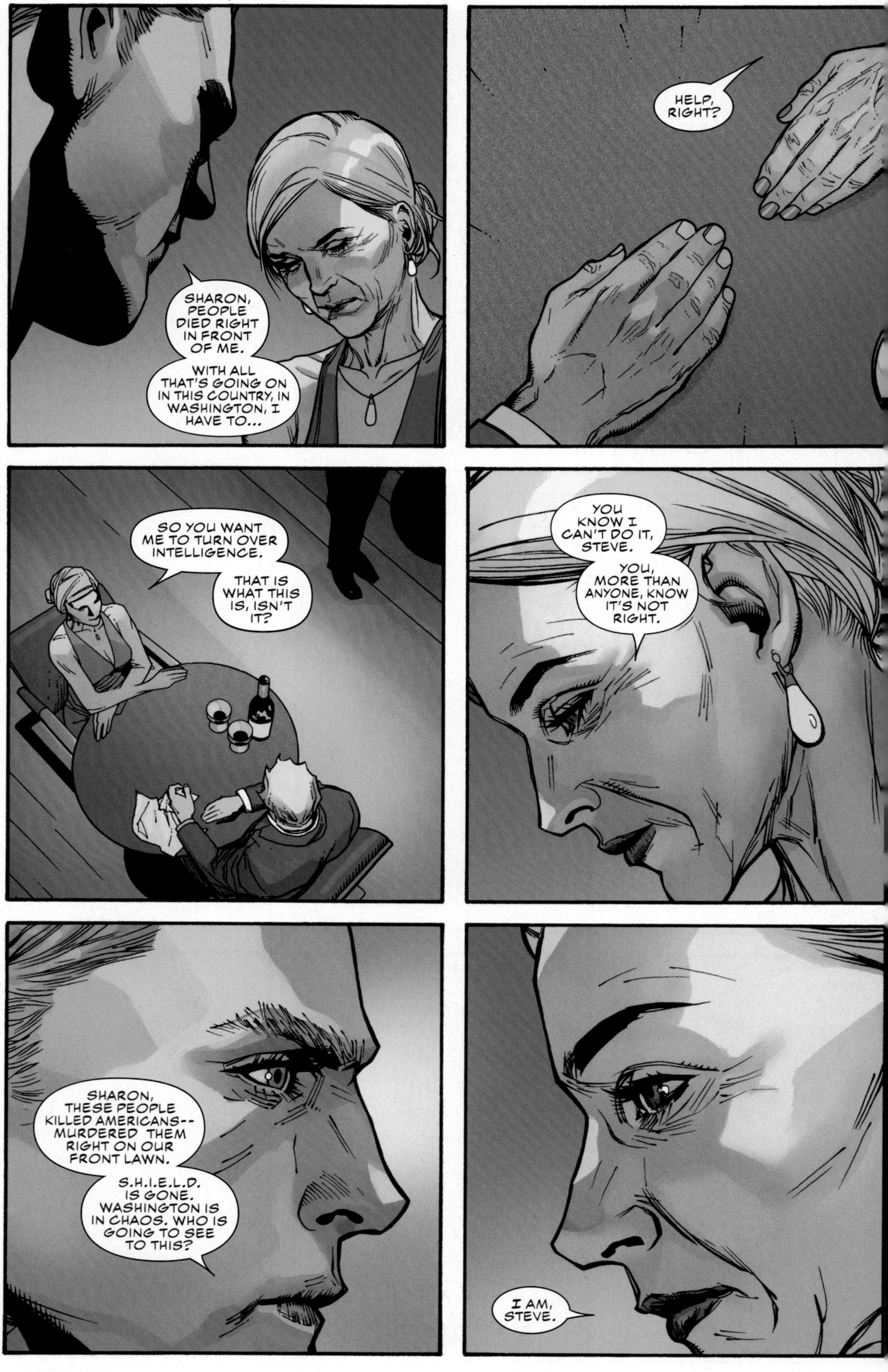
SHARON, PEOPLE DIED RIGHT IN FRONT OF ME.
WITH ALL THAT'S GOING ON IN THIS COUNTRY, IN WASHINGTON, I HAVE TO...
HELP, RIGHT?
SO YOU WANT ME TO TURN OVER INTELLIGENCE.
THAT IS WHAT THIS IS, ISN'T IT?
YOU KNOW I CAN'T DO IT, STEVE.
YOU, MORE THAN ANYONE, KNOW IT'S NOT RIGHT.
SHARON, THESE PEOPLE KILLED AMERICANS-- MURDERED THEM RIGHT ON OUR FRONT LAWN.
S.H.I.E.L.D. IS GONE. WASHINGTON IS IN CHAOS. WHO IS GOING TO SEE TO THIS?
I AM, STEVE.

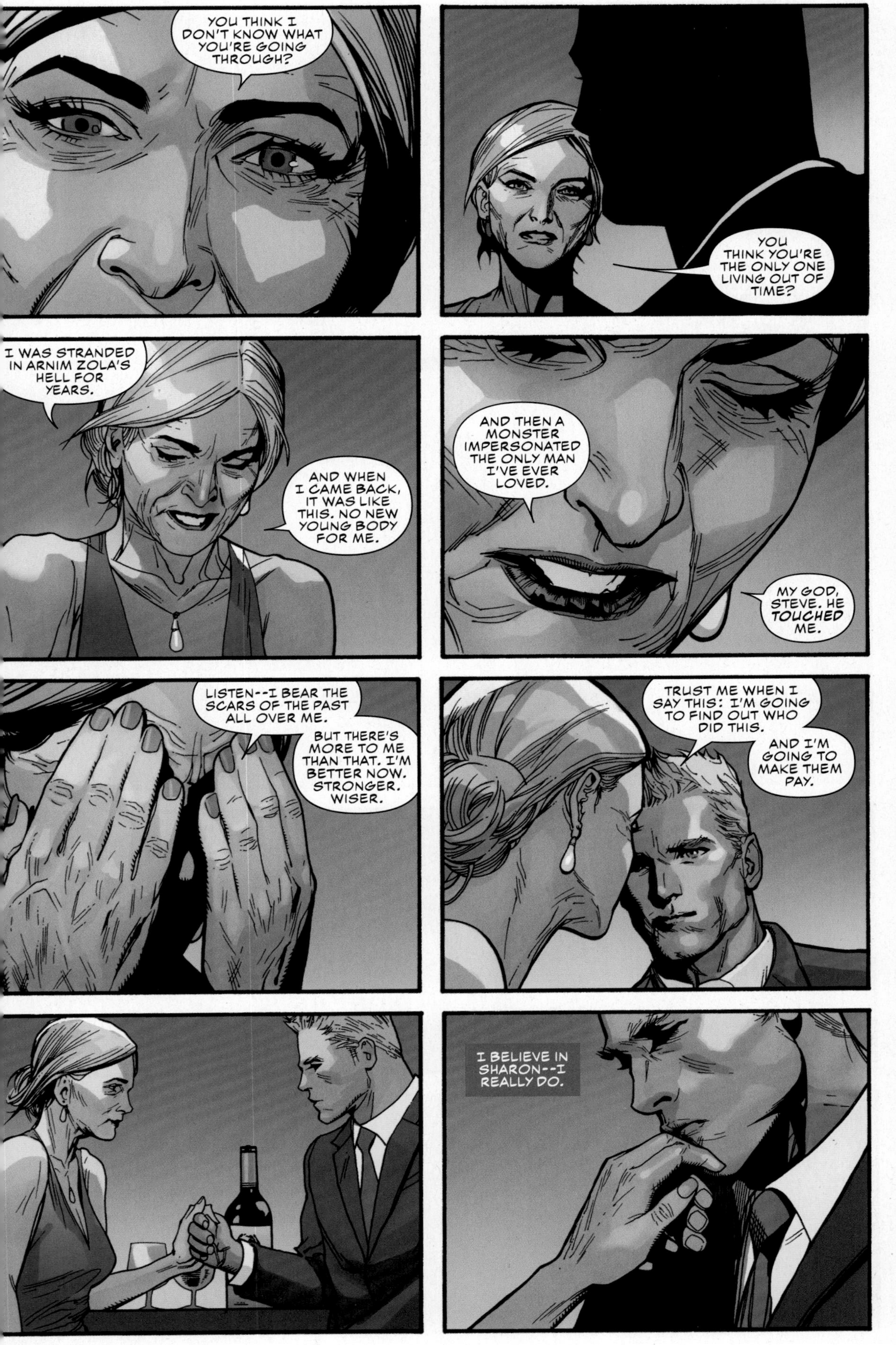
YOU THINK I DON'T KNOW WHAT YOU'RE GOING THROUGH?
YOU THINK YOU'RE THE ONLY ONE LIVING OUT OF TIME?
I WAS STRANDED IN ARNIM ZOLA'S HELL FOR YEARS.
AND WHEN I CAME BACK, IT WAS LIKE THIS. NO NEW YOUNG BODY FOR ME.
AND THEN A MONSTER IMPERSONATED THE ONLY MAN I'VE EVER LOVED.
MY GOD, STEVE. HE TOUCHED ME.
LISTEN--I BEAR THE SCARS OF THE PAST ALL OVER ME.
BUT THERE'S MORE TO ME THAN THAT. I'M BETTER NOW. STRONGER. WISER.
TRUST ME WHEN I SAY THIS: I'M GOING TO FIND OUT WHO DID THIS.
AND I'M GOING TO MAKE THEM PAY.
I BELIEVE IN SHARON--I REALLY DO.

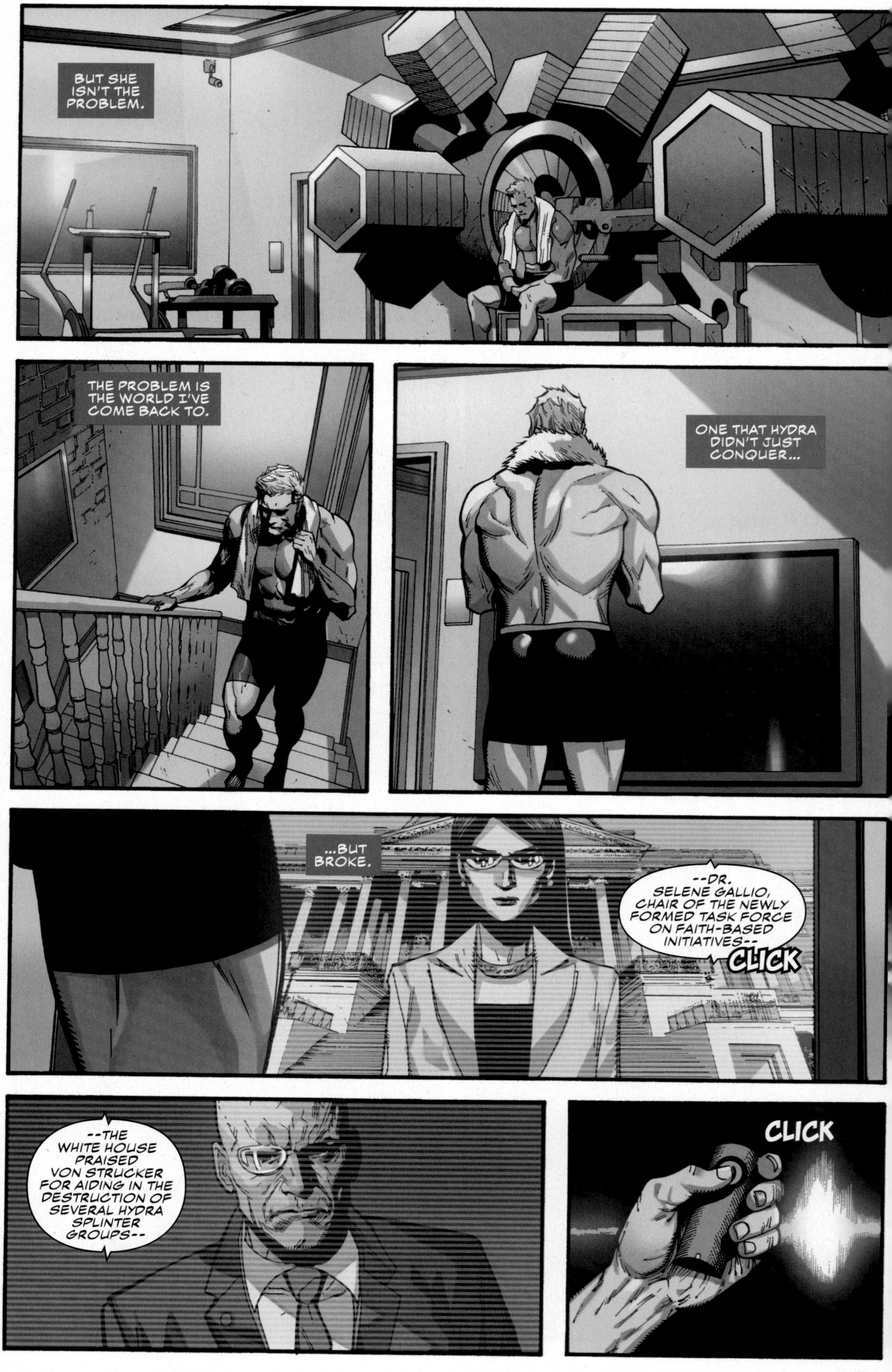
BUT SHE ISN'T THE PROBLEM.
THE PROBLEM IS THE WORLD I'VE COME BACK TO.
ONE THAT HYDRA DIDN'T JUST CONQUER...
...BUT BROKE.
--DR. SELENE GALLIO, CHAIR OF THE NEWLY FORMED TASK FORCE ON FAITH-BASED INITIATIVES--
CLICK
--THE WHITE HOUSE PRAISED VON STRUCKER FOR AIDING IN THE DESTRUCTION OF SEVERAL HYDRA SPLINTER GROUPS--
CLICK

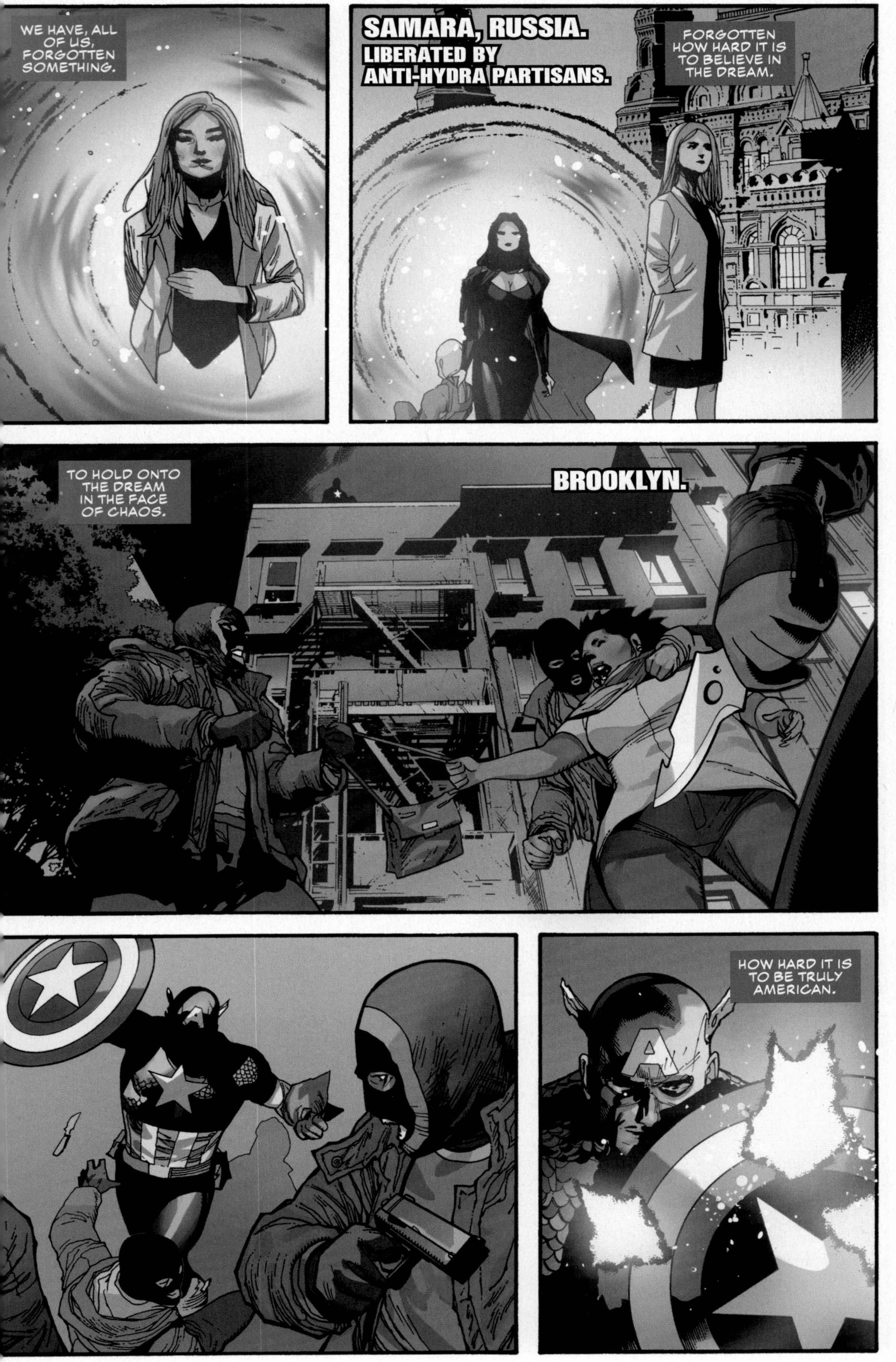
WE HAVE, ALL OF US, FORGOTTEN SOMETHING.
SAMARA, RUSSIA. LIBERATED BY ANTI-HYDRA PARTISANS.
FORGOTTEN HOW HARD IT IS TO BELIEVE IN THE DREAM.
TO HOLD ONTO THE DREAM IN THE FACE OF CHAOS.
BROOKLYN.
HOW HARD IT IS TO BE TRULY AMERICAN.

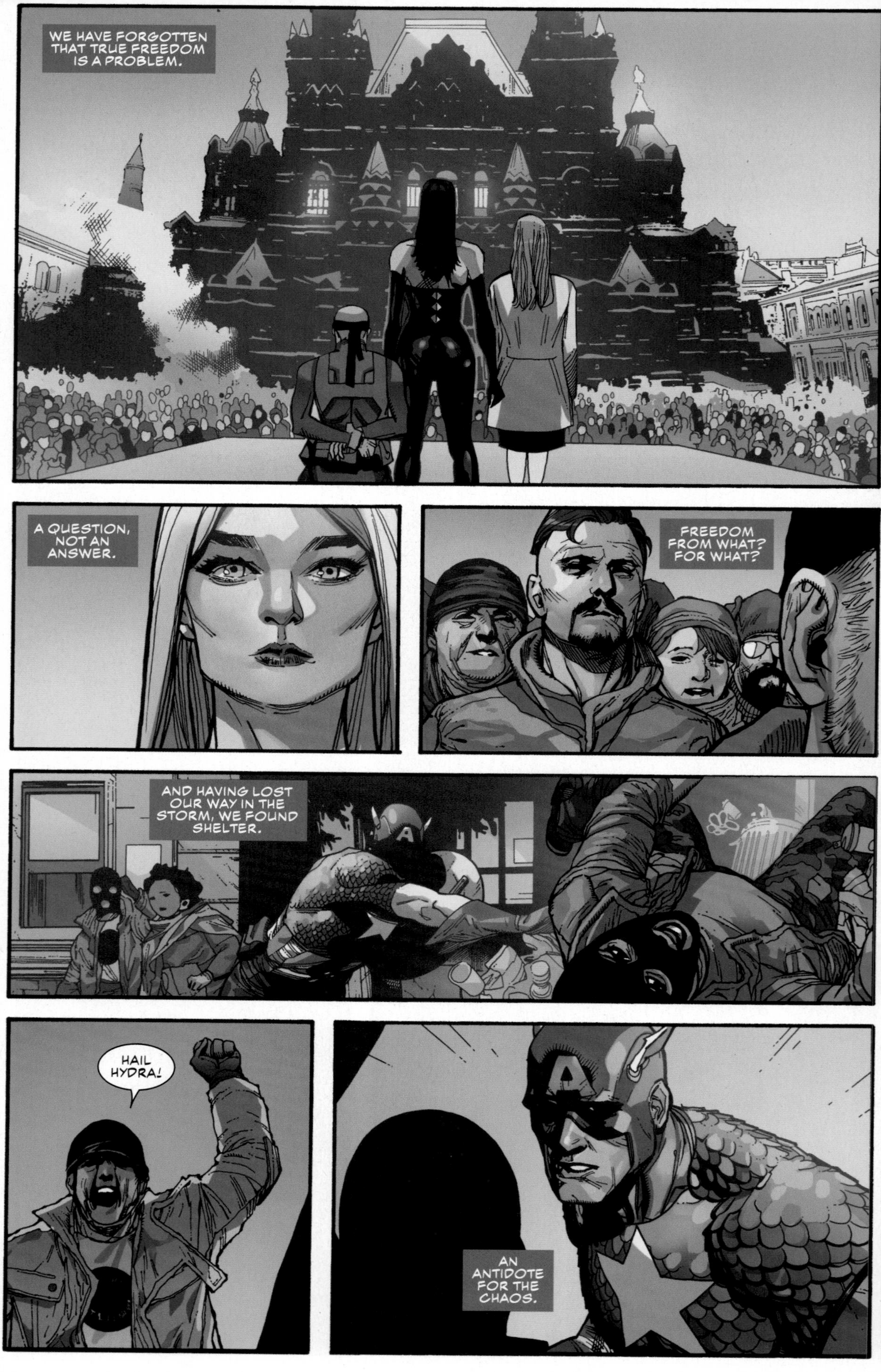
WE HAVE FORGOTTEN THAT TRUE FREEDOM IS A PROBLEM.
A QUESTION, NOT AN ANSWER.
FREEDOM FROM WHAT? FOR WHAT?
AND HAVING LOST OUR WAY IN THE STORM, WE FOUND SHELTER.
HAIL HYDRA!
AN ANTIDOTE FOR THE CHAOS.

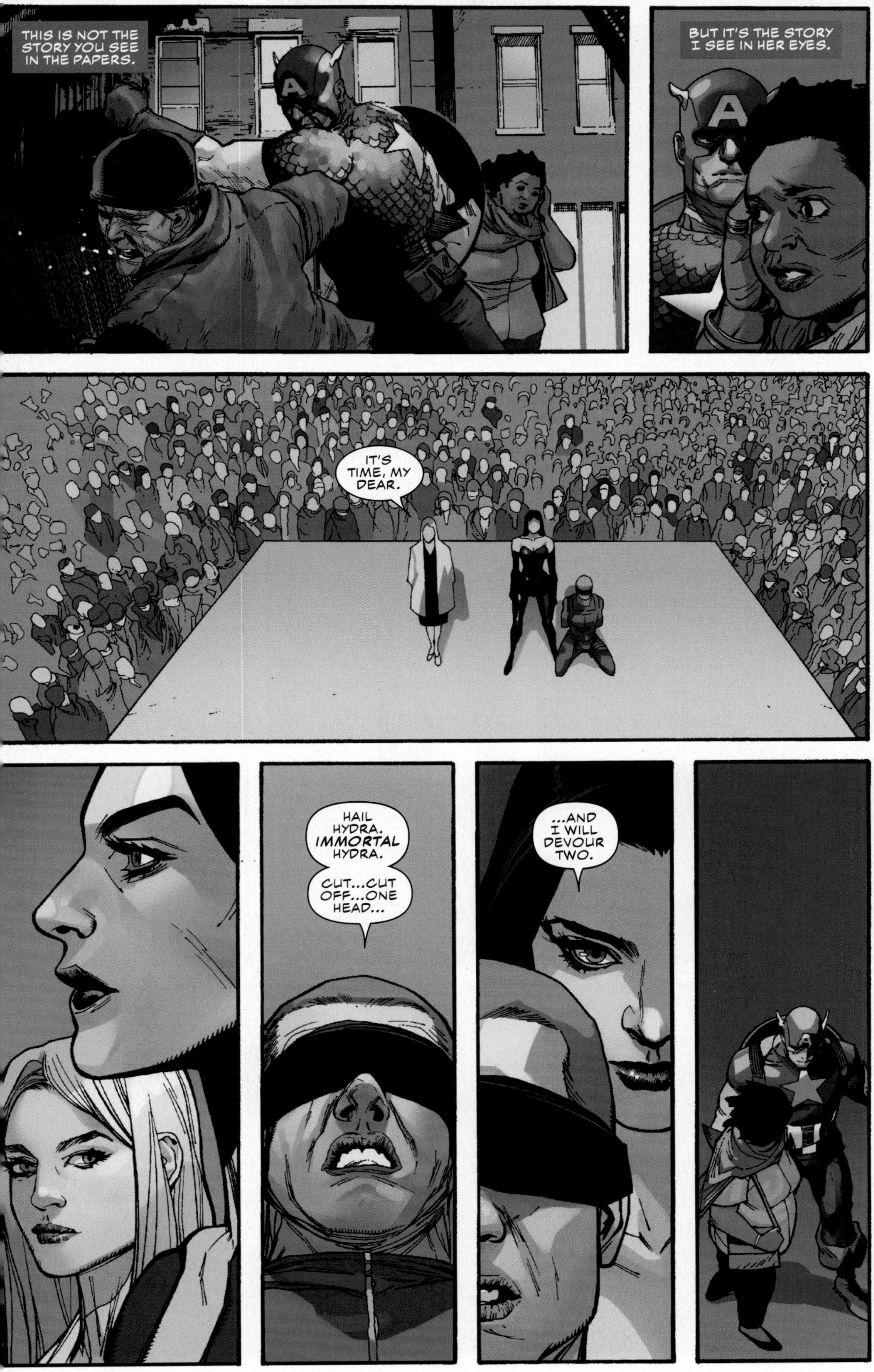
THIS IS NOT THE STORY YOU SEE IN THE PAPERS.
BUT IT'S THE STORY I SEE IN HER EYES.
IT'S TIME, MY DEAR.
HAIL HYDRA. IMMORTAL HYDRA.
CUT...CUT OFF...ONE HEAD...
...AND I WILL DEVOUR TWO.

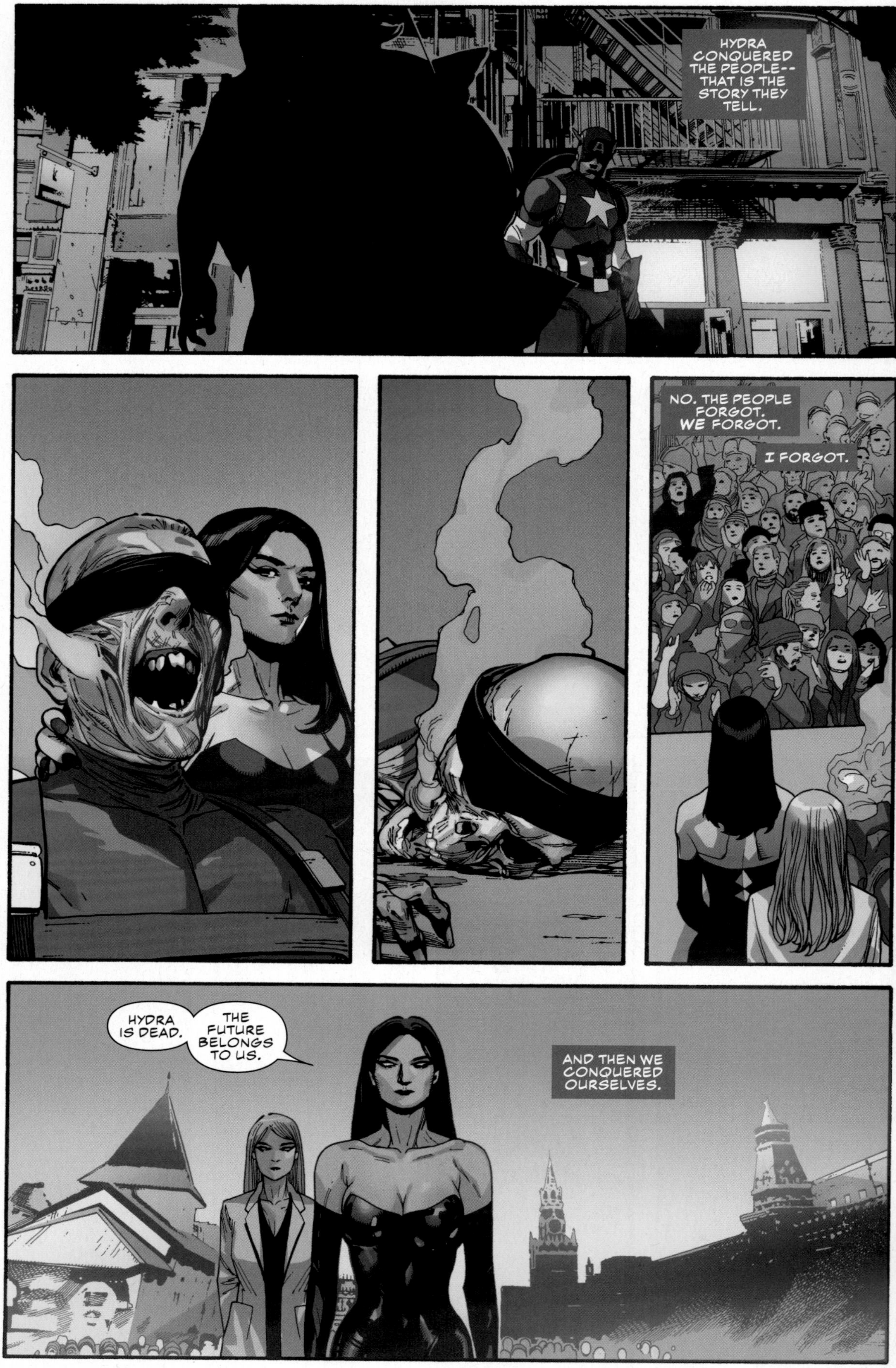
HYDRA CONQUERED THE PEOPLE-- THAT IS THE STORY THEY TELL.
NO. THE PEOPLE FORGOT. WE FORGOT.
I FORGOT.
HYDRA IS DEAD.
THE FUTURE BELONGS TO US.
AND THEN WE CONQUERED OURSELVES.

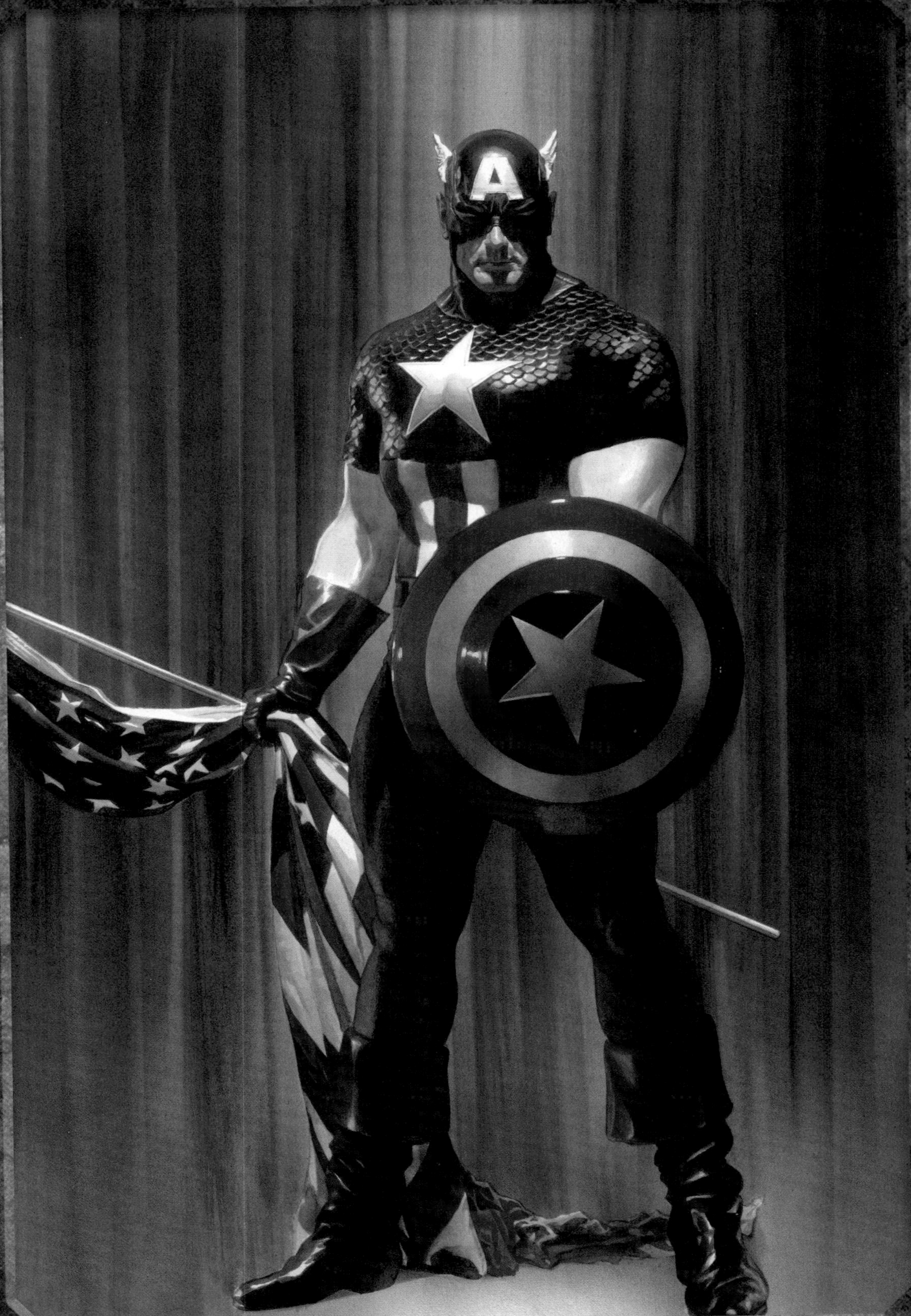

2

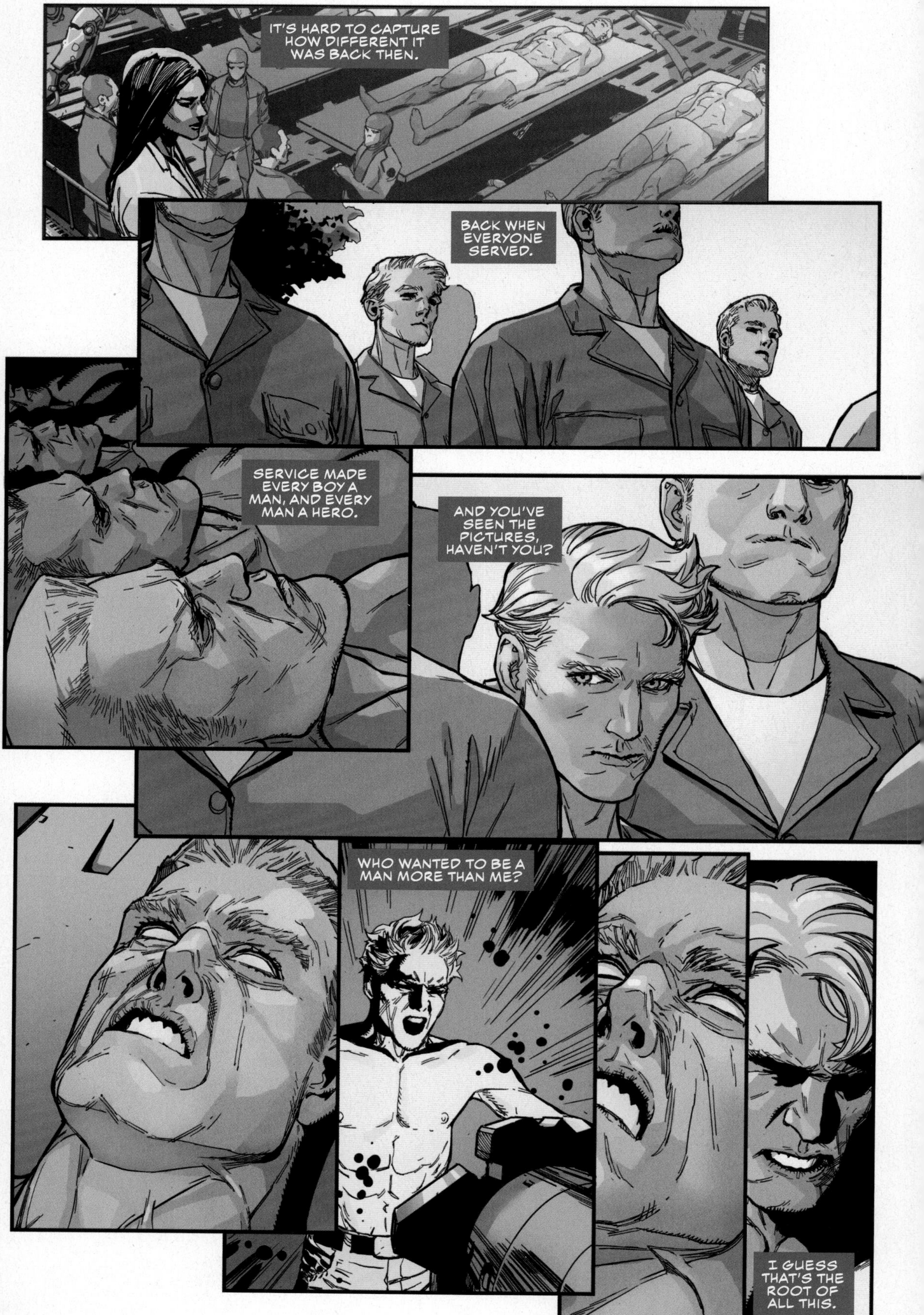

IT'S HARD TO CAPTURE HOW DIFFERENT IT WAS BACK THEN.
BACK WHEN EVERYONE SERVED.
SERVICE MADE EVERY BOY A MAN, AND EVERY MAN A HERO.
AND YOU'VE SEEN THE PICTURES, HAVEN'T YOU?
WHO WANTED TO BE A MAN MORE THAN ME?
I GUESS THAT'S THE ROOT OF ALL THIS.

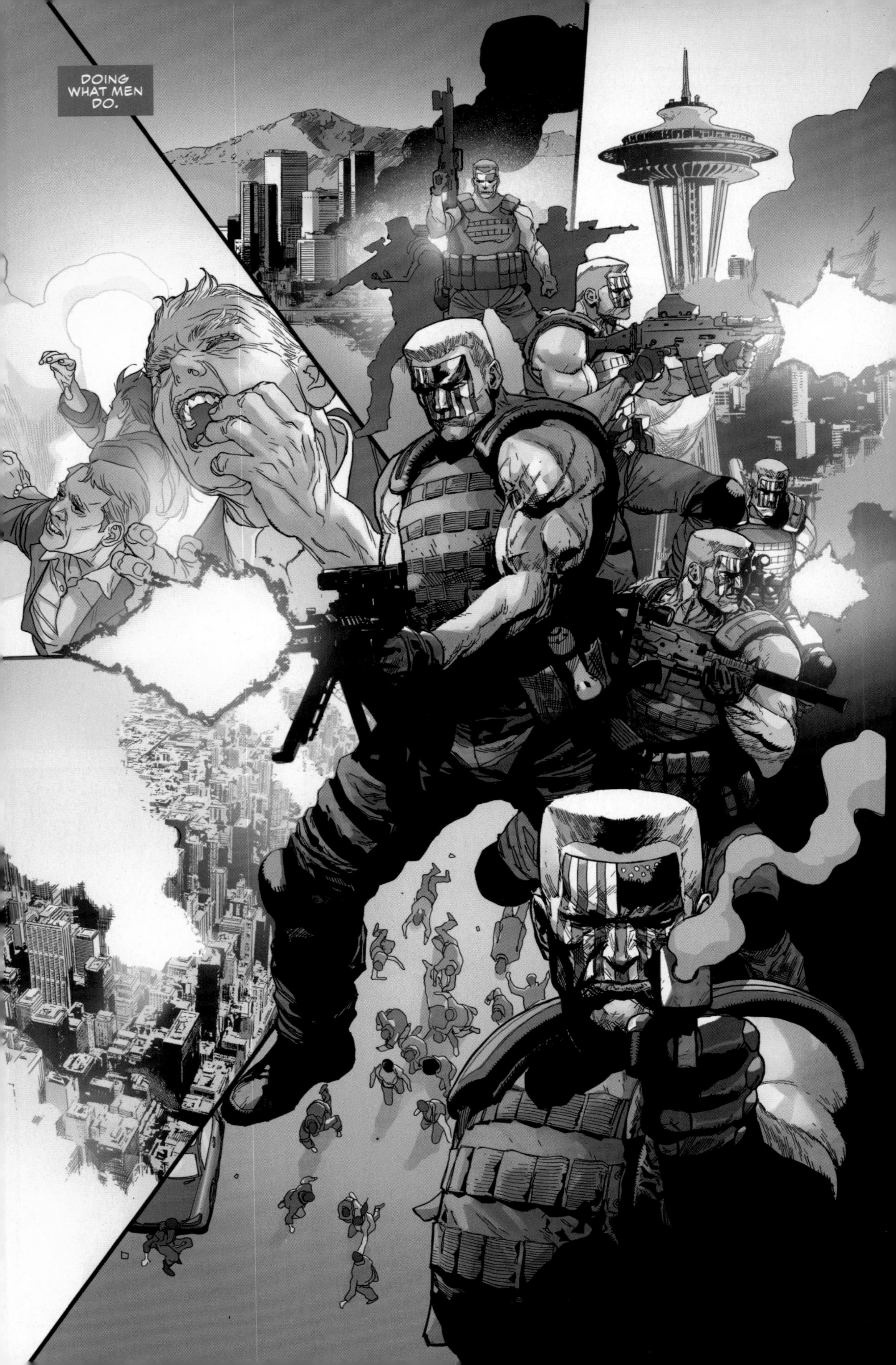
DOING WHAT MEN DO.

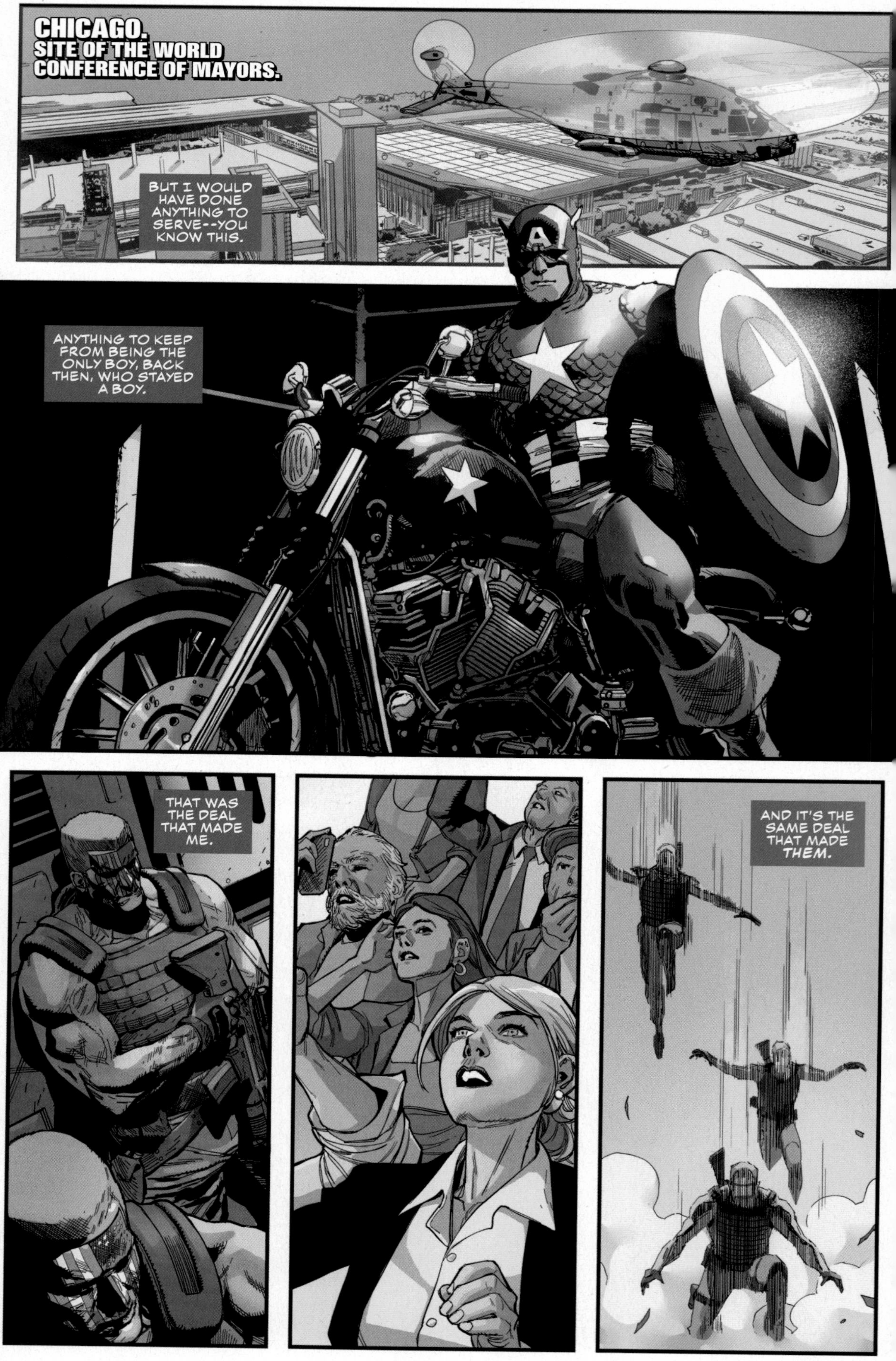
CHICAGO.
SITE OF THE WORLD CONFERENCE OF MAYORS.
BUT I WOULD HAVE DONE ANYTHING TO SERVE--YOU KNOW THIS.
ANYTHING TO KEEP FROM BEING THE ONLY BOY, BACK THEN, WHO STAYED A BOY.
THAT WAS THE DEAL THAT MADE ME.
AND IT'S THE SAME DEAL THAT MADE THEM.

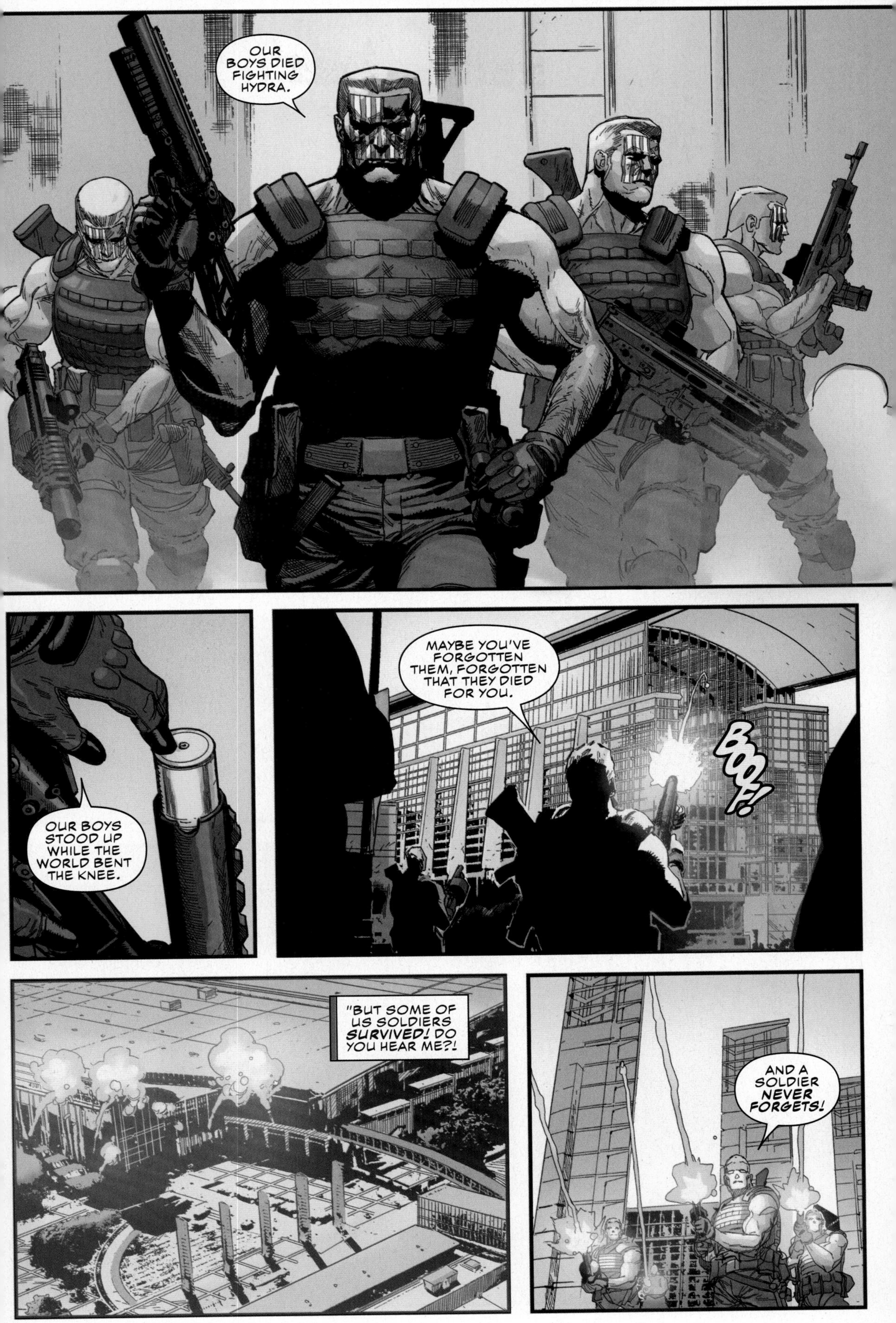
OUR BOYS DIED FIGHTING HYDRA.
OUR BOYS STOOD UP WHILE THE WORLD BENT THE KNEE.
MAYBE YOU'VE FORGOTTEN THEM, FORGOTTEN THAT THEY DIED FOR YOU.
BOOF!
"BUT SOME OF US SOLDIERS SURVIVED! DO YOU HEAR ME?!
AND A SOLDIER NEVER FORGETS!

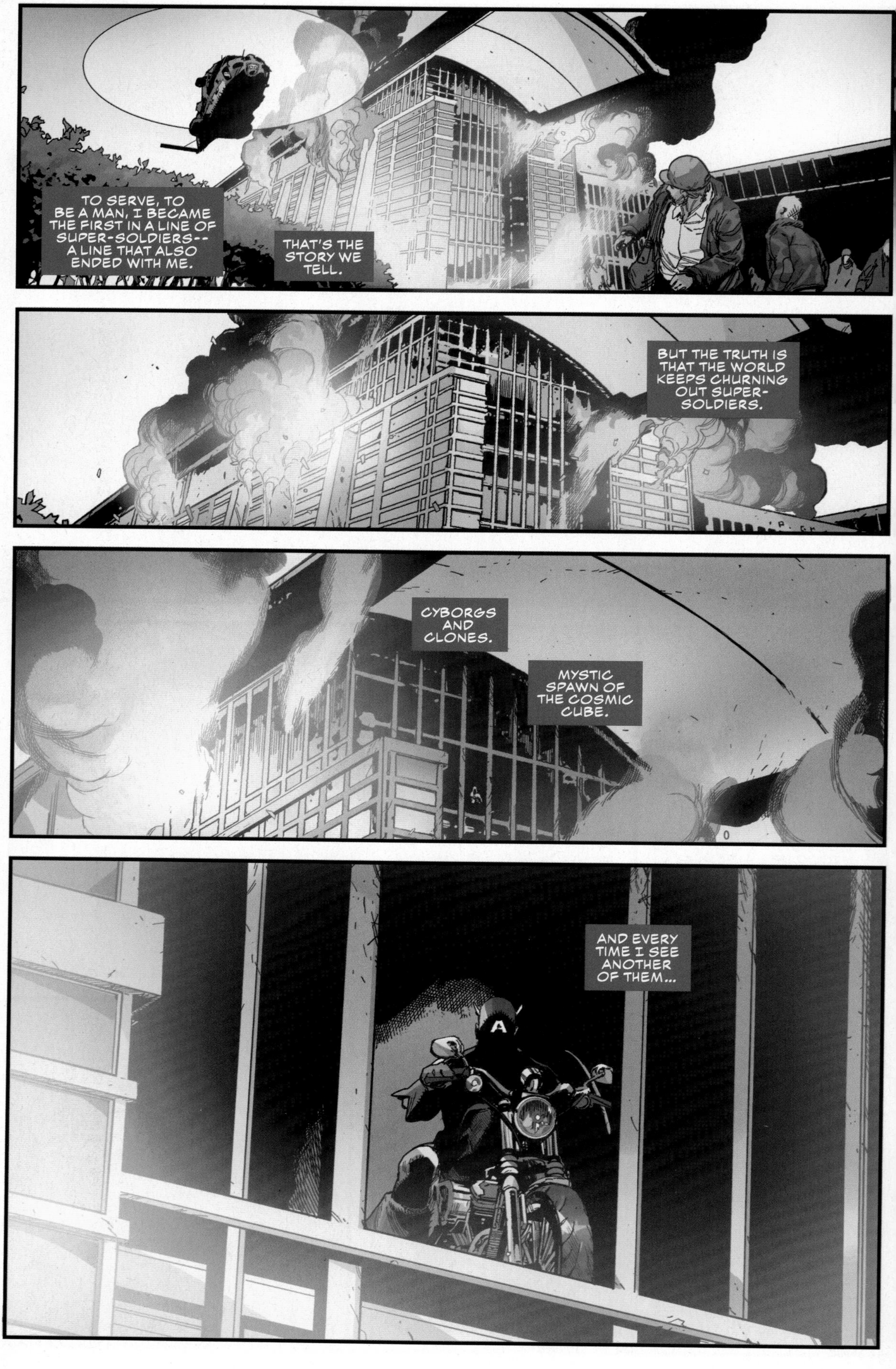

TO SERVE, TO BE A MAN, I BECAME THE FIRST IN A LINE OF SUPER-SOLDIERS-- A LINE THAT ALSO ENDED WITH ME.
THAT'S THE STORY WE TELL.
BUT THE TRUTH IS THAT THE WORLD KEEPS CHURNING OUT SUPER-SOLDIERS.
CYBORGS AND CLONES.
MYSTIC SPAWN OF THE COSMIC CUBE.
AND EVERY TIME I SEE ANOTHER OF THEM...

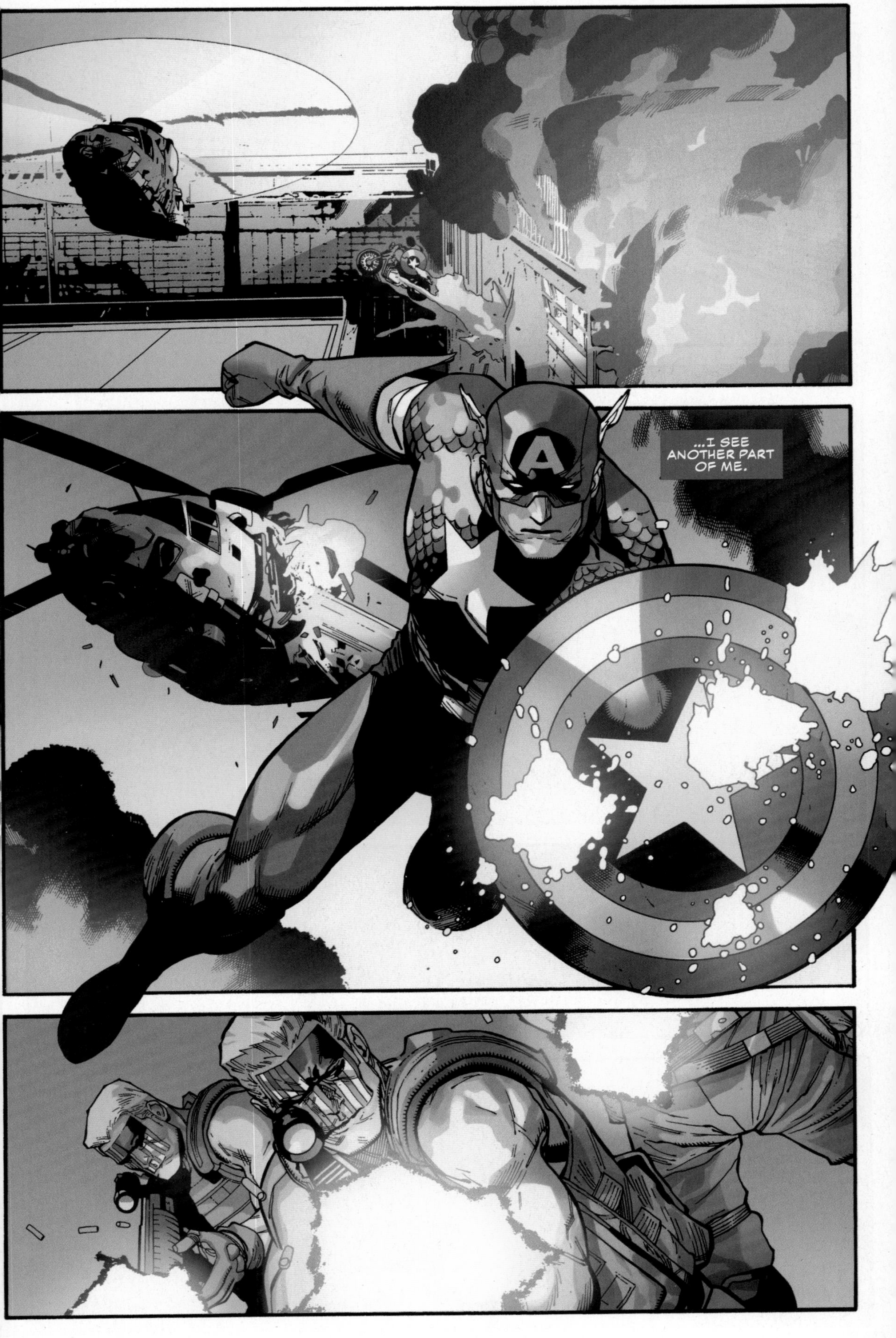
...I SEE
ANOTHER PART
OF ME.

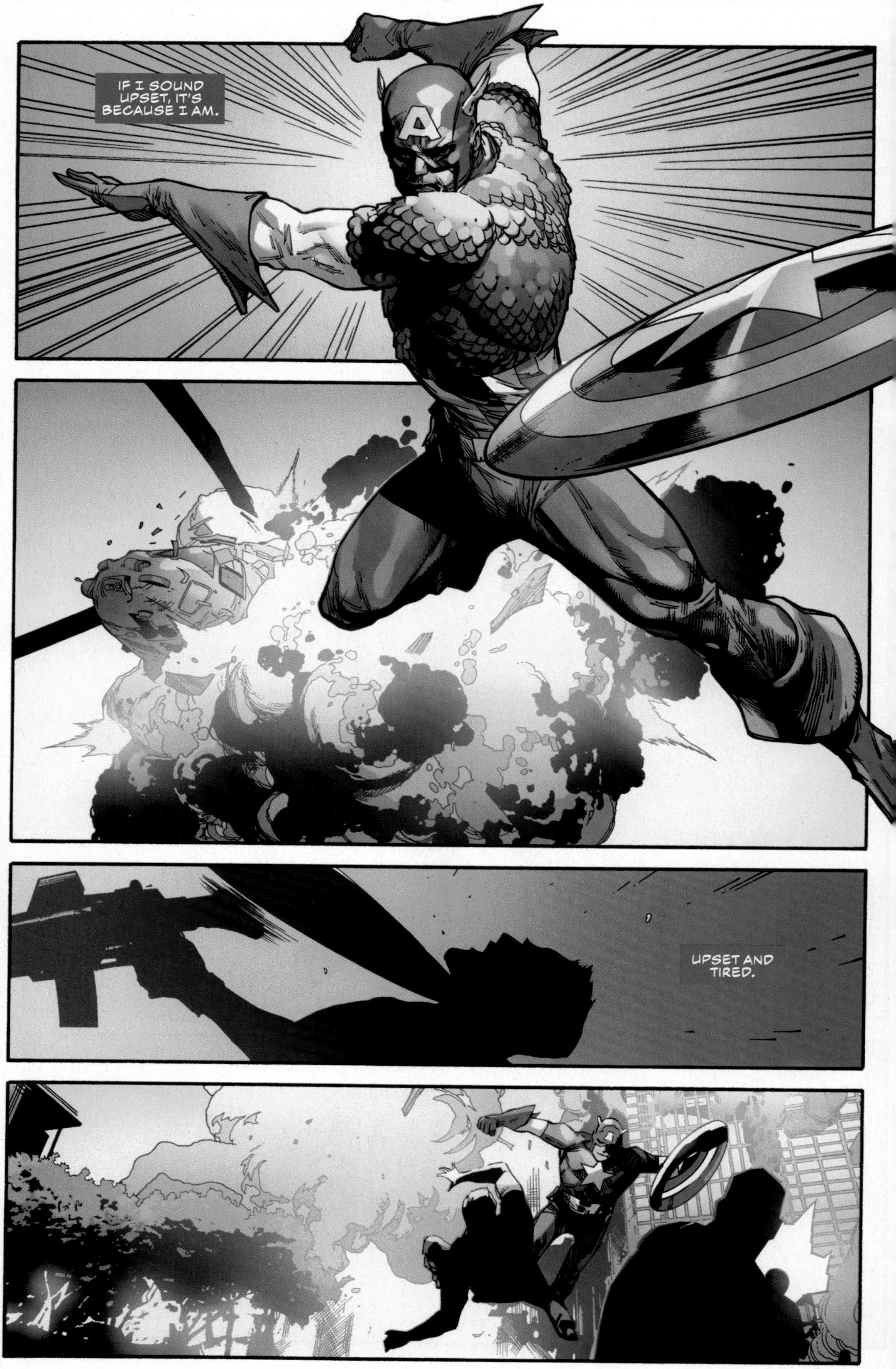
IF I SOUND UPSET, IT'S BECAUSE I AM.
UPSET AND TIRED.

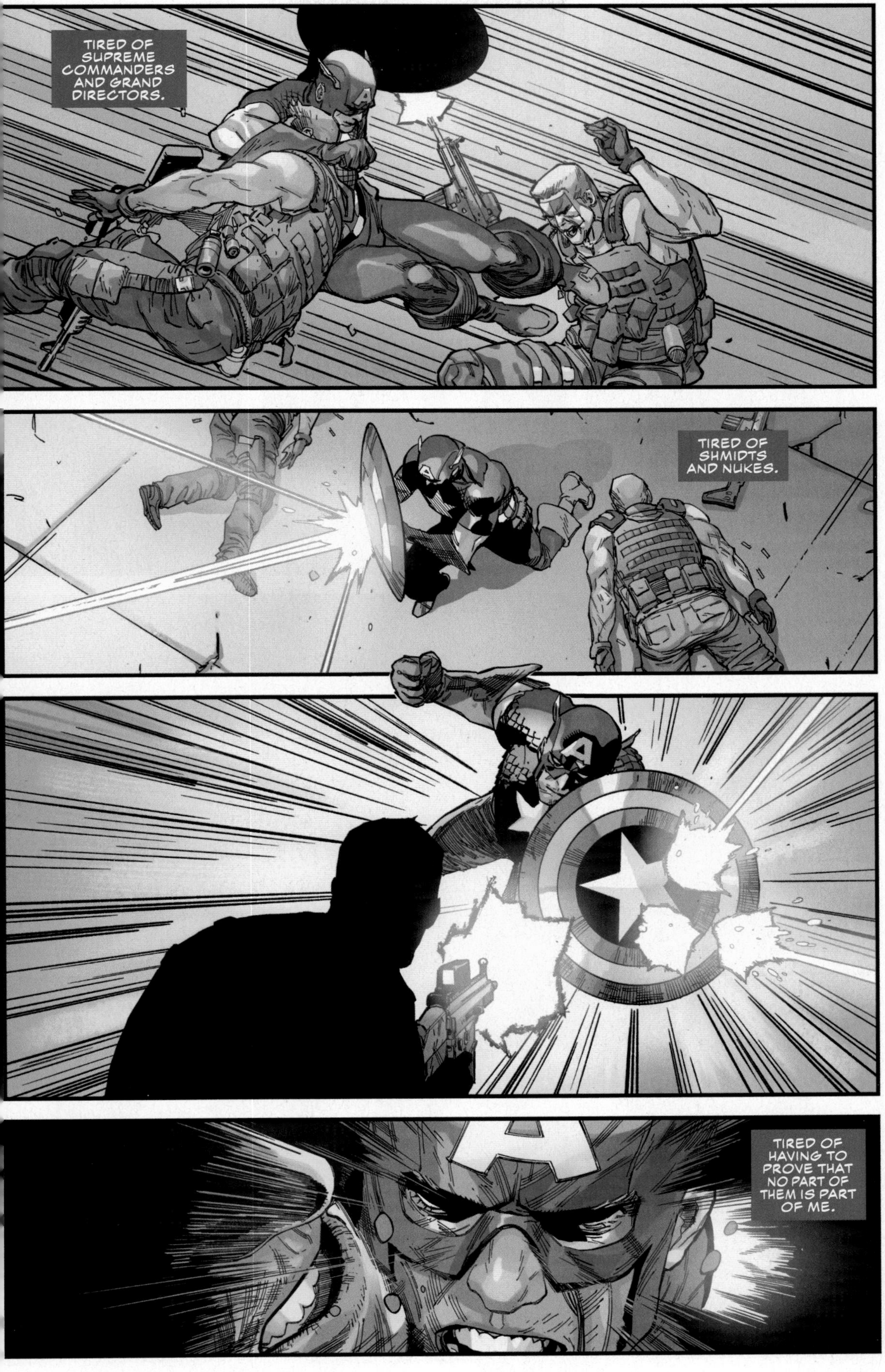
TIRED OF SUPREME COMMANDERS AND GRAND DIRECTORS.
TIRED OF SHMIDTS AND NUKES.
TIRED OF HAVING TO PROVE THAT NO PART OF THEM IS PART OF ME.

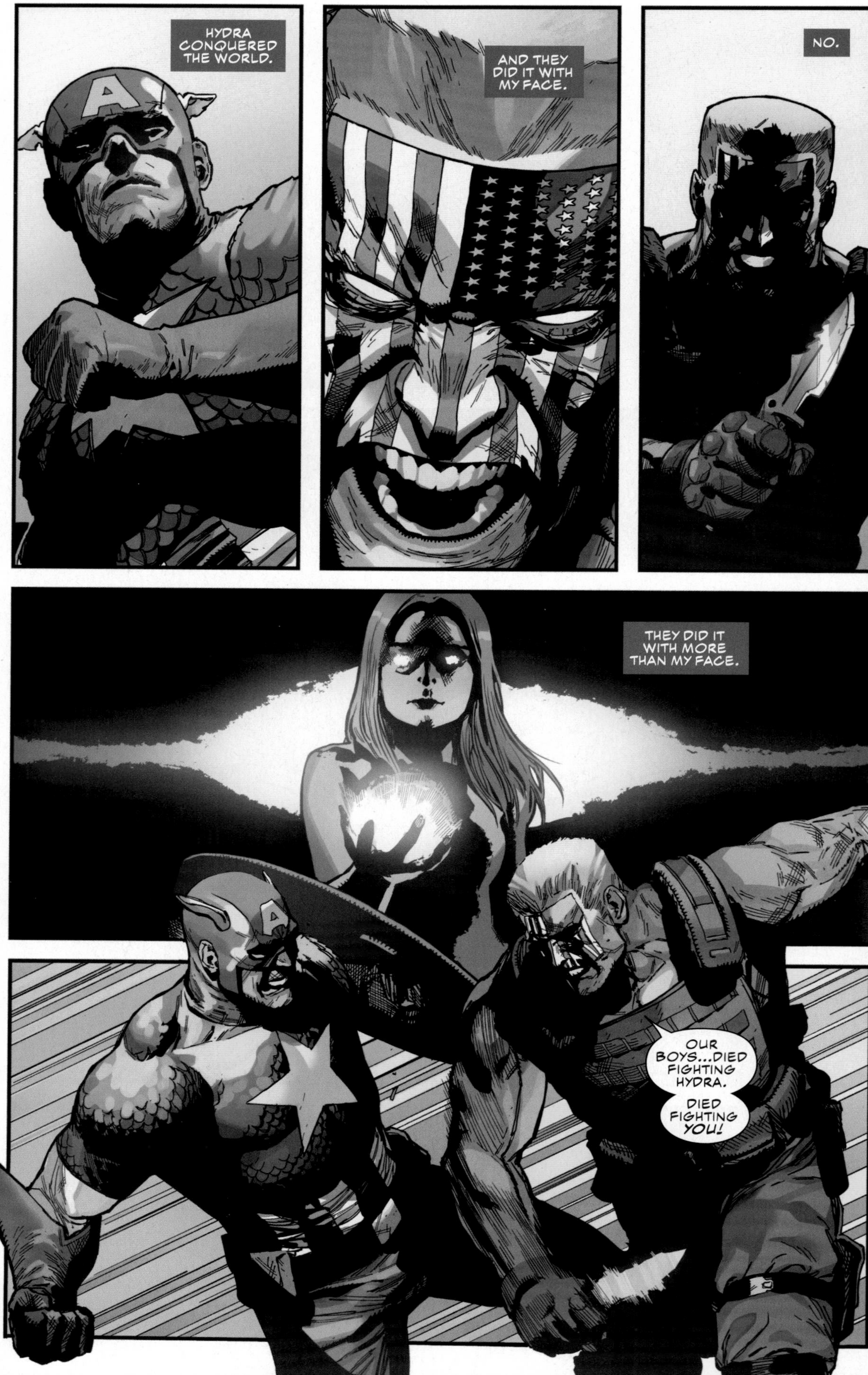
HYDRA CONQUERED THE WORLD.
AND THEY DID IT WITH MY FACE.
NO.
THEY DID IT WITH MORE THAN MY FACE.
OUR BOYS...DIED FIGHTING HYDRA.
DIED FIGHTING YOU!

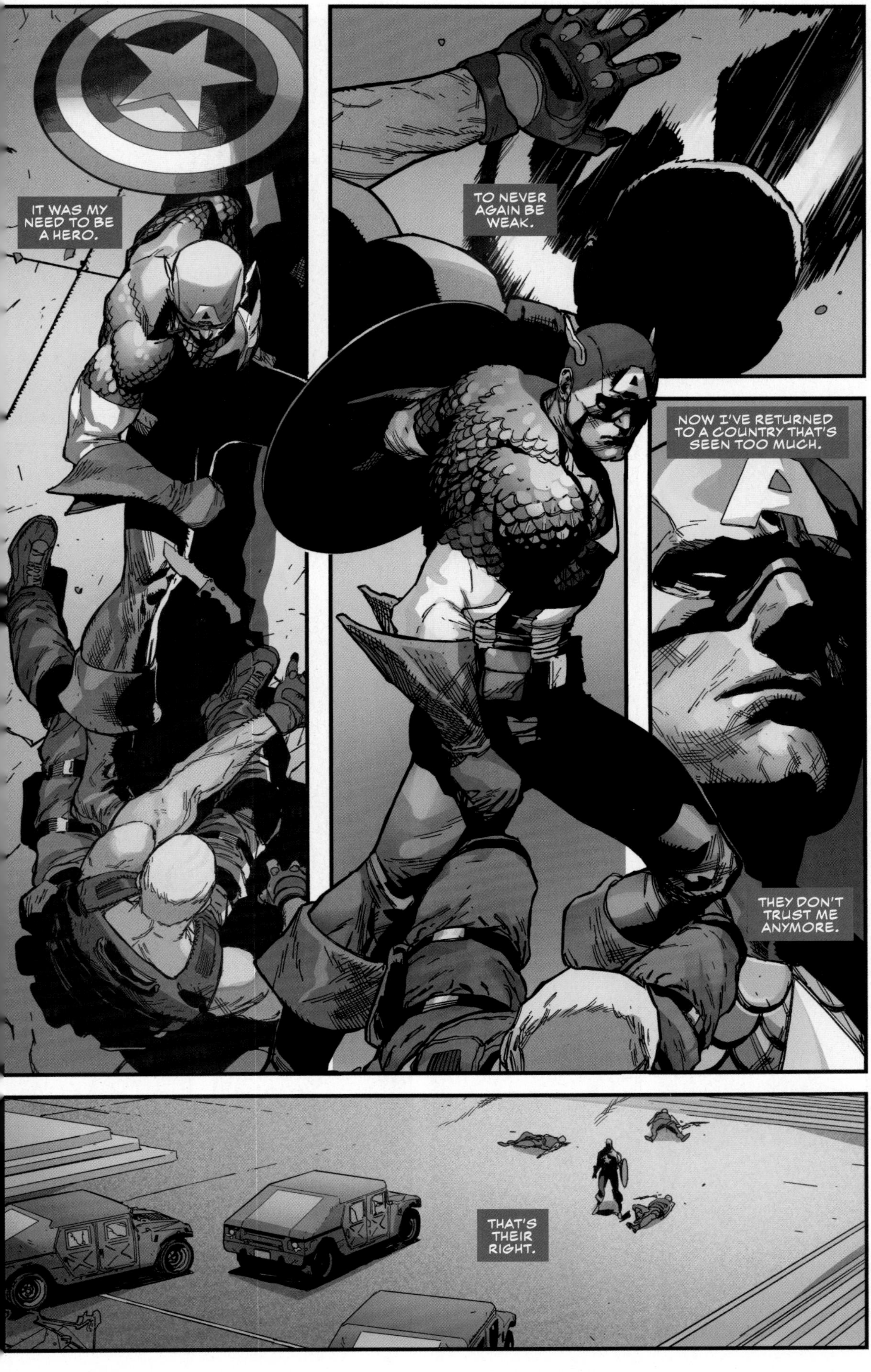
IT WAS MY NEED TO BE A HERO.
TO NEVER AGAIN BE WEAK.
NOW I'VE RETURNED TO A COUNTRY THAT'S SEEN TOO MUCH.
THEY DON'T TRUST ME ANYMORE.
THAT'S THEIR RIGHT.

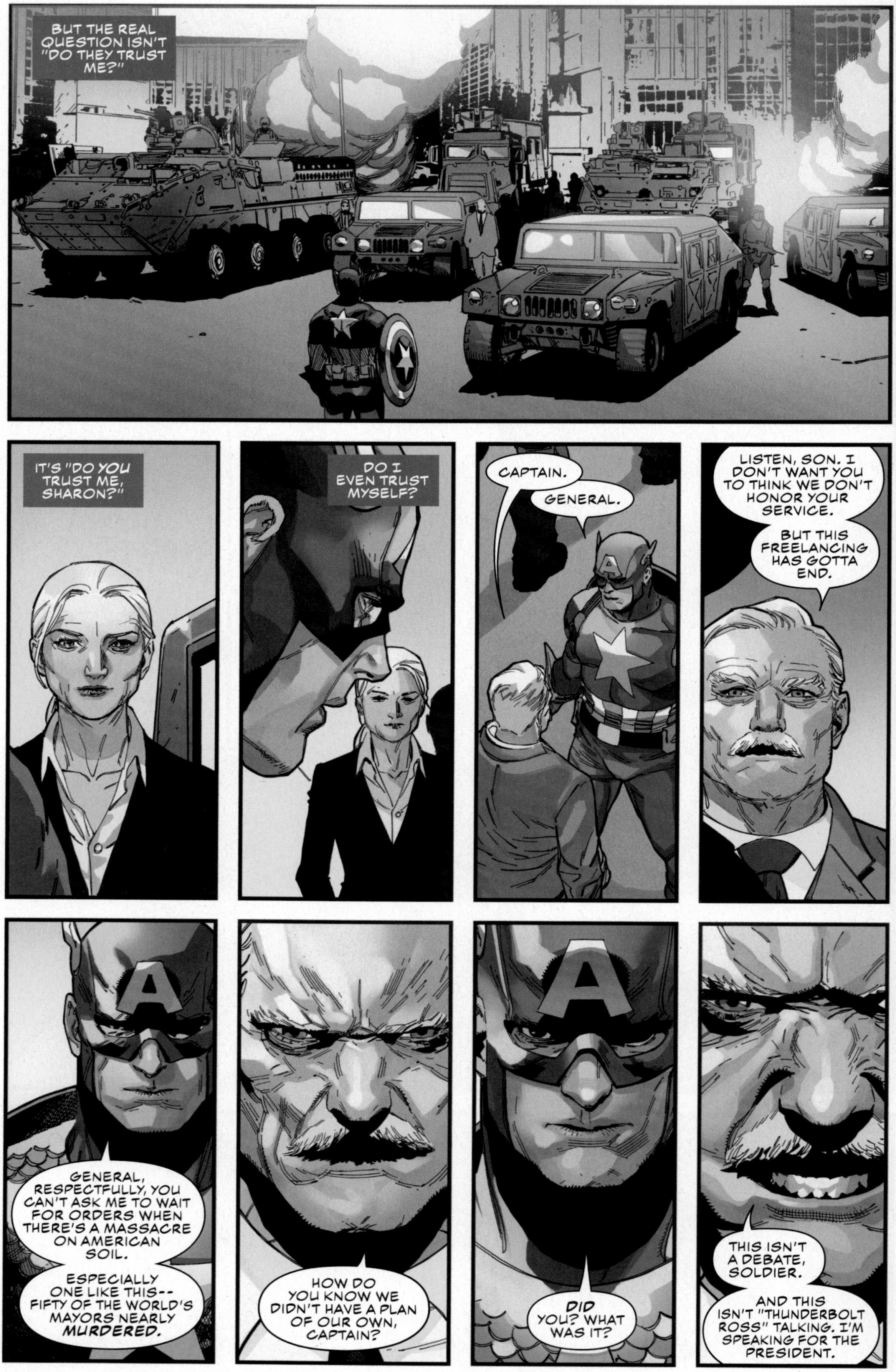
BUT THE REAL QUESTION ISN'T "DO THEY TRUST ME?"
IT'S "DO *YOU* TRUST ME, SHARON?"
DO I EVEN TRUST MYSELF?
CAPTAIN.
GENERAL.
LISTEN, SON. I DON'T WANT YOU TO THINK WE DON'T HONOR YOUR SERVICE.
BUT THIS FREELANCING HAS GOTTA END.
GENERAL, RESPECTFULLY, YOU CAN'T ASK ME TO WAIT FOR ORDERS WHEN THERE'S A MASSACRE ON AMERICAN SOIL.
ESPECIALLY ONE LIKE THIS-- FIFTY OF THE WORLD'S MAYORS NEARLY ***MURDERED.***
HOW DO YOU KNOW WE DIDN'T HAVE A PLAN OF OUR OWN, CAPTAIN?
DID YOU? WHAT WAS IT?
THIS ISN'T A DEBATE, SOLDIER.
AND THIS ISN'T "THUNDERBOLT ROSS" TALKING. I'M SPEAKING FOR THE PRESIDENT.

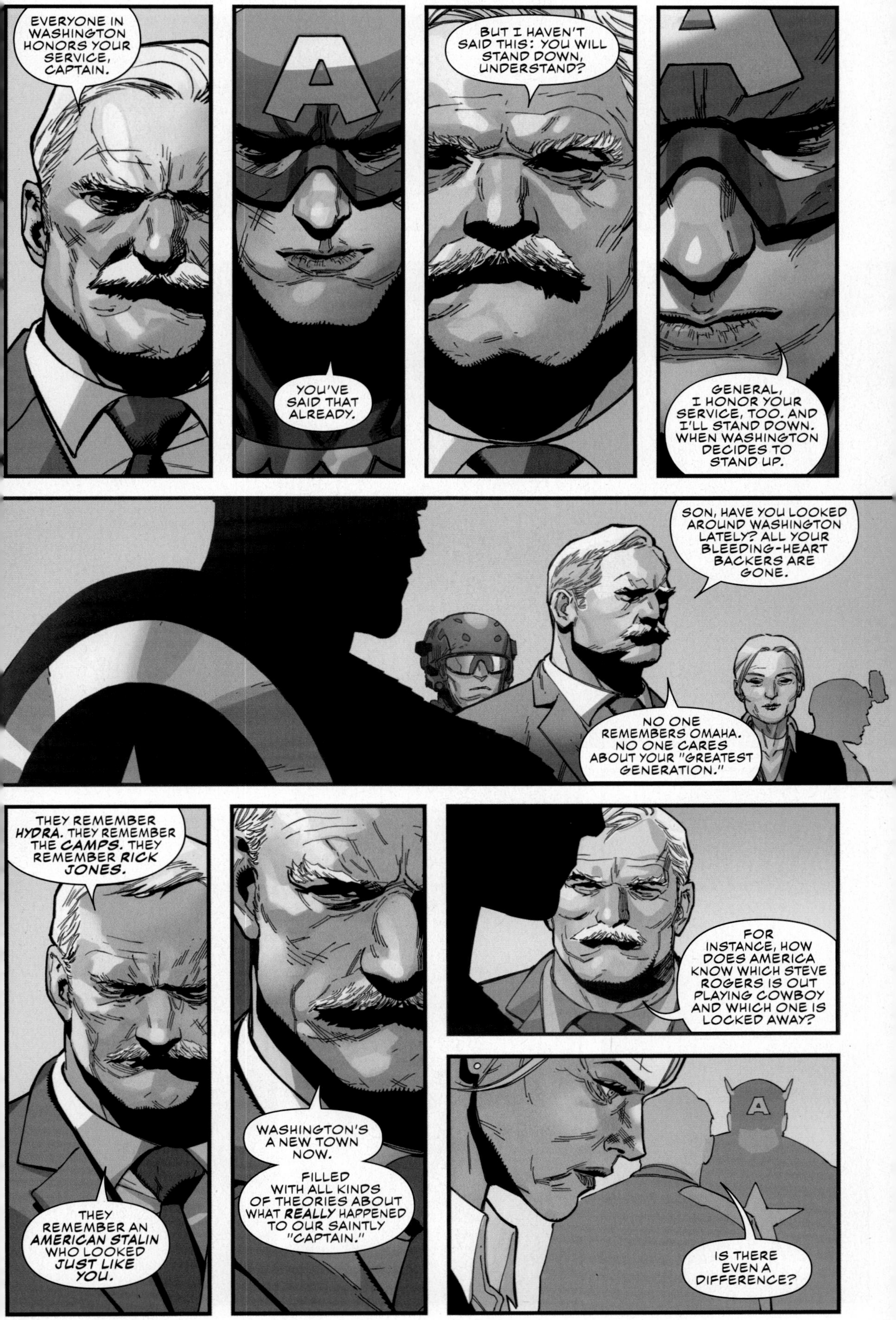
EVERYONE IN WASHINGTON HONORS YOUR SERVICE, CAPTAIN.
YOU'VE SAID THAT ALREADY.
BUT I HAVEN'T SAID THIS: YOU WILL STAND DOWN, UNDERSTAND?
GENERAL, I HONOR YOUR SERVICE, TOO. AND I'LL STAND DOWN. WHEN WASHINGTON DECIDES TO STAND UP.
SON, HAVE YOU LOOKED AROUND WASHINGTON LATELY? ALL YOUR BLEEDING-HEART BACKERS ARE GONE.
NO ONE REMEMBERS OMAHA. NO ONE CARES ABOUT YOUR "GREATEST GENERATION."
THEY REMEMBER HYDRA. THEY REMEMBER THE CAMPS. THEY REMEMBER RICK JONES.
THEY REMEMBER AN AMERICAN STALIN WHO LOOKED JUST LIKE YOU.
WASHINGTON'S A NEW TOWN NOW.
FILLED WITH ALL KINDS OF THEORIES ABOUT WHAT REALLY HAPPENED TO OUR SAINTLY "CAPTAIN."
FOR INSTANCE, HOW DOES AMERICA KNOW WHICH STEVE ROGERS IS OUT PLAYING COWBOY AND WHICH ONE IS LOCKED AWAY?
IS THERE EVEN A DIFFERENCE?

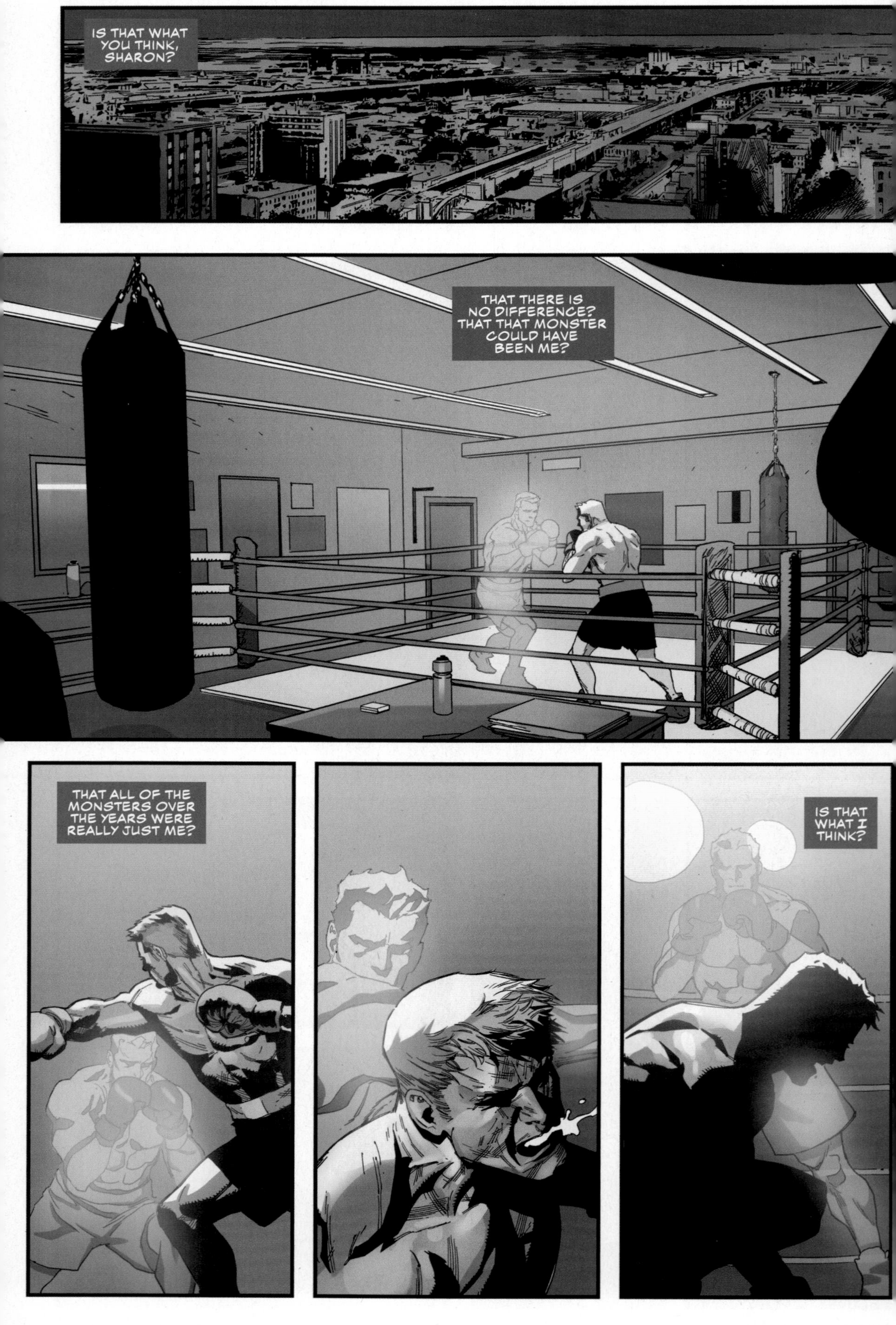
IS THAT WHAT YOU THINK, SHARON?
THAT THERE IS NO DIFFERENCE? THAT THAT MONSTER COULD HAVE BEEN ME?
THAT ALL OF THE MONSTERS OVER THE YEARS WERE REALLY JUST ME?
IS THAT WHAT I THINK?

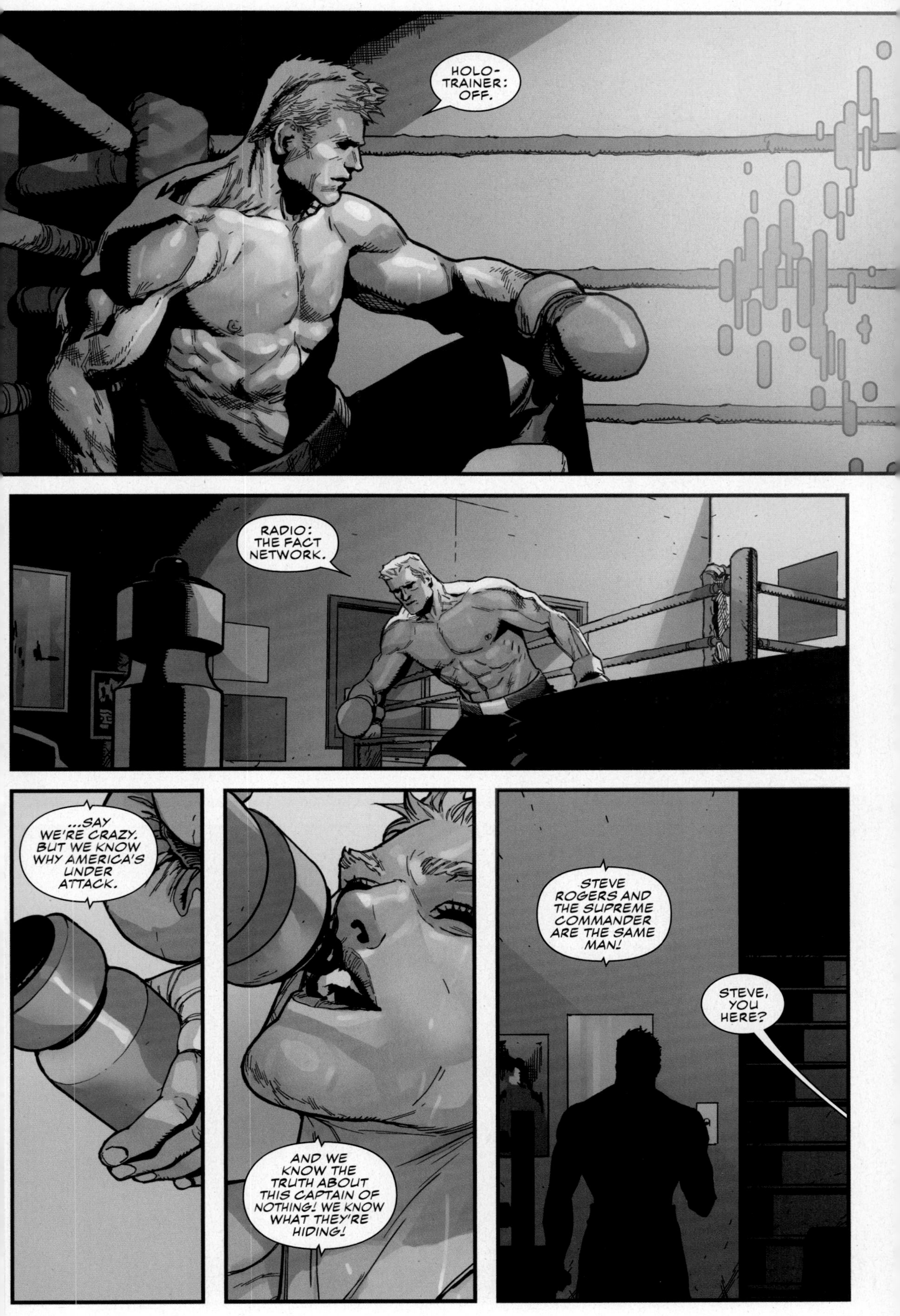
HOLO-
TRAINER:
OFF.
RADIO:
THE FACT
NETWORK.
...SAY
WE'RE CRAZY.
BUT WE KNOW
WHY AMERICA'S
UNDER
ATTACK.
AND WE
KNOW THE
TRUTH ABOUT
THIS CAPTAIN OF
NOTHING! WE KNOW
WHAT THEY'RE
HIDING!
STEVE
ROGERS AND
THE SUPREME
COMMANDER
ARE THE SAME
MAN!
STEVE,
YOU
HERE?

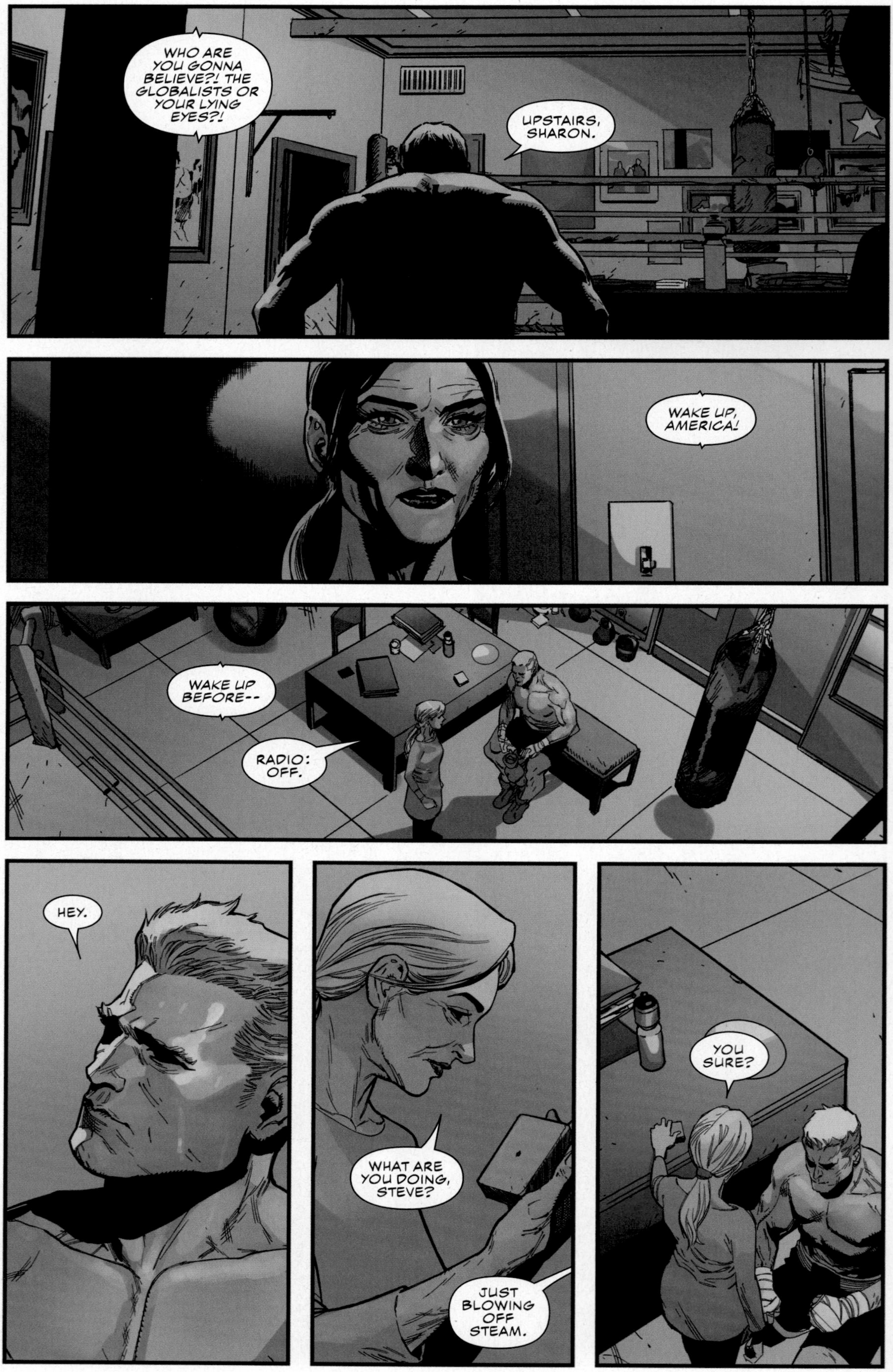
WHO ARE YOU GONNA BELIEVE?! THE GLOBALISTS OR YOUR LYING EYES?!
UPSTAIRS, SHARON.
WAKE UP, AMERICA!
WAKE UP BEFORE--
RADIO: OFF.
HEY.
WHAT ARE YOU DOING, STEVE?
JUST BLOWING OFF STEAM.
YOU SURE?

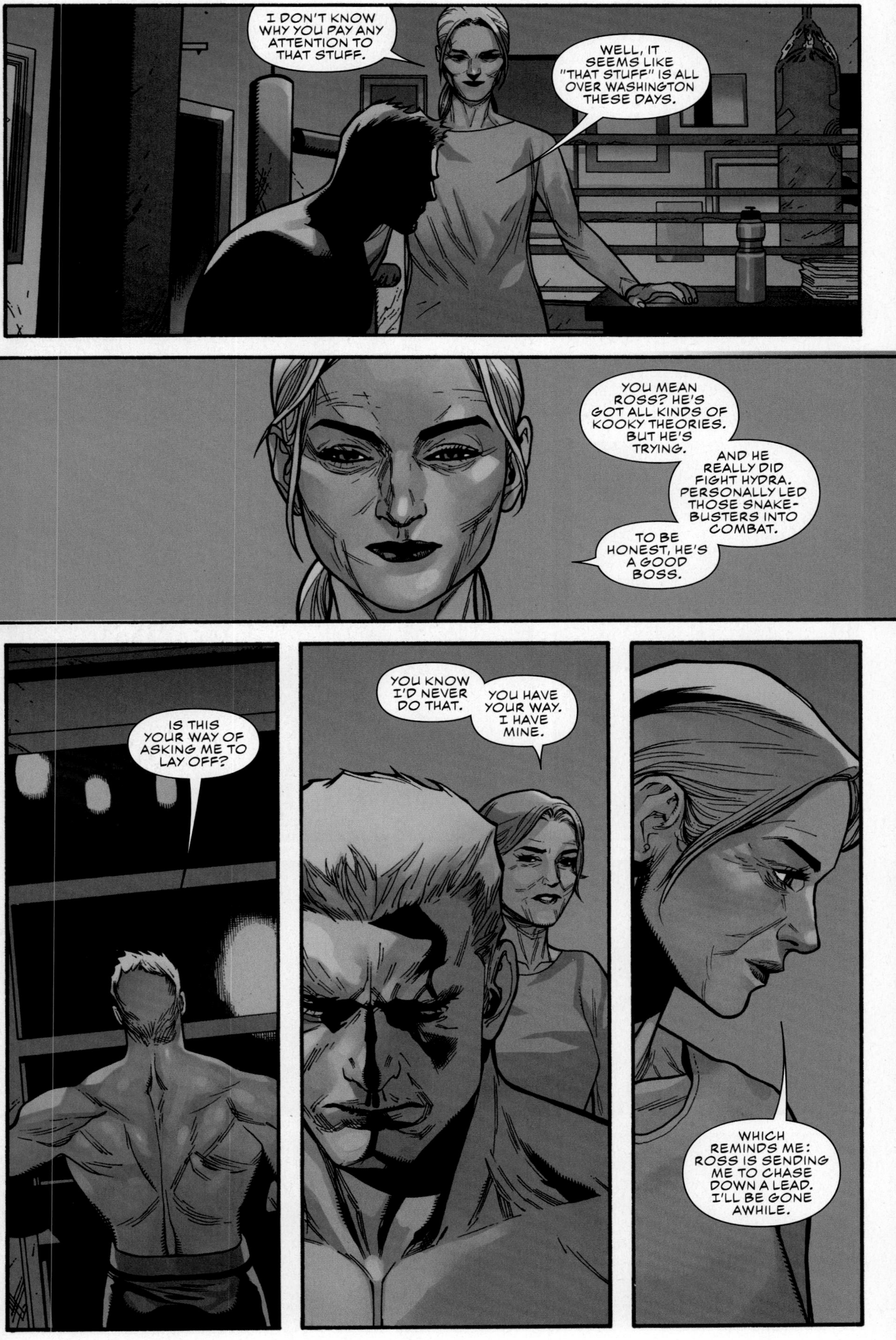
I DON'T KNOW WHY YOU PAY ANY ATTENTION TO THAT STUFF.
WELL, IT SEEMS LIKE "THAT STUFF" IS ALL OVER WASHINGTON THESE DAYS.
YOU MEAN ROSS? HE'S GOT ALL KINDS OF KOOKY THEORIES. BUT HE'S TRYING.
AND HE REALLY DID FIGHT HYDRA. PERSONALLY LED THOSE SNAKE-BUSTERS INTO COMBAT.
TO BE HONEST, HE'S A GOOD BOSS.
IS THIS YOUR WAY OF ASKING ME TO LAY OFF?
YOU KNOW I'D NEVER DO THAT.
YOU HAVE YOUR WAY. I HAVE MINE.
WHICH REMINDS ME: ROSS IS SENDING ME TO CHASE DOWN A LEAD. I'LL BE GONE AWHILE.

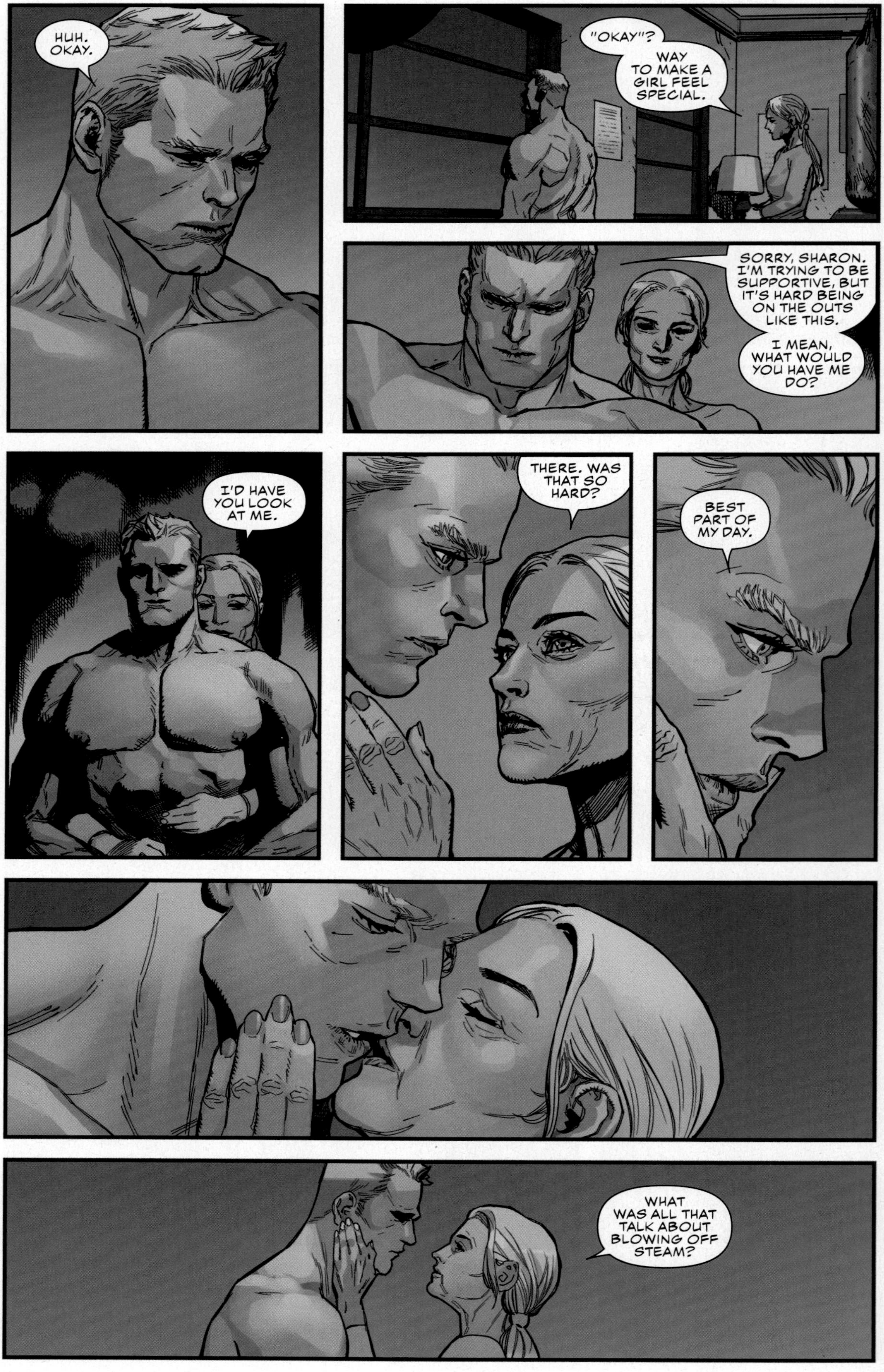
HUH. OKAY.
"OKAY"?
WAY TO MAKE A GIRL FEEL SPECIAL.
SORRY, SHARON. I'M TRYING TO BE SUPPORTIVE, BUT IT'S HARD BEING ON THE OUTS LIKE THIS.
I MEAN, WHAT WOULD YOU HAVE ME DO?
I'D HAVE YOU LOOK AT ME.
THERE. WAS THAT SO HARD?
BEST PART OF MY DAY.
WHAT WAS ALL THAT TALK ABOUT BLOWING OFF STEAM?

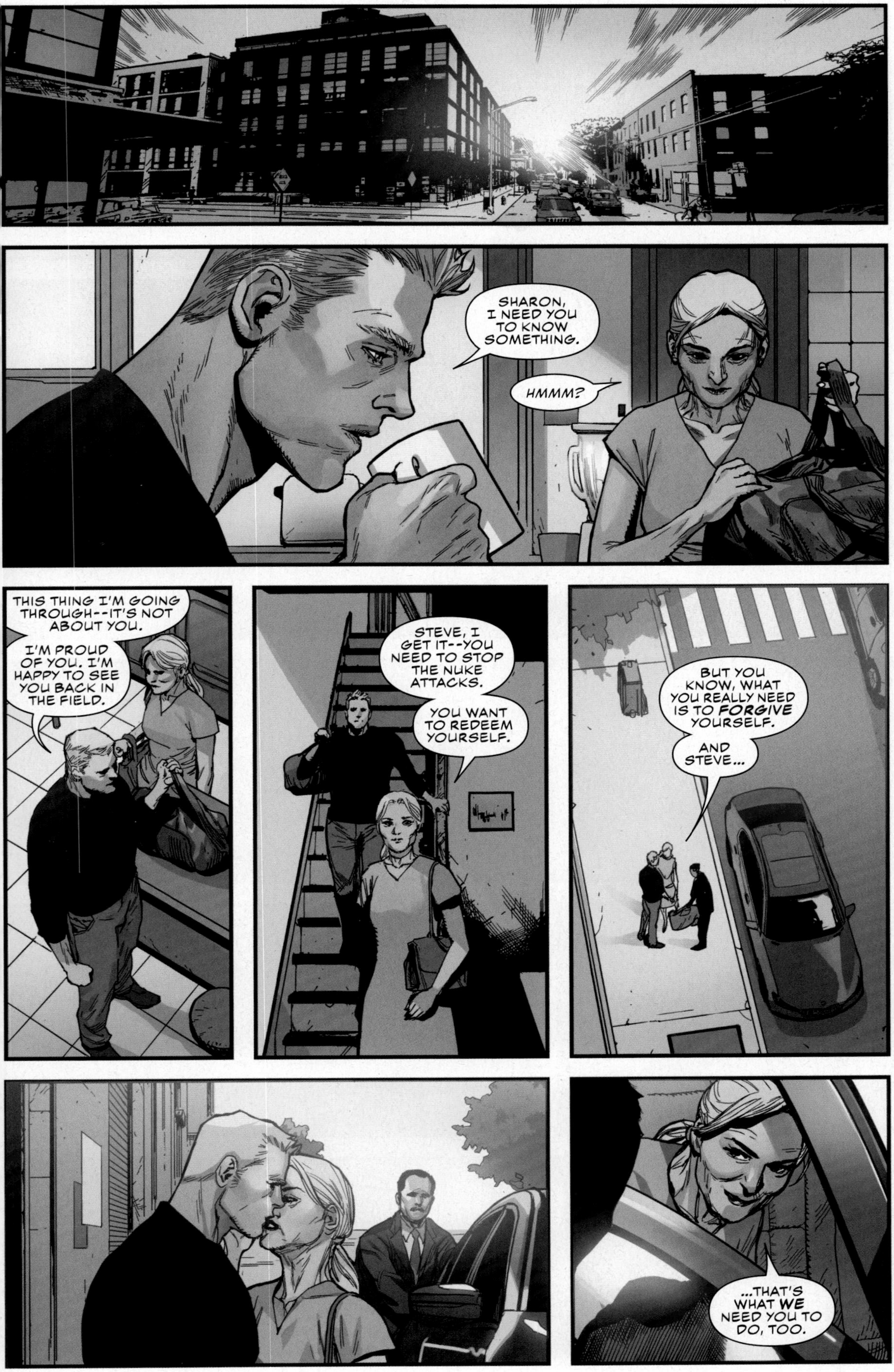
SHARON, I NEED YOU TO KNOW SOMETHING.
HMMM?
THIS THING I'M GOING THROUGH--IT'S NOT ABOUT YOU.
I'M PROUD OF YOU. I'M HAPPY TO SEE YOU BACK IN THE FIELD.
STEVE, I GET IT--YOU NEED TO STOP THE NUKE ATTACKS.
YOU WANT TO REDEEM YOURSELF.
BUT YOU KNOW, WHAT YOU REALLY NEED IS TO *FORGIVE* YOURSELF.
AND STEVE...
...THAT'S WHAT **WE** NEED YOU TO DO, TOO.

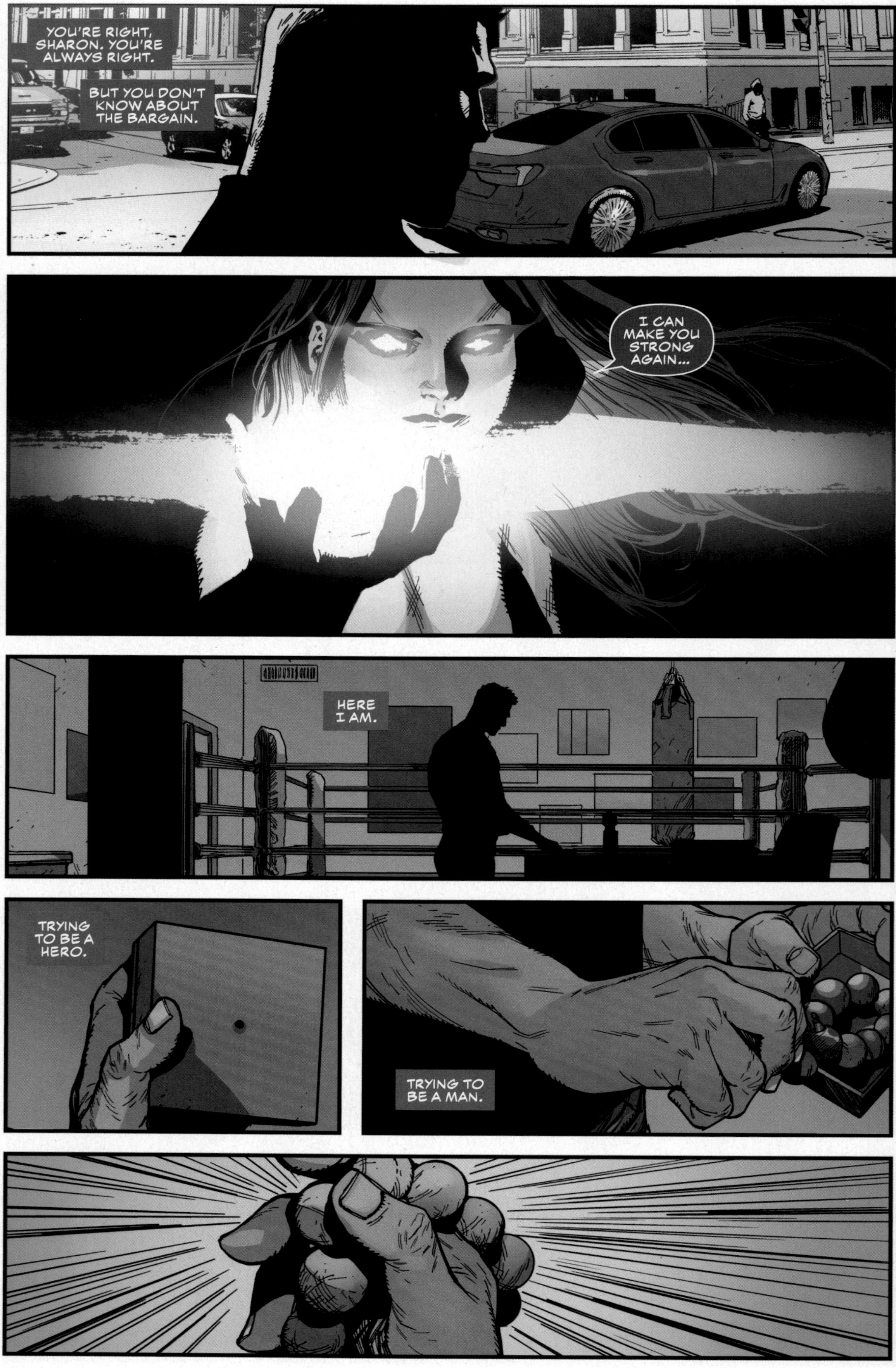
YOU'RE RIGHT, SHARON. YOU'RE ALWAYS RIGHT.
BUT YOU DON'T KNOW ABOUT THE BARGAIN.
I CAN MAKE YOU STRONG AGAIN...
HERE I AM.
TRYING TO BE A HERO.
TRYING TO BE A MAN.

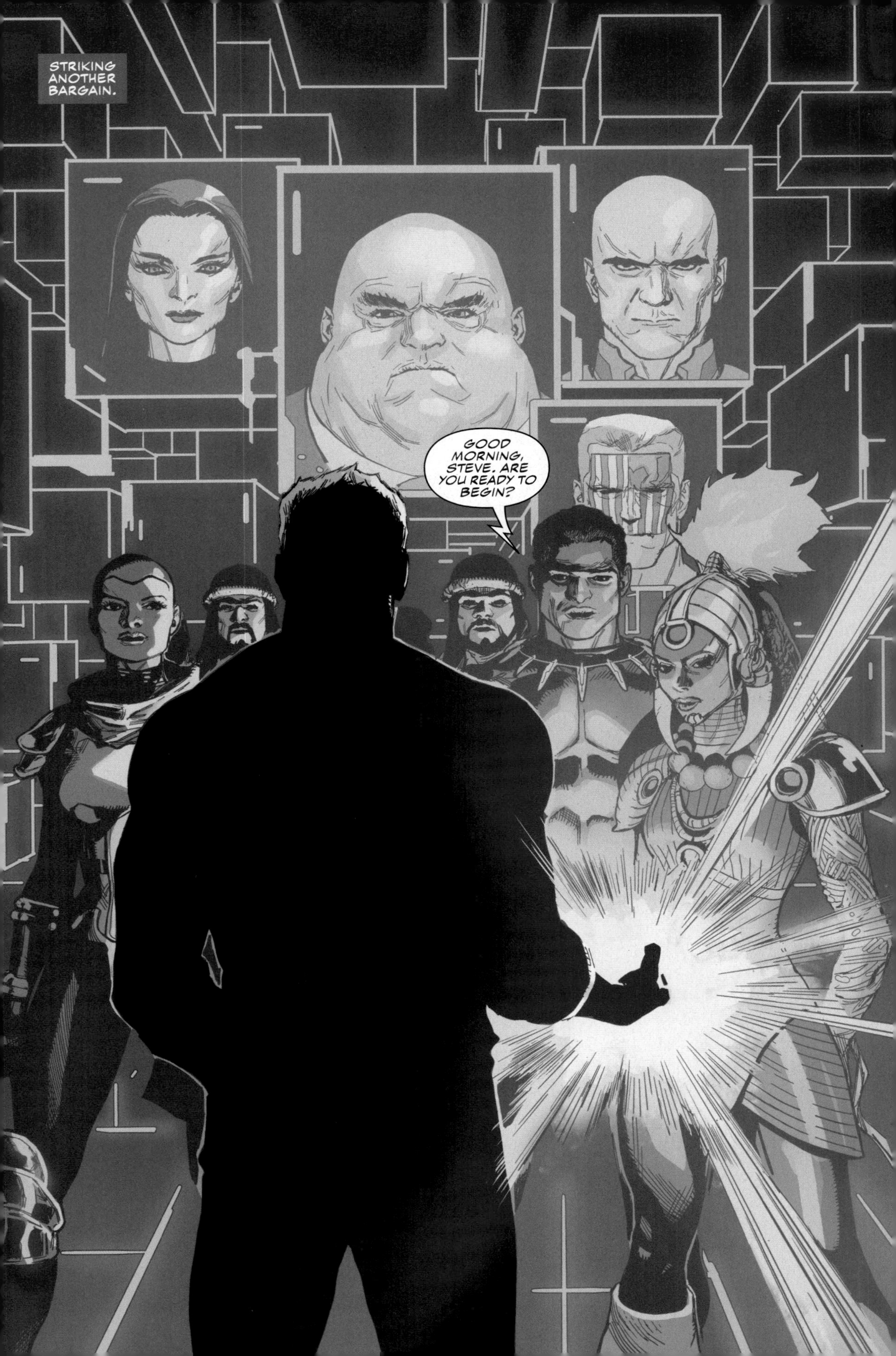
STRIKING ANOTHER BARGAIN.
GOOD MORNING, STEVE. ARE YOU READY TO BEGIN?

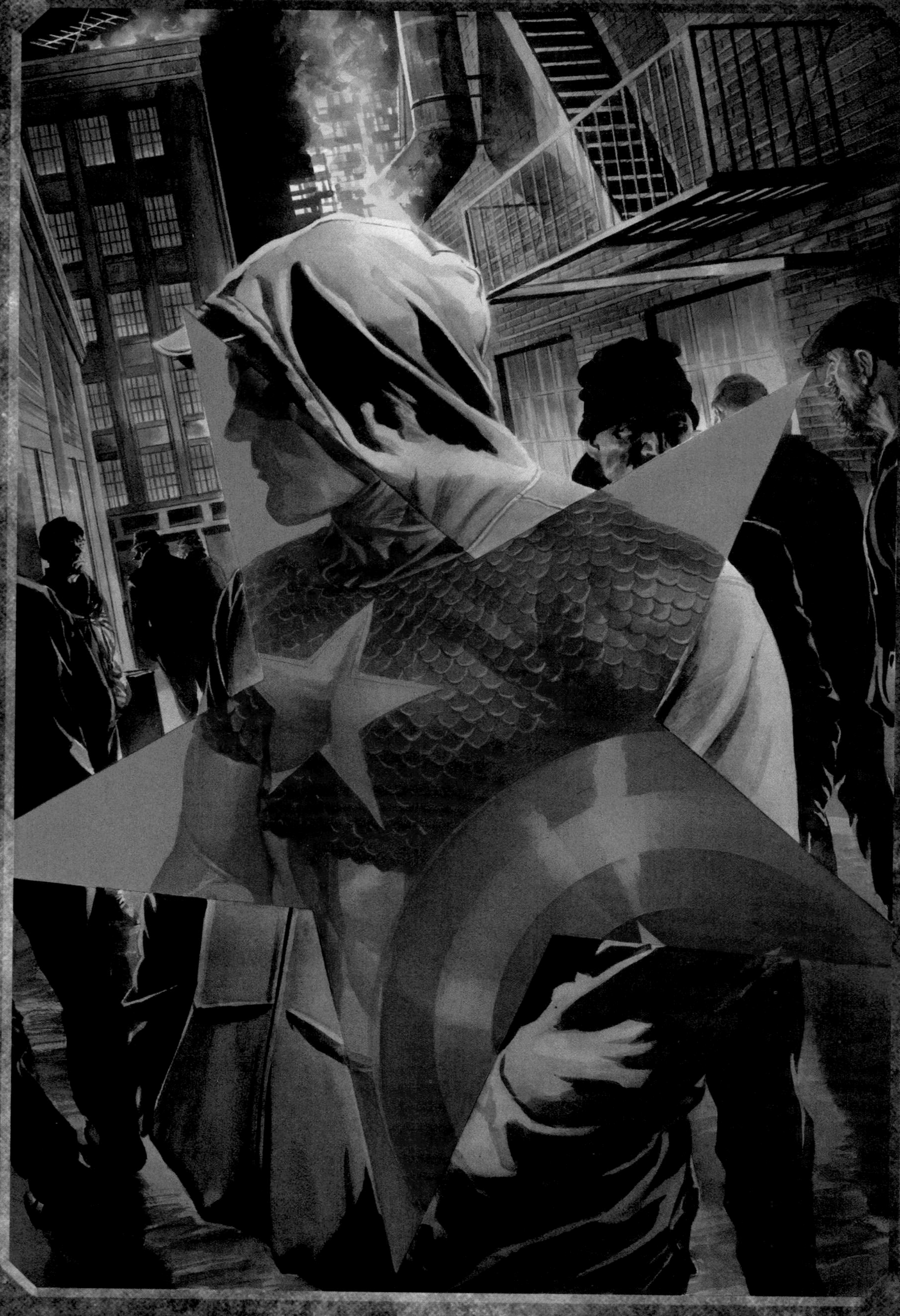

3

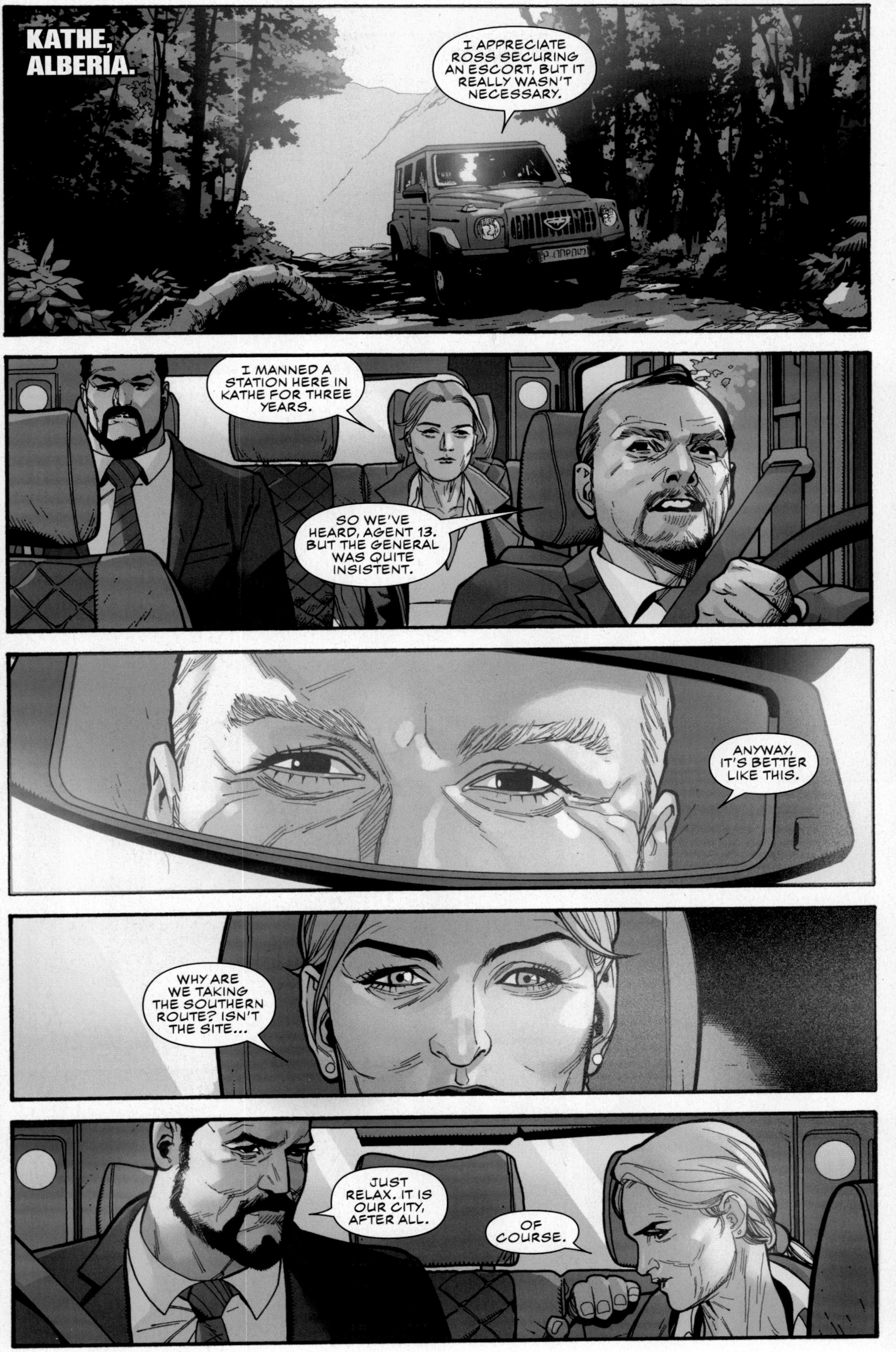
KATHE, ALBERIA.
I APPRECIATE ROSS SECURING AN ESCORT, BUT IT REALLY WASN'T NECESSARY.
I MANNED A STATION HERE IN KATHE FOR THREE YEARS.
SO WE'VE HEARD, AGENT 13. BUT THE GENERAL WAS QUITE INSISTENT.
ANYWAY, IT'S BETTER LIKE THIS.
WHY ARE WE TAKING THE SOUTHERN ROUTE? ISN'T THE SITE...
JUST RELAX. IT IS OUR CITY, AFTER ALL.
OF COURSE.

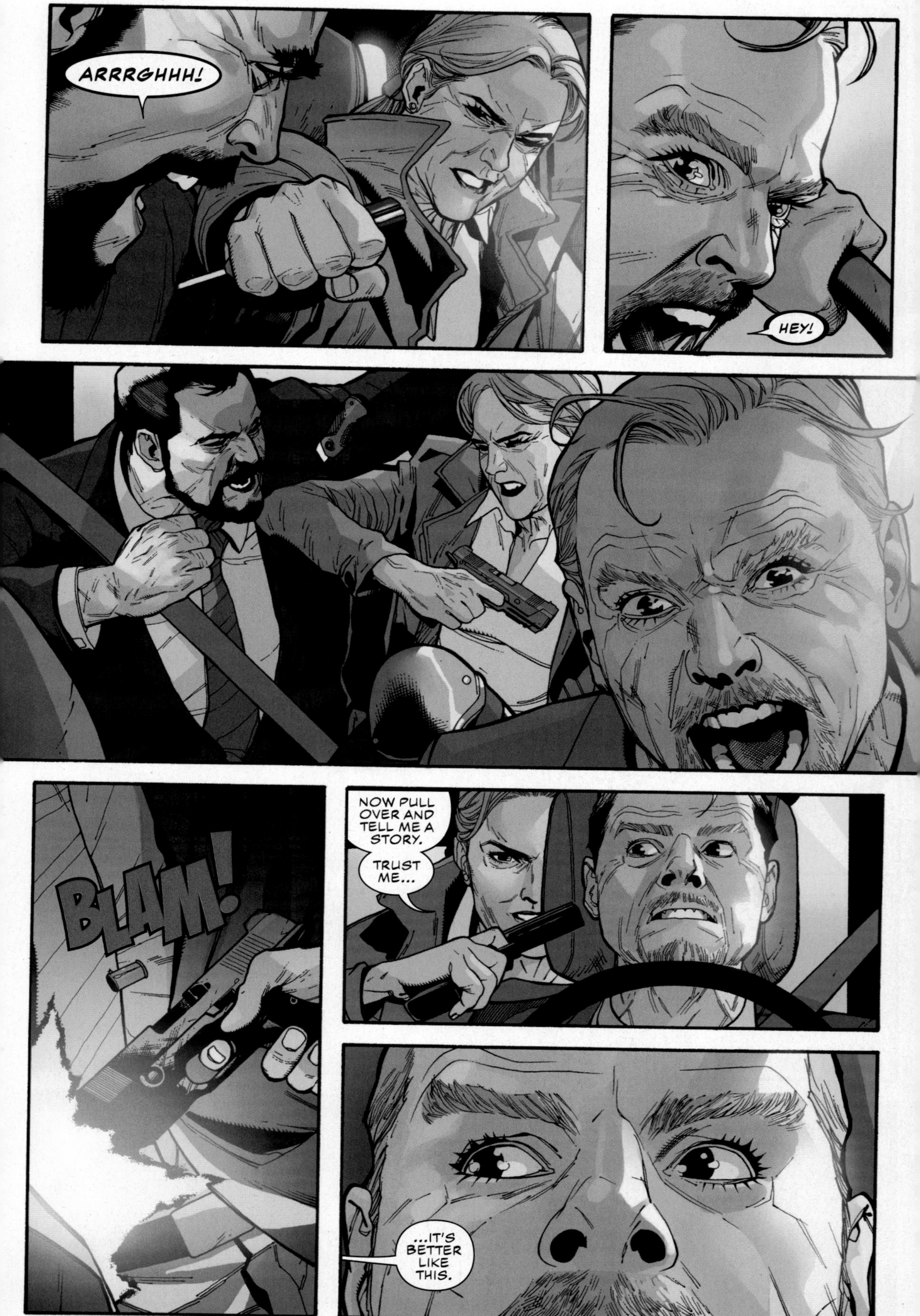
ARRRGHHH!
HEY!
BLAM!
NOW PULL OVER AND TELL ME A STORY.
TRUST ME...
...IT'S BETTER LIKE THIS.

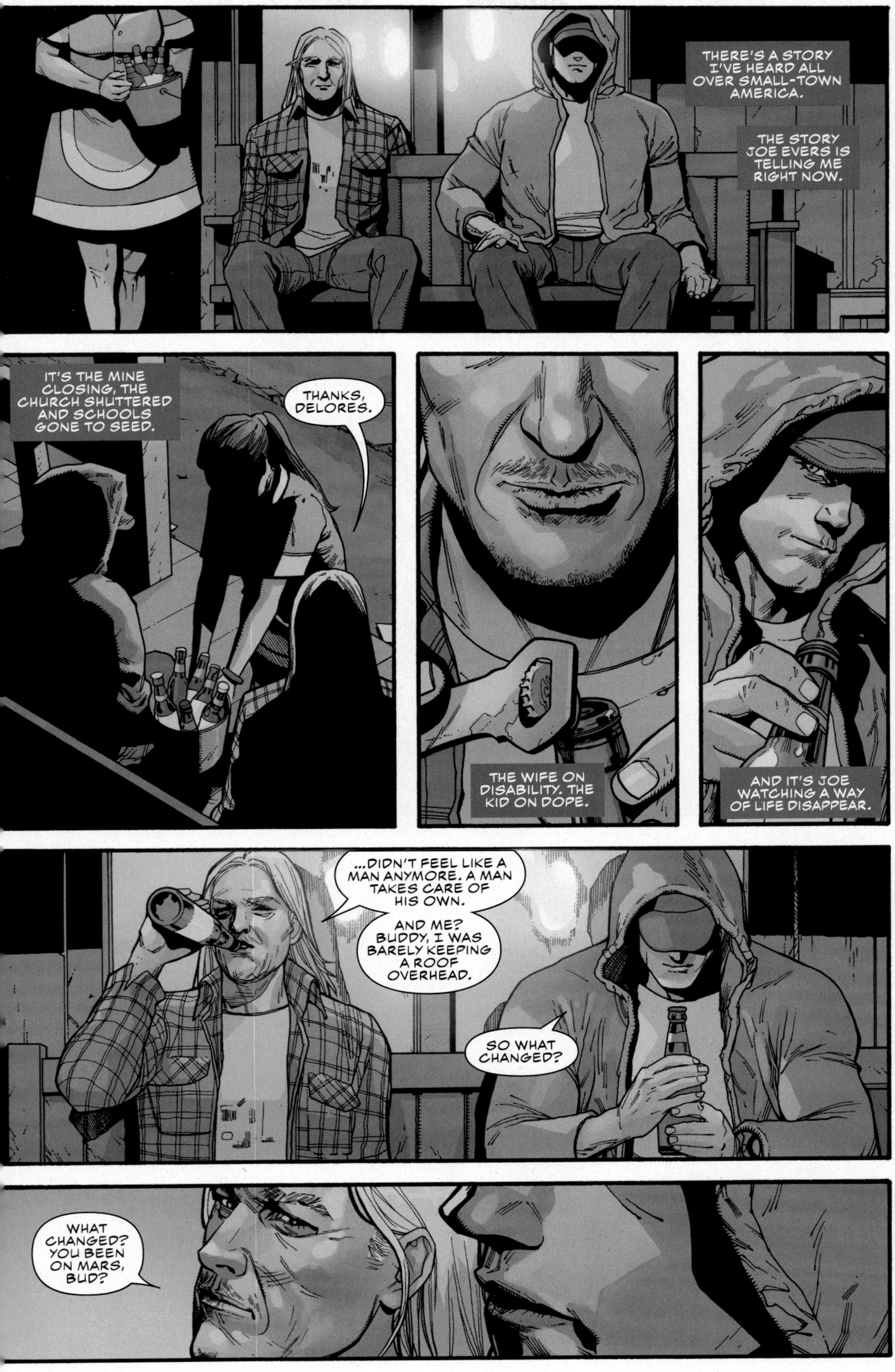
THERE'S A STORY I'VE HEARD ALL OVER SMALL-TOWN AMERICA.
THE STORY JOE EVERS IS TELLING ME RIGHT NOW.
IT'S THE MINE CLOSING, THE CHURCH SHUTTERED AND SCHOOLS GONE TO SEED.
THANKS, DELORES.
THE WIFE ON DISABILITY. THE KID ON DOPE.
AND IT'S JOE WATCHING A WAY OF LIFE DISAPPEAR.
...DIDN'T FEEL LIKE A MAN ANYMORE. A MAN TAKES CARE OF HIS OWN.
AND ME? BUDDY, I WAS BARELY KEEPING A ROOF OVERHEAD.
SO WHAT CHANGED?
WHAT CHANGED? YOU BEEN ON MARS, BUD?

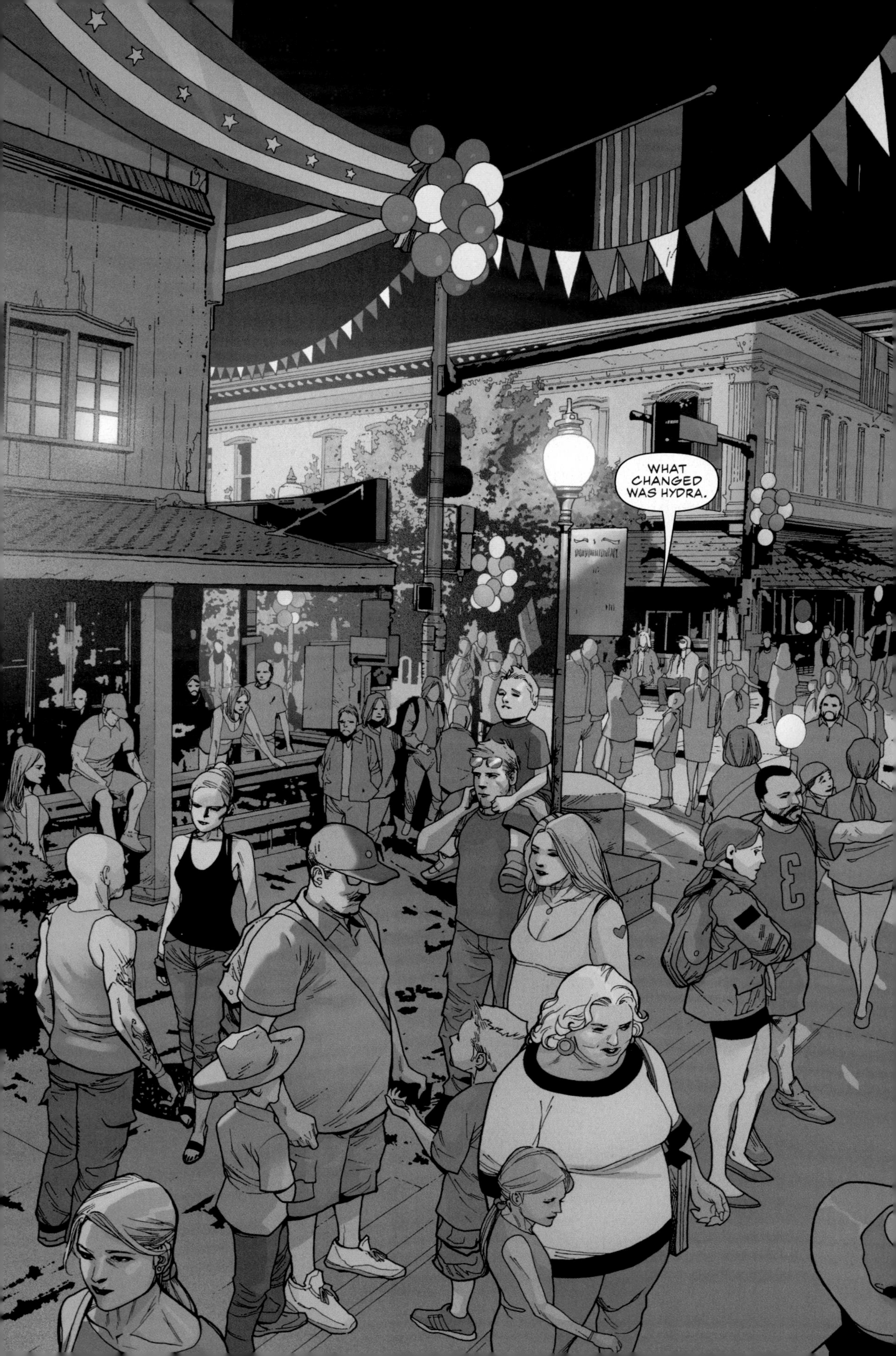
WHAT CHANGED WAS HYDRA.

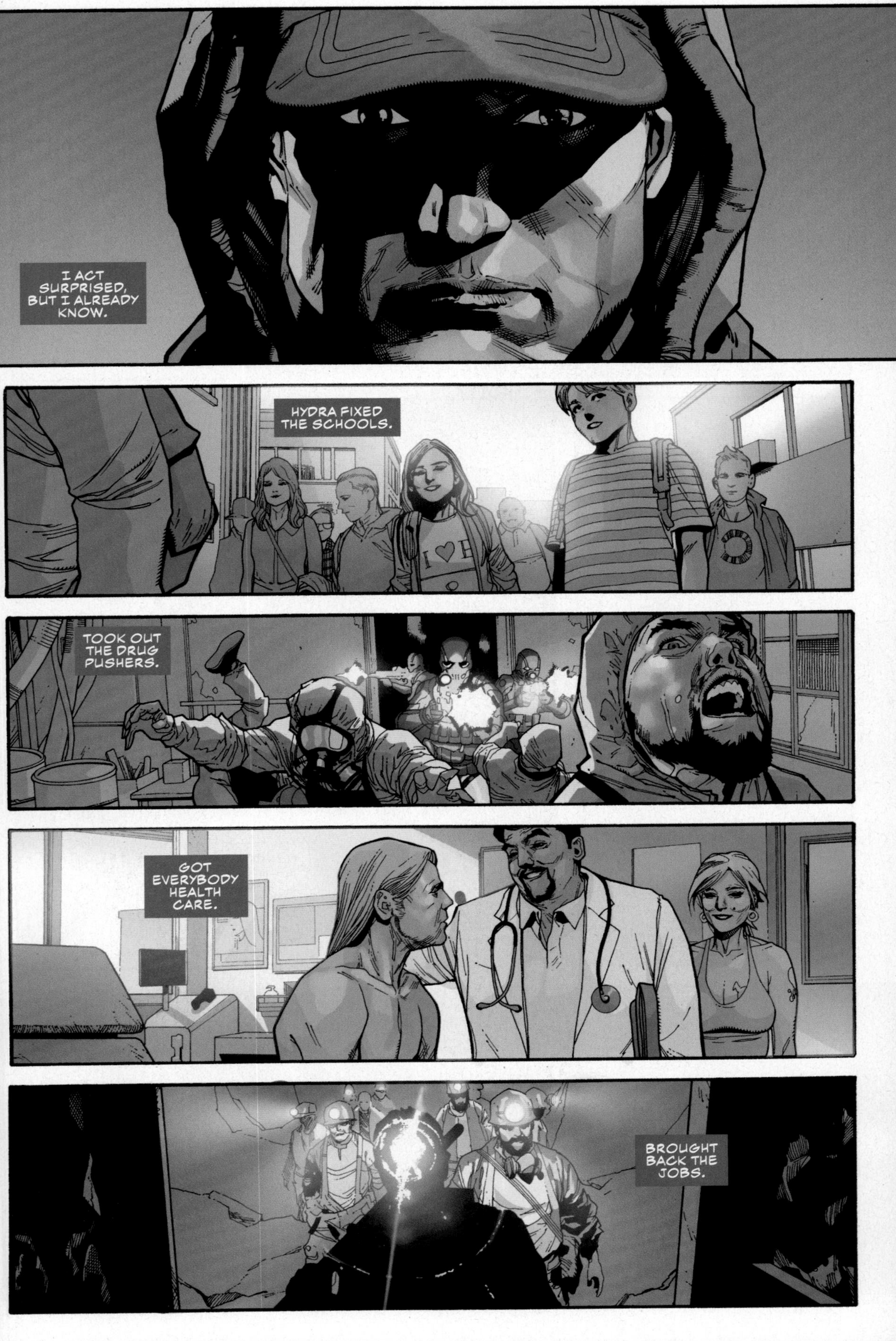
I ACT SURPRISED, BUT I ALREADY KNOW.
HYDRA FIXED THE SCHOOLS.
TOOK OUT THE DRUG PUSHERS.
GOT EVERYBODY HEALTH CARE.
BROUGHT BACK THE JOBS.

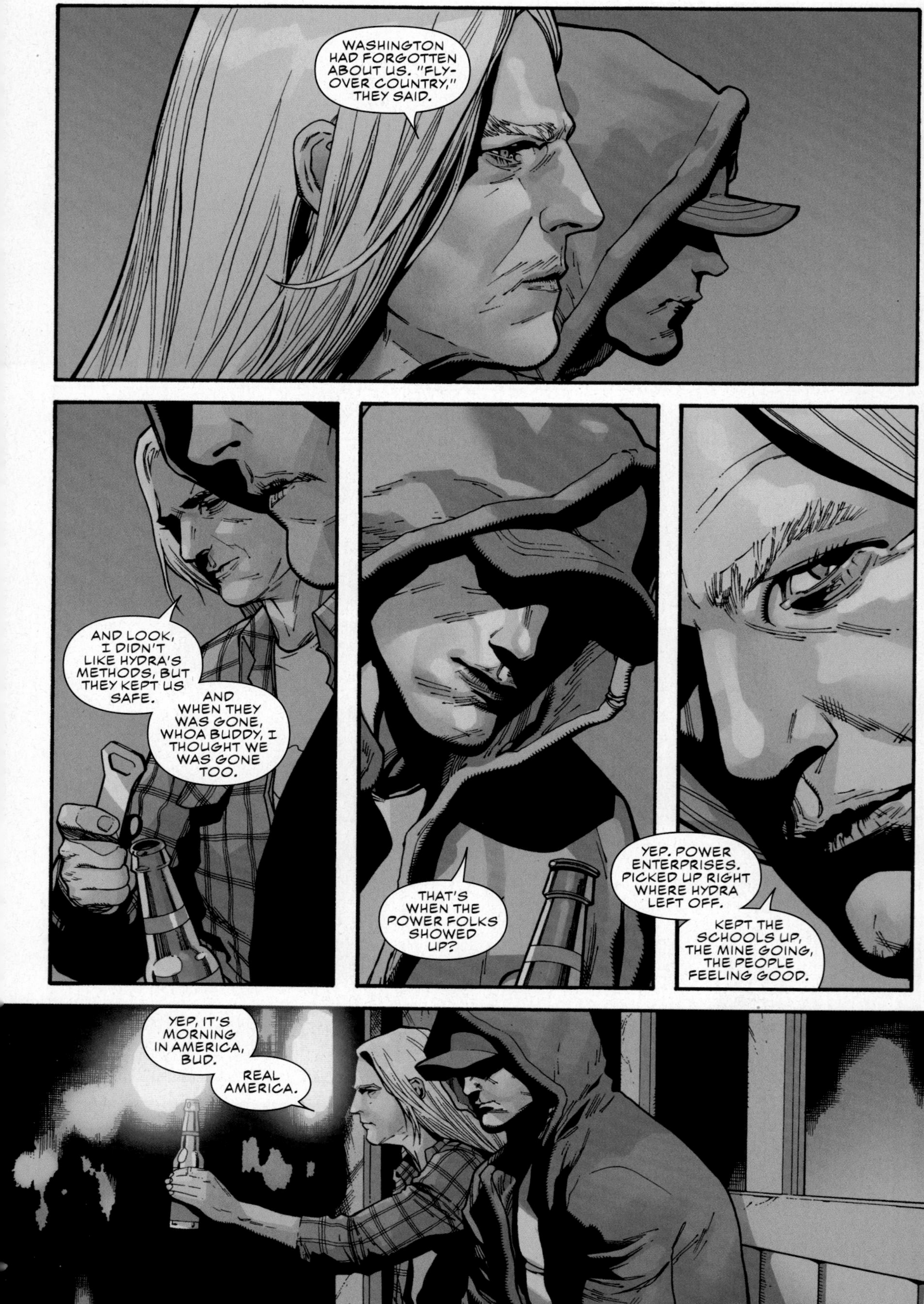
WASHINGTON HAD FORGOTTEN ABOUT US. "FLY-OVER COUNTRY," THEY SAID.
AND LOOK, I DIDN'T LIKE HYDRA'S METHODS, BUT THEY KEPT US SAFE.
AND WHEN THEY WAS GONE, WHOA BUDDY, I THOUGHT WE WAS GONE TOO.
THAT'S WHEN THE POWER FOLKS SHOWED UP?
YEP. POWER ENTERPRISES. PICKED UP RIGHT WHERE HYDRA LEFT OFF.
KEPT THE SCHOOLS UP, THE MINE GOING, THE PEOPLE FEELING GOOD.
YEP, IT'S MORNING IN AMERICA, BUD.
REAL AMERICA.

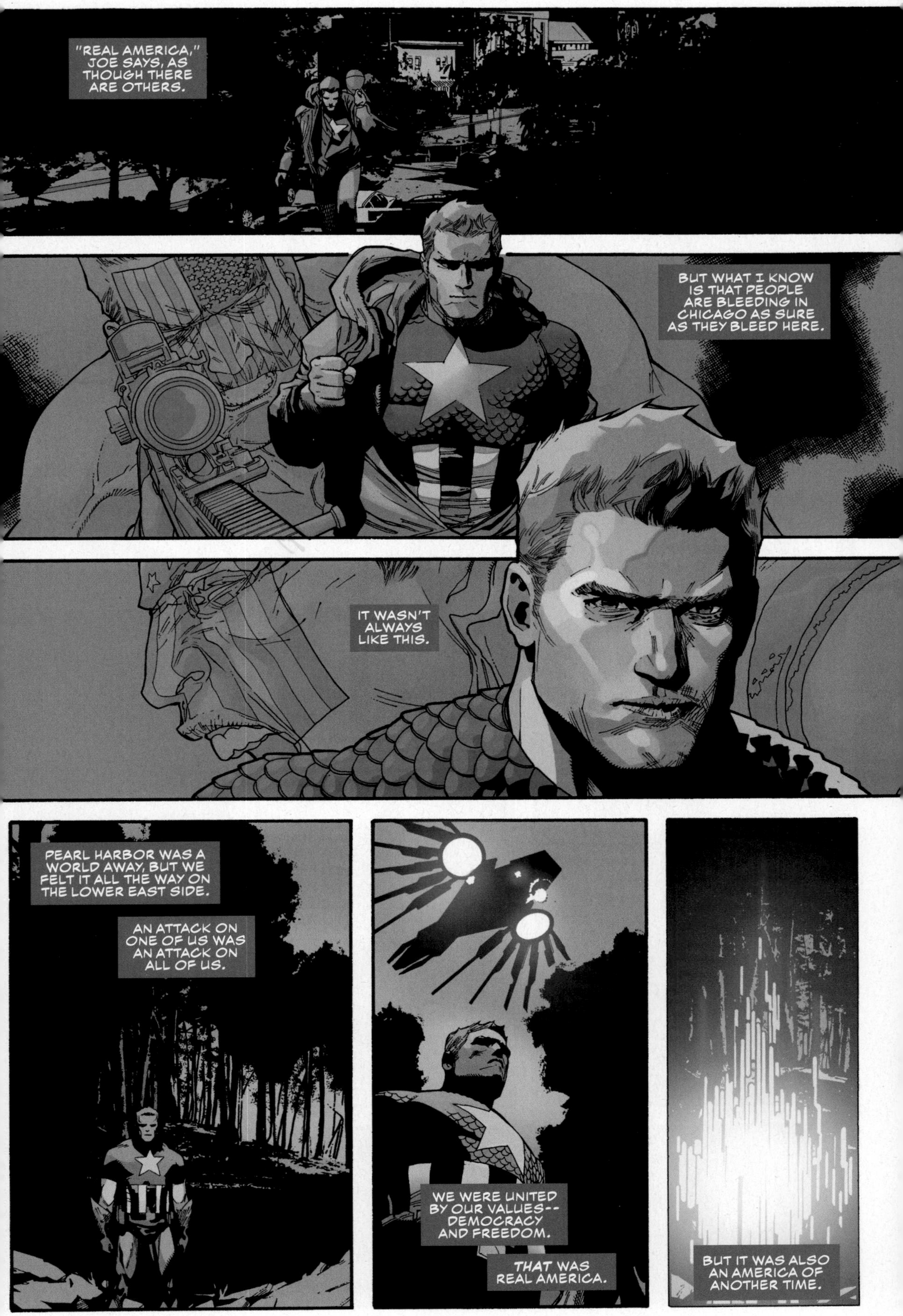
"REAL AMERICA," JOE SAYS, AS THOUGH THERE ARE OTHERS.
BUT WHAT I KNOW IS THAT PEOPLE ARE BLEEDING IN CHICAGO AS SURE AS THEY BLEED HERE.
IT WASN'T ALWAYS LIKE THIS.
PEARL HARBOR WAS A WORLD AWAY, BUT WE FELT IT ALL THE WAY ON THE LOWER EAST SIDE.
AN ATTACK ON ONE OF US WAS AN ATTACK ON ALL OF US.
WE WERE UNITED BY OUR VALUES--DEMOCRACY AND FREEDOM.
THAT WAS REAL AMERICA.
BUT IT WAS ALSO AN AMERICA OF ANOTHER TIME.

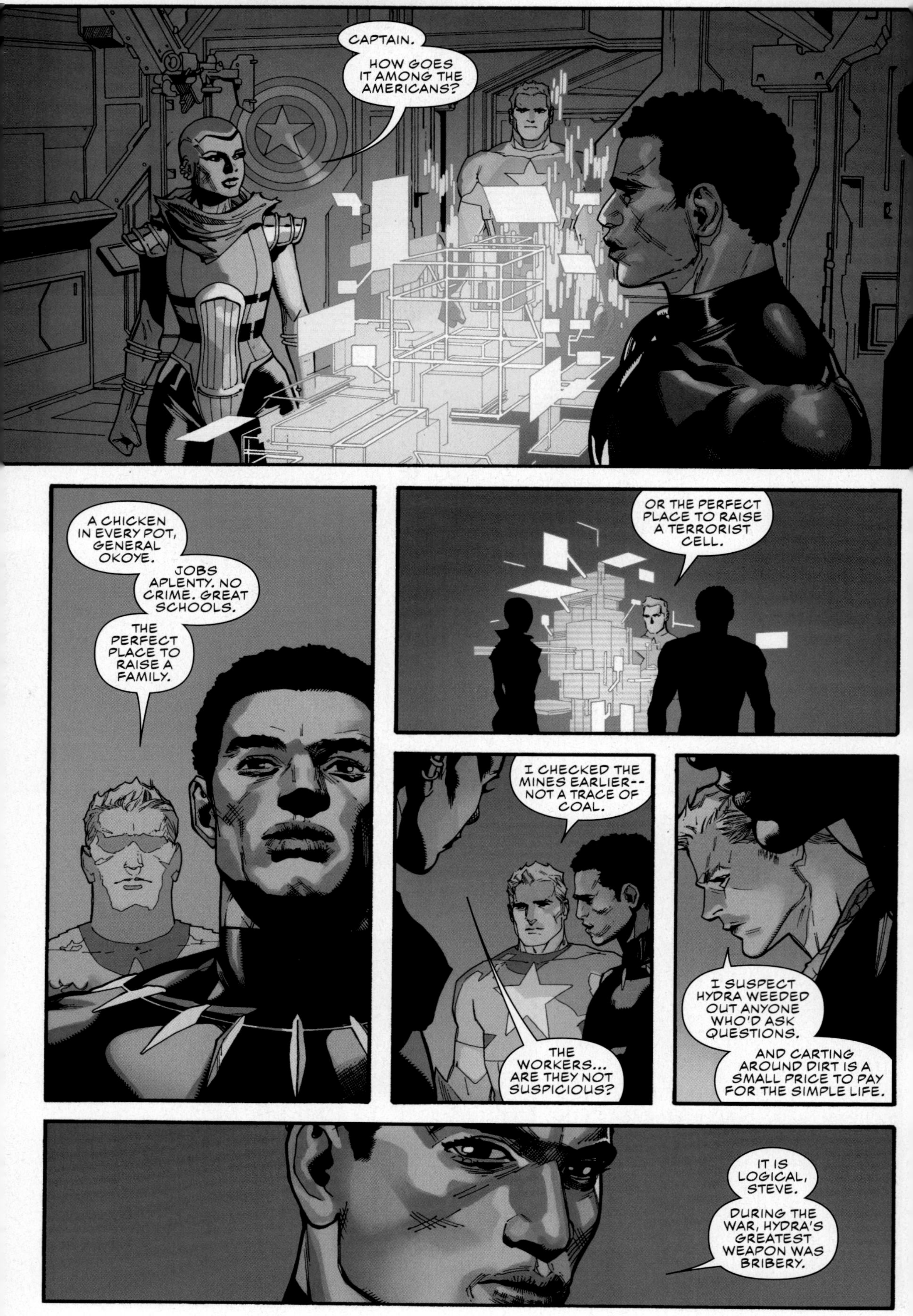
CAPTAIN.
HOW GOES IT AMONG THE AMERICANS?
A CHICKEN IN EVERY POT, GENERAL OKOYE.
JOBS APLENTY. NO CRIME. GREAT SCHOOLS.
THE PERFECT PLACE TO RAISE A FAMILY.
OR THE PERFECT PLACE TO RAISE A TERRORIST CELL.
I CHECKED THE MINES EARLIER-- NOT A TRACE OF COAL.
THE WORKERS... ARE THEY NOT SUSPICIOUS?
I SUSPECT HYDRA WEEDED OUT ANYONE WHO'D ASK QUESTIONS.
AND CARTING AROUND DIRT IS A SMALL PRICE TO PAY FOR THE SIMPLE LIFE.
IT IS LOGICAL, STEVE.
DURING THE WAR, HYDRA'S GREATEST WEAPON WAS BRIBERY.

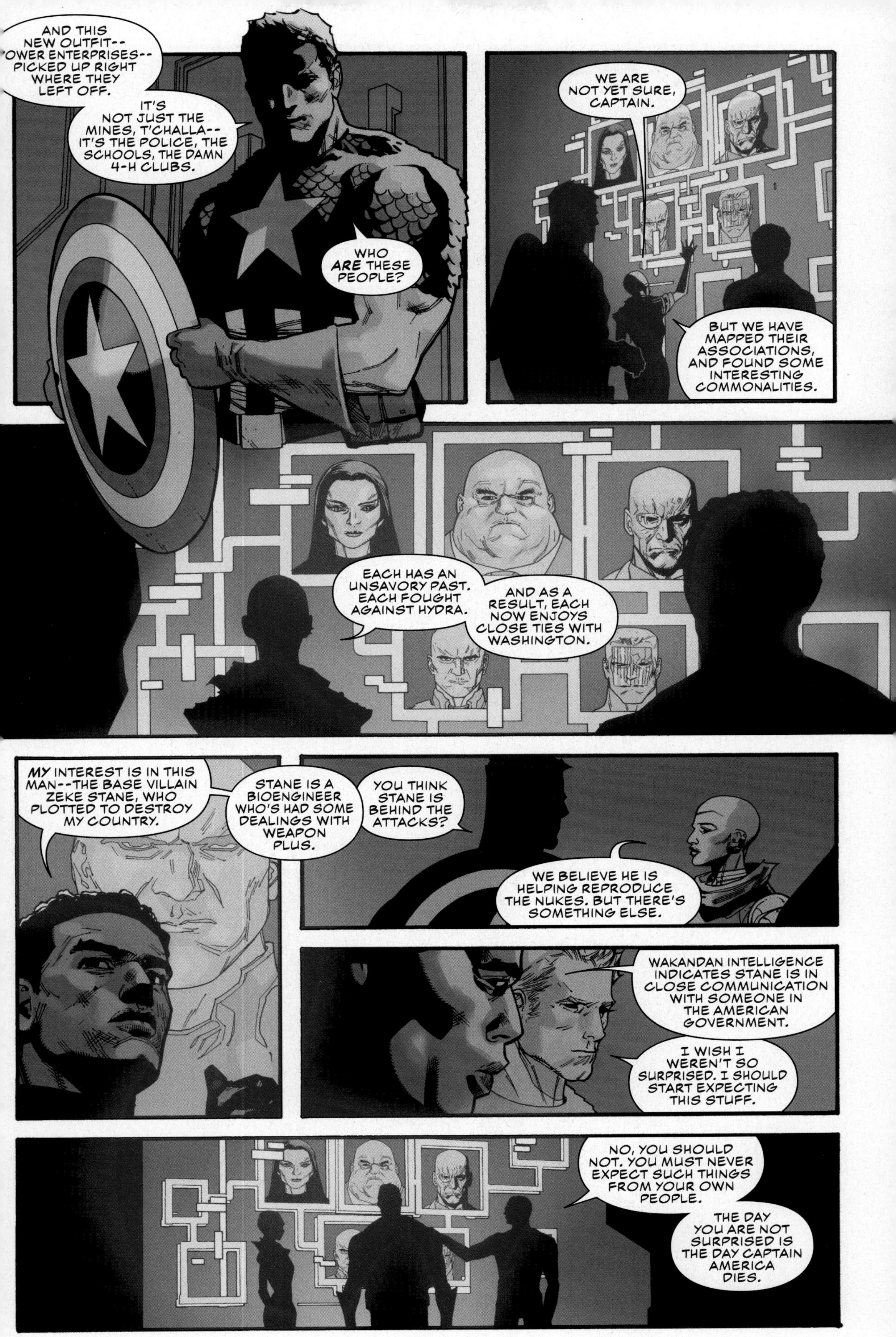

AND THIS NEW OUTFIT-- OWER ENTERPRISES-- PICKED UP RIGHT WHERE THEY LEFT OFF.
IT'S NOT JUST THE MINES, T'CHALLA-- IT'S THE POLICE, THE SCHOOLS, THE DAMN 4-H CLUBS.
WHO ARE THESE PEOPLE?
WE ARE NOT YET SURE, CAPTAIN.
BUT WE HAVE MAPPED THEIR ASSOCIATIONS, AND FOUND SOME INTERESTING COMMONALITIES.
EACH HAS AN UNSAVORY PAST. EACH FOUGHT AGAINST HYDRA.
AND AS A RESULT, EACH NOW ENJOYS CLOSE TIES WITH WASHINGTON.
MY INTEREST IS IN THIS MAN--THE BASE VILLAIN ZEKE STANE, WHO PLOTTED TO DESTROY MY COUNTRY.
STANE IS A BIOENGINEER WHO'S HAD SOME DEALINGS WITH WEAPON PLUS.
YOU THINK STANE IS BEHIND THE ATTACKS?
WE BELIEVE HE IS HELPING REPRODUCE THE NUKES. BUT THERE'S SOMETHING ELSE.
WAKANDAN INTELLIGENCE INDICATES STANE IS IN CLOSE COMMUNICATION WITH SOMEONE IN THE AMERICAN GOVERNMENT.
I WISH I WEREN'T SO SURPRISED. I SHOULD START EXPECTING THIS STUFF.
NO, YOU SHOULD NOT. YOU MUST NEVER EXPECT SUCH THINGS FROM YOUR OWN PEOPLE.
THE DAY YOU ARE NOT SURPRISED IS THE DAY CAPTAIN AMERICA DIES.

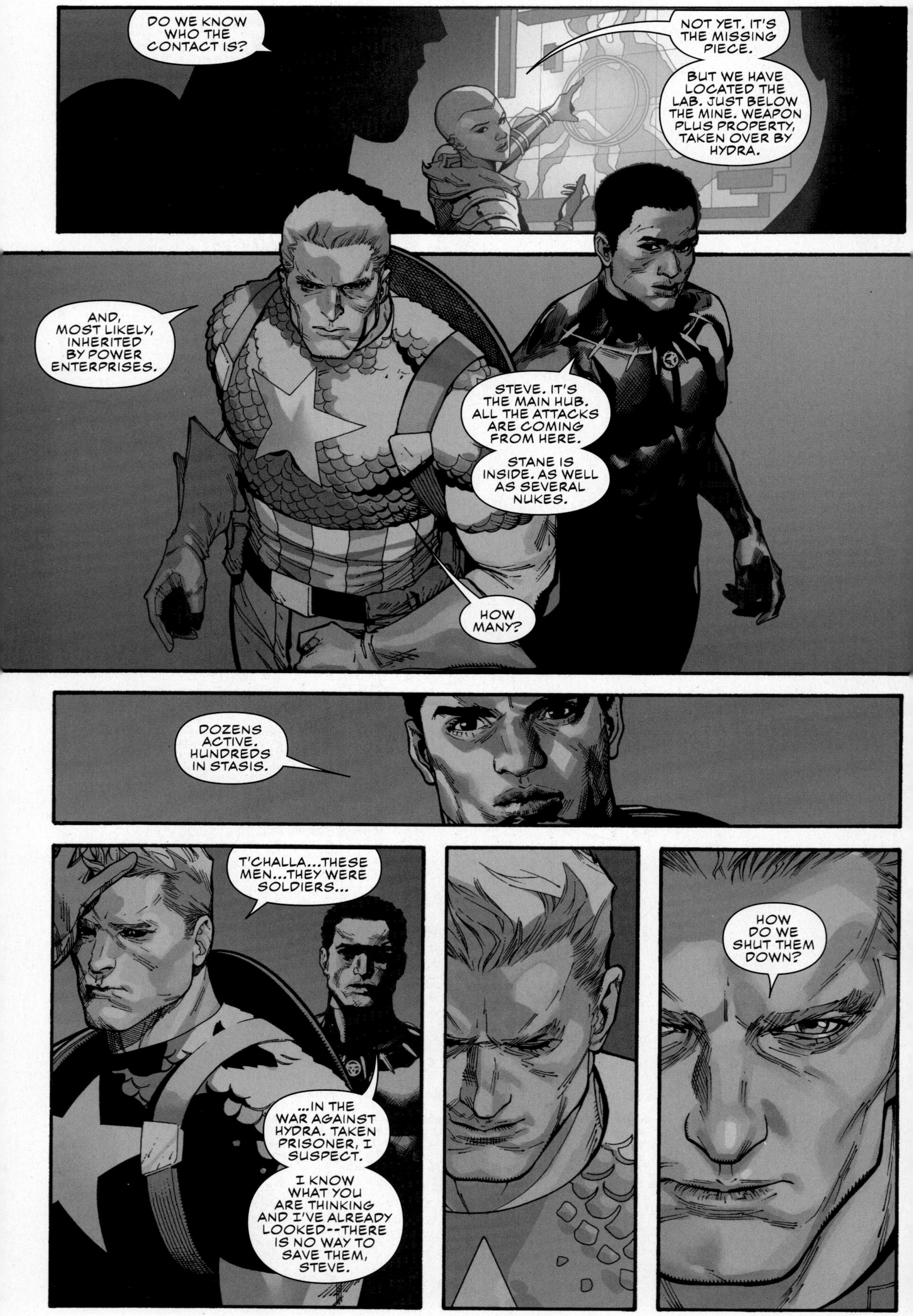
DO WE KNOW WHO THE CONTACT IS?
NOT YET. IT'S THE MISSING PIECE.
BUT WE HAVE LOCATED THE LAB. JUST BELOW THE MINE. WEAPON PLUS PROPERTY, TAKEN OVER BY HYDRA.
AND, MOST LIKELY, INHERITED BY POWER ENTERPRISES.
STEVE. IT'S THE MAIN HUB. ALL THE ATTACKS ARE COMING FROM HERE.
STANE IS INSIDE. AS WELL AS SEVERAL NUKES.
HOW MANY?
DOZENS ACTIVE. HUNDREDS IN STASIS.
T'CHALLA...THESE MEN...THEY WERE SOLDIERS...
...IN THE WAR AGAINST HYDRA. TAKEN PRISONER, I SUSPECT.
I KNOW WHAT YOU ARE THINKING AND I'VE ALREADY LOOKED--THERE IS NO WAY TO SAVE THEM, STEVE.
HOW DO WE SHUT THEM DOWN?

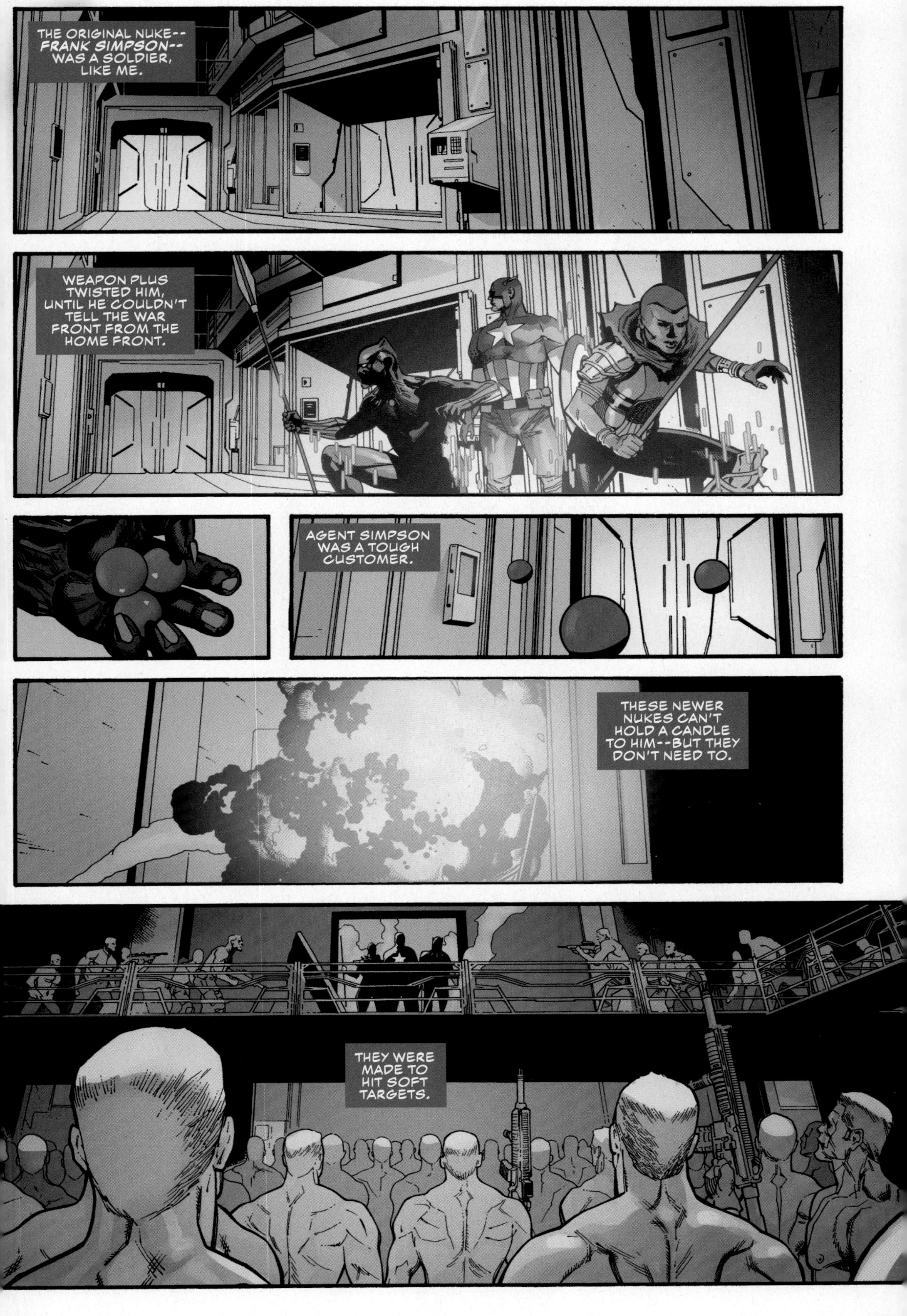
THE ORIGINAL NUKE-- FRANK SIMPSON-- WAS A SOLDIER, LIKE ME.
WEAPON PLUS TWISTED HIM, UNTIL HE COULDN'T TELL THE WAR FRONT FROM THE HOME FRONT.
AGENT SIMPSON WAS A TOUGH CUSTOMER.
THESE NEWER NUKES CAN'T HOLD A CANDLE TO HIM--BUT THEY DON'T NEED TO.
THEY WERE MADE TO HIT SOFT TARGETS.

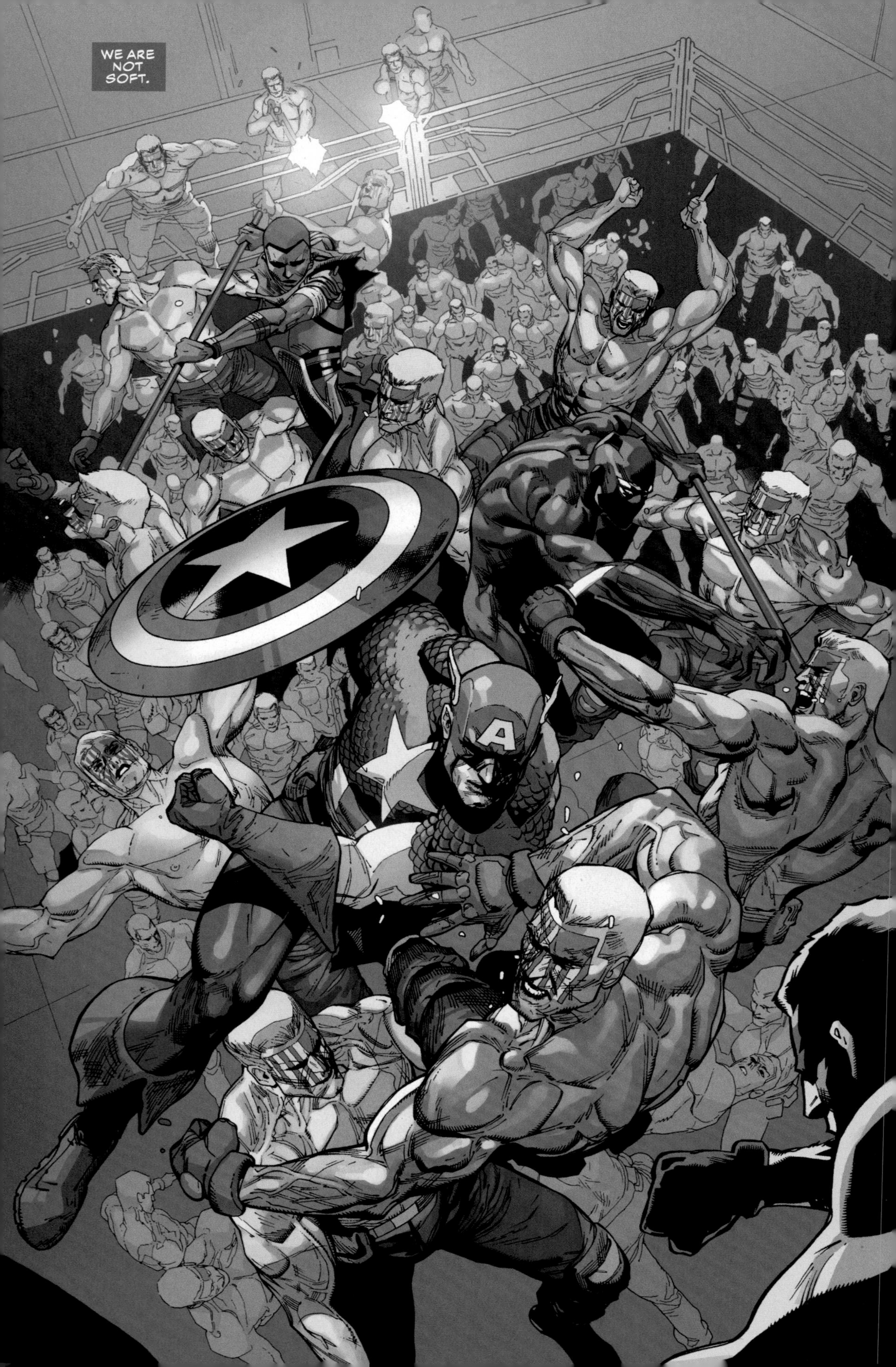
WE ARE NOT SOFT.

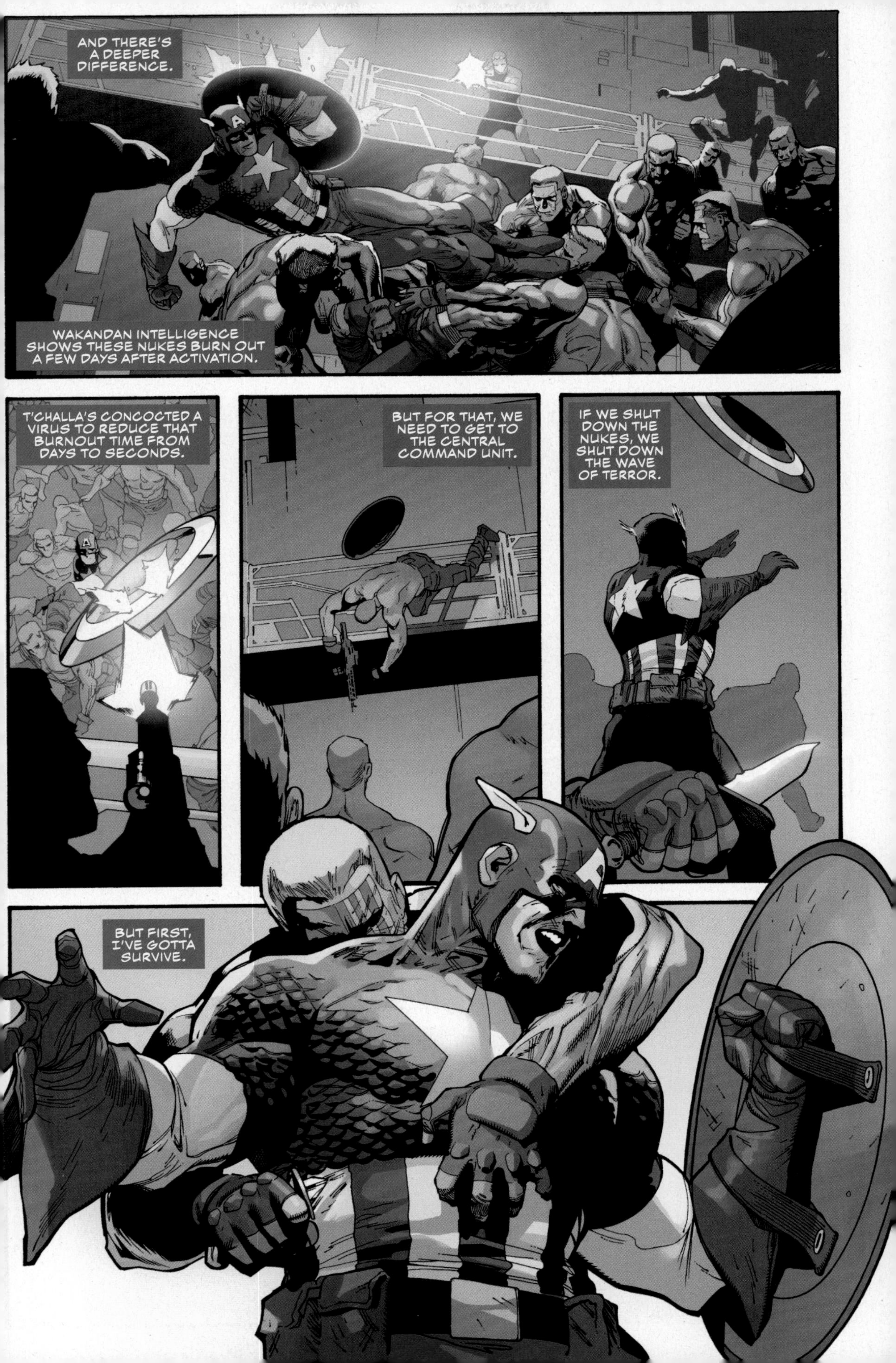
AND THERE'S A DEEPER DIFFERENCE.
WAKANDAN INTELLIGENCE SHOWS THESE NUKES BURN OUT A FEW DAYS AFTER ACTIVATION.
T'CHALLA'S CONCOCTED A VIRUS TO REDUCE THAT BURNOUT TIME FROM DAYS TO SECONDS.
BUT FOR THAT, WE NEED TO GET TO THE CENTRAL COMMAND UNIT.
IF WE SHUT DOWN THE NUKES, WE SHUT DOWN THE WAVE OF TERROR.
BUT FIRST, I'VE GOTTA SURVIVE.

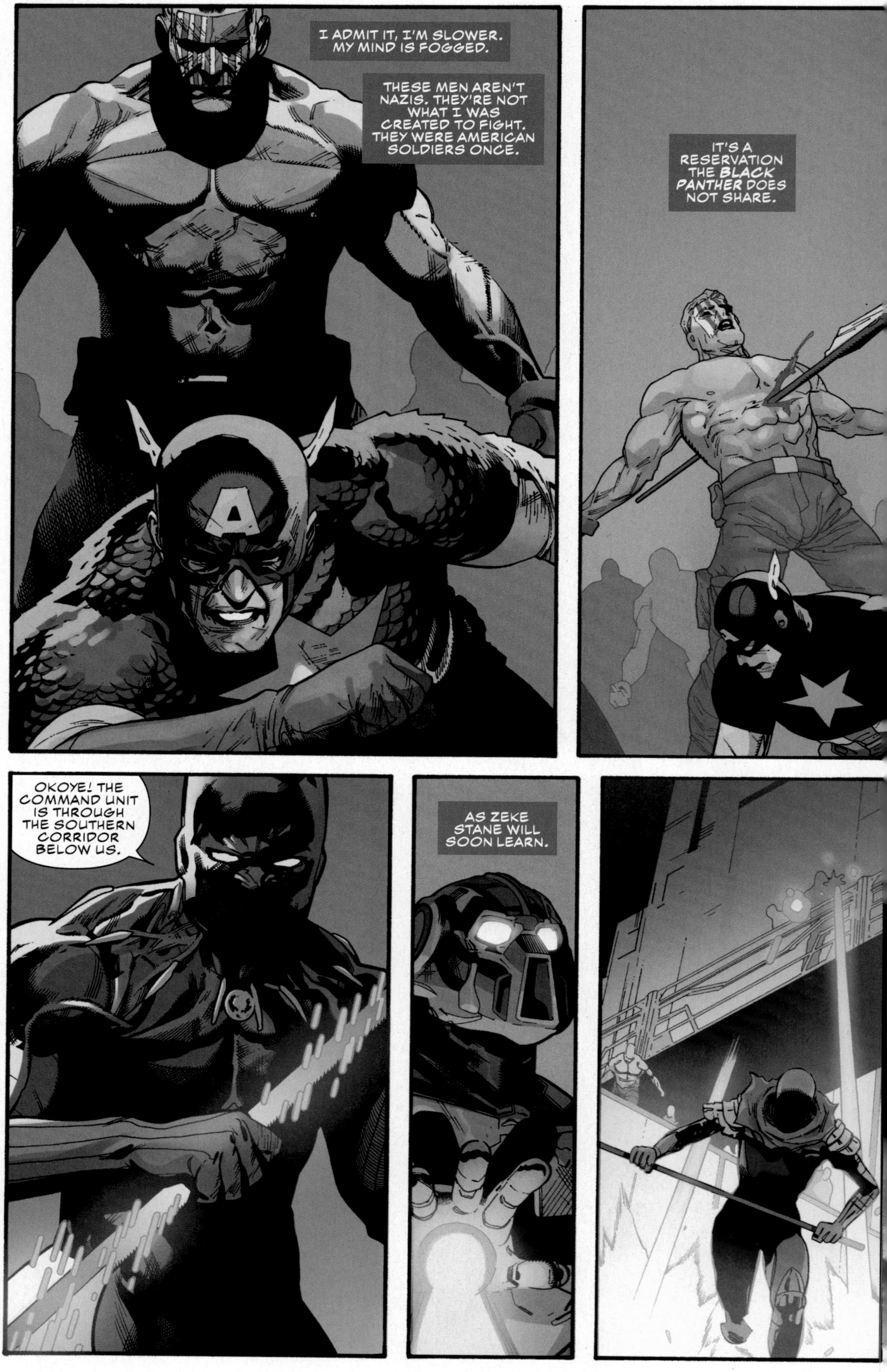
I ADMIT IT, I'M SLOWER. MY MIND IS FOGGED.
THESE MEN AREN'T NAZIS. THEY'RE NOT WHAT I WAS CREATED TO FIGHT. THEY WERE AMERICAN SOLDIERS ONCE.
IT'S A RESERVATION THE BLACK PANTHER DOES NOT SHARE.
OKOYE! THE COMMAND UNIT IS THROUGH THE SOUTHERN CORRIDOR BELOW US.
AS ZEKE STANE WILL SOON LEARN.

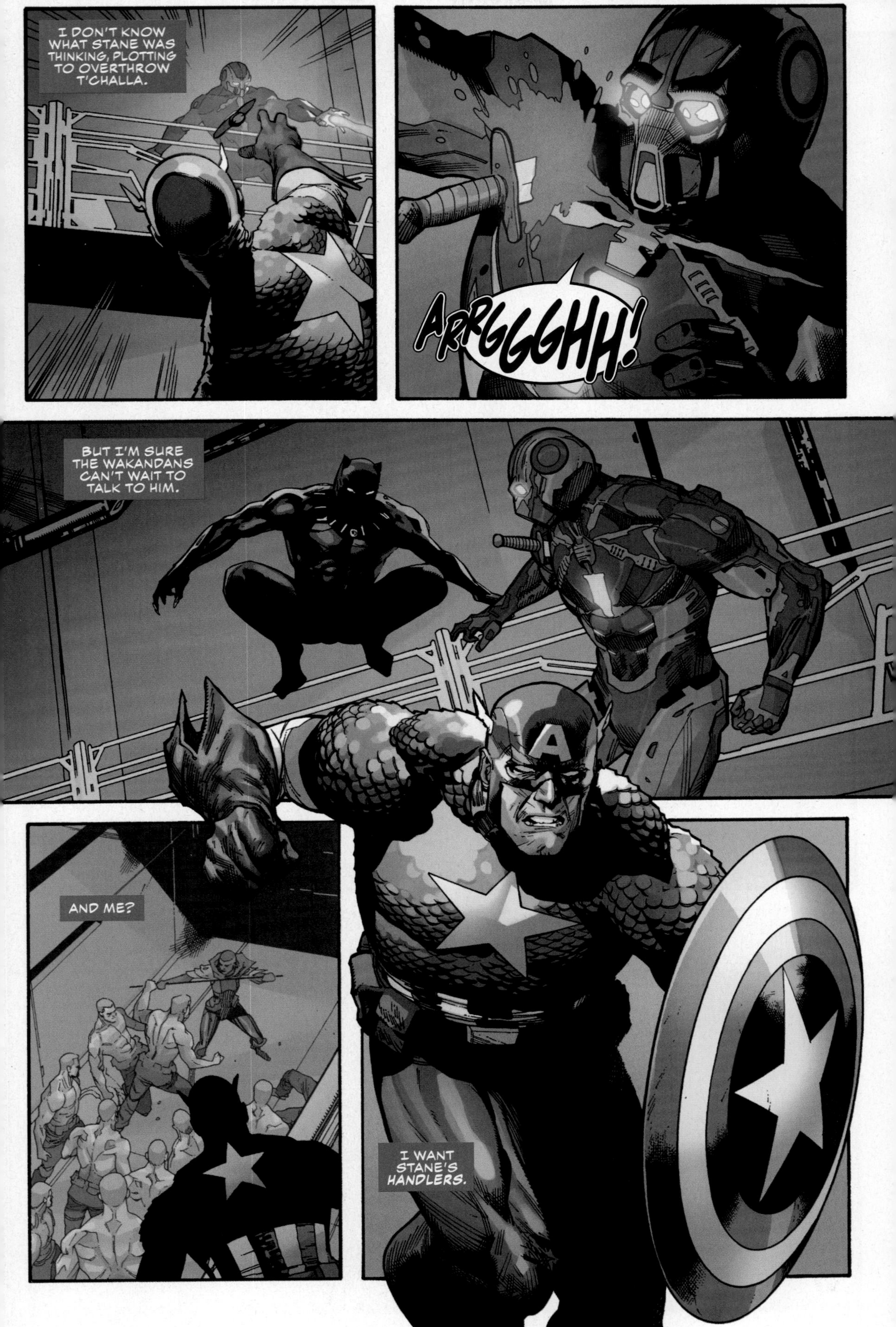
I DON'T KNOW WHAT STANE WAS THINKING, PLOTTING TO OVERTHROW T'CHALLA.
ARRRGGGHH!
BUT I'M SURE THE WAKANDANS CAN'T WAIT TO TALK TO HIM.
AND ME?
I WANT STANE'S HANDLERS.

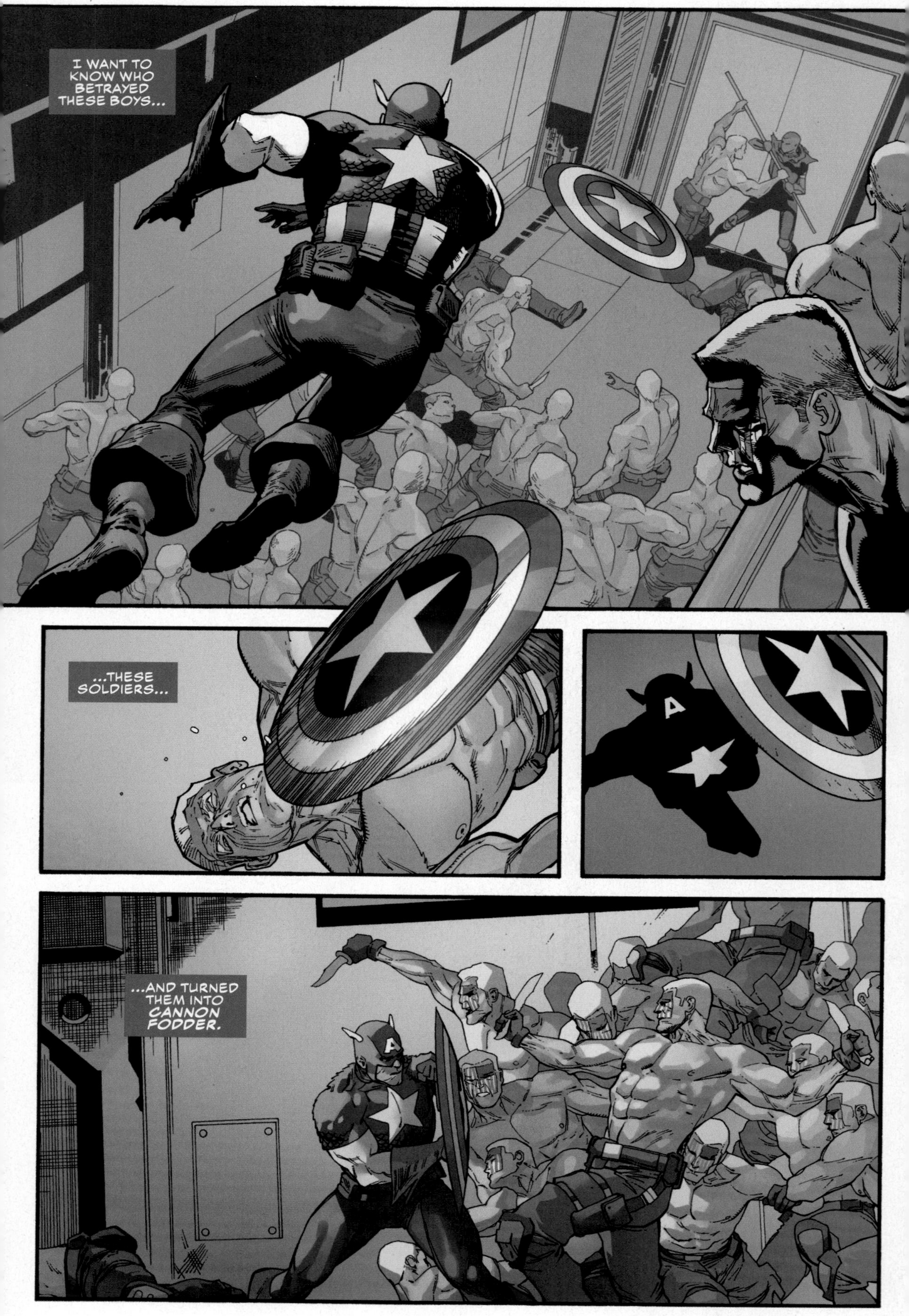
I WANT TO KNOW WHO BETRAYED THESE BOYS...
...THESE SOLDIERS...
...AND TURNED THEM INTO CANNON FODDER.

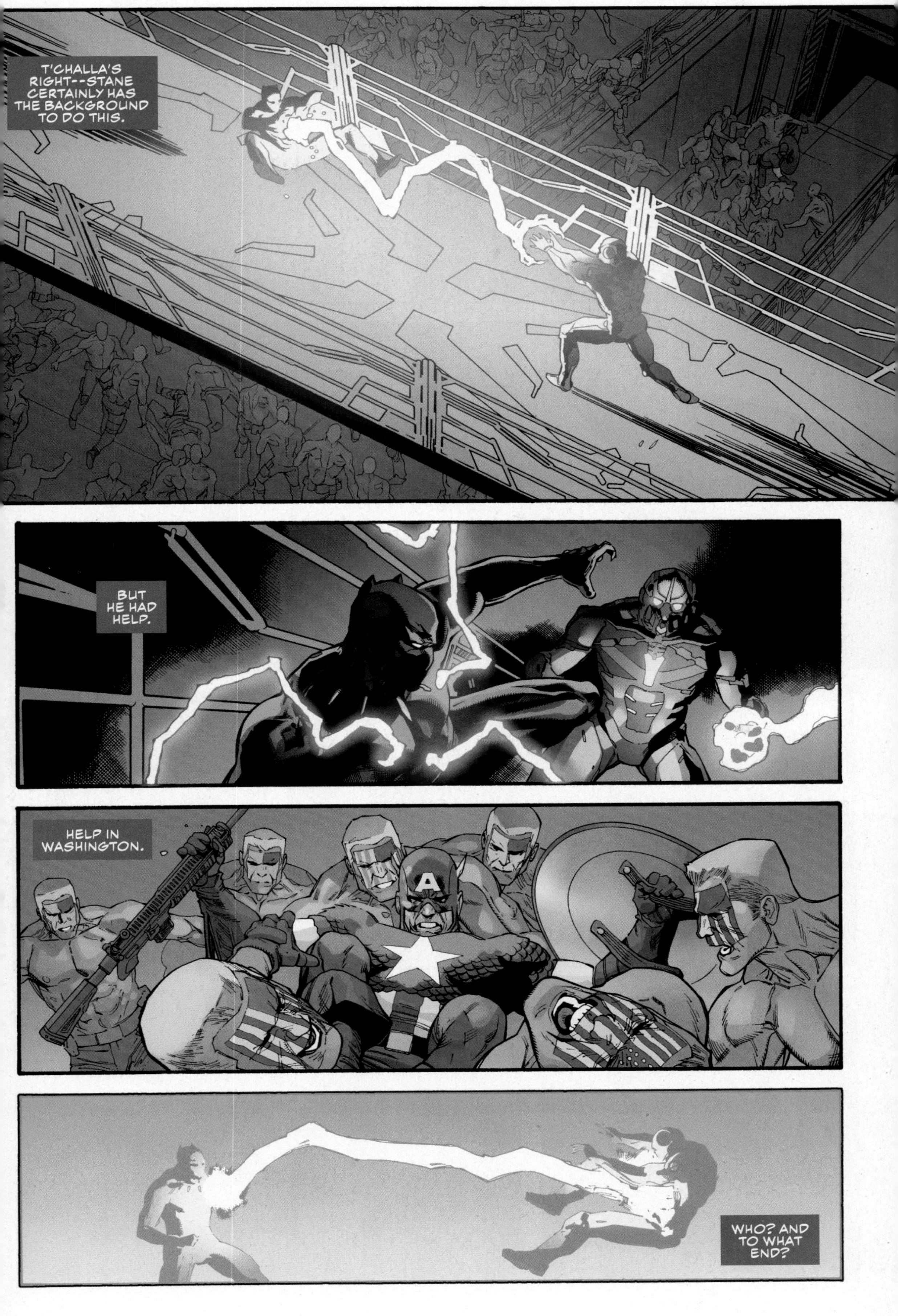
T'CHALLA'S RIGHT--STANE CERTAINLY HAS THE BACKGROUND TO DO THIS.
BUT HE HAD HELP.
HELP IN WASHINGTON.
WHO? AND TO WHAT END?

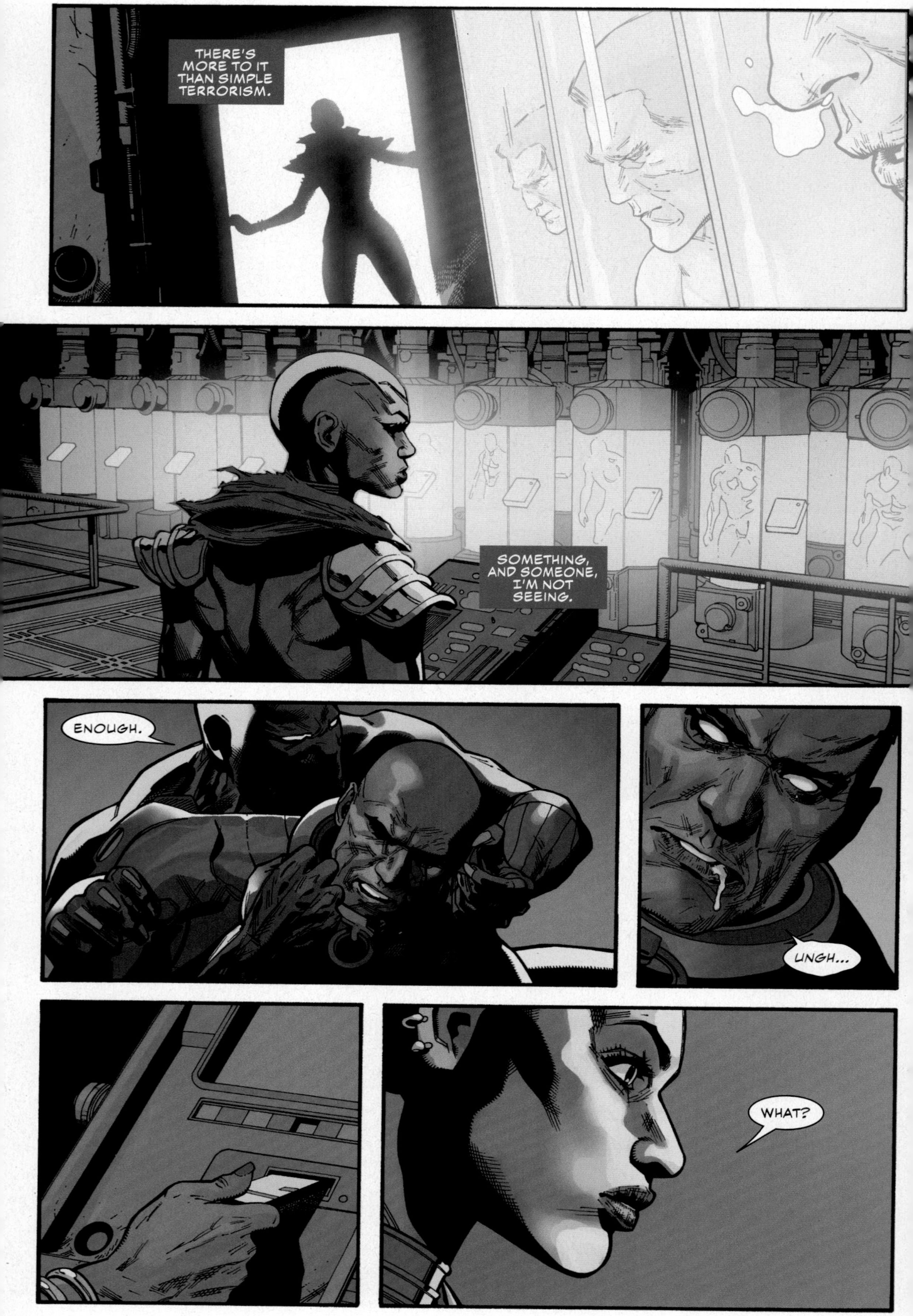
THERE'S MORE TO IT THAN SIMPLE TERRORISM.
SOMETHING, AND SOMEONE, I'M NOT SEEING.
ENOUGH.
UNGH...
WHAT?

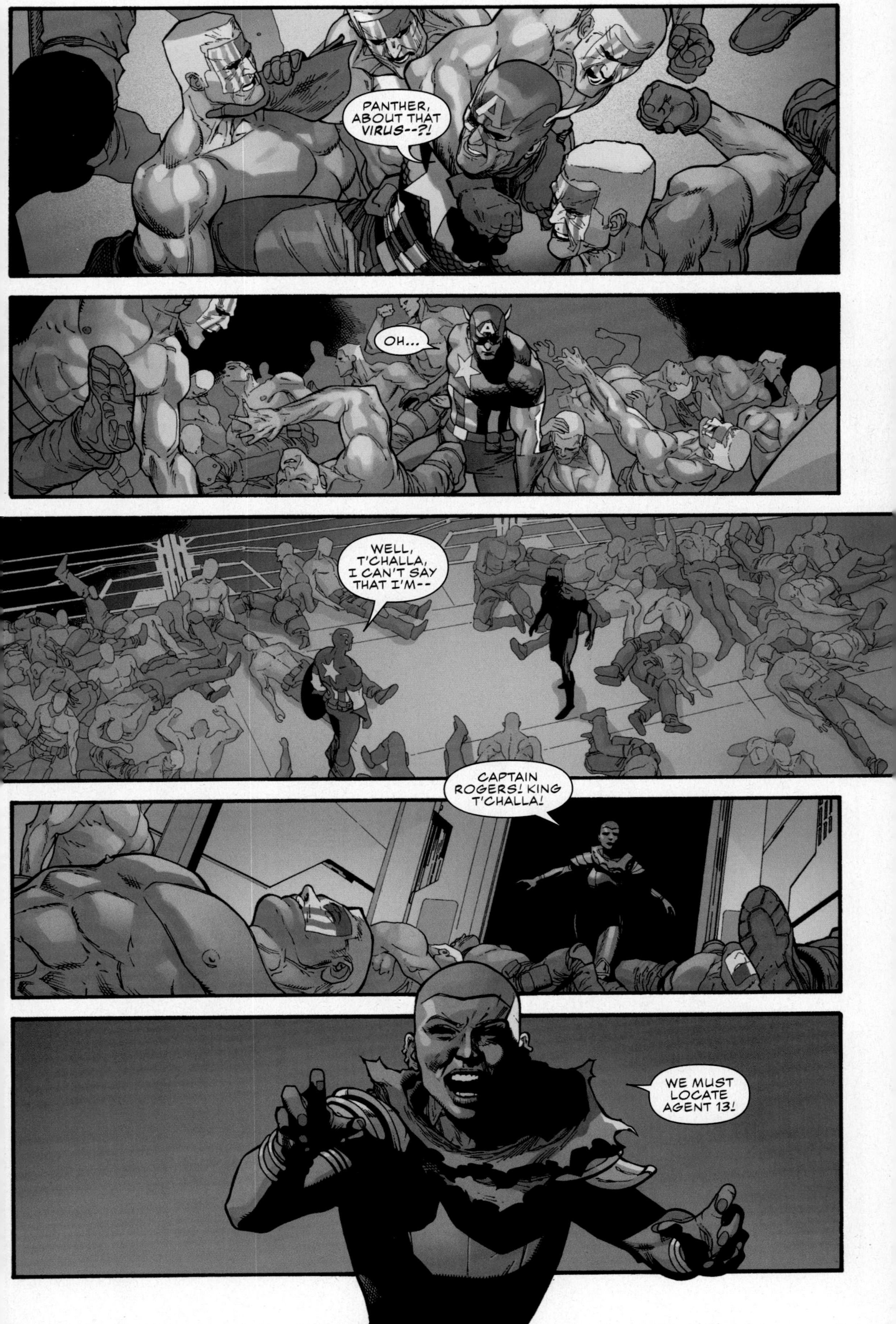
PANTHER, ABOUT THAT VIRUS--?!
OH...
WELL, T'CHALLA, I CAN'T SAY THAT I'M--
CAPTAIN ROGERS! KING T'CHALLA!
WE MUST LOCATE AGENT 13!

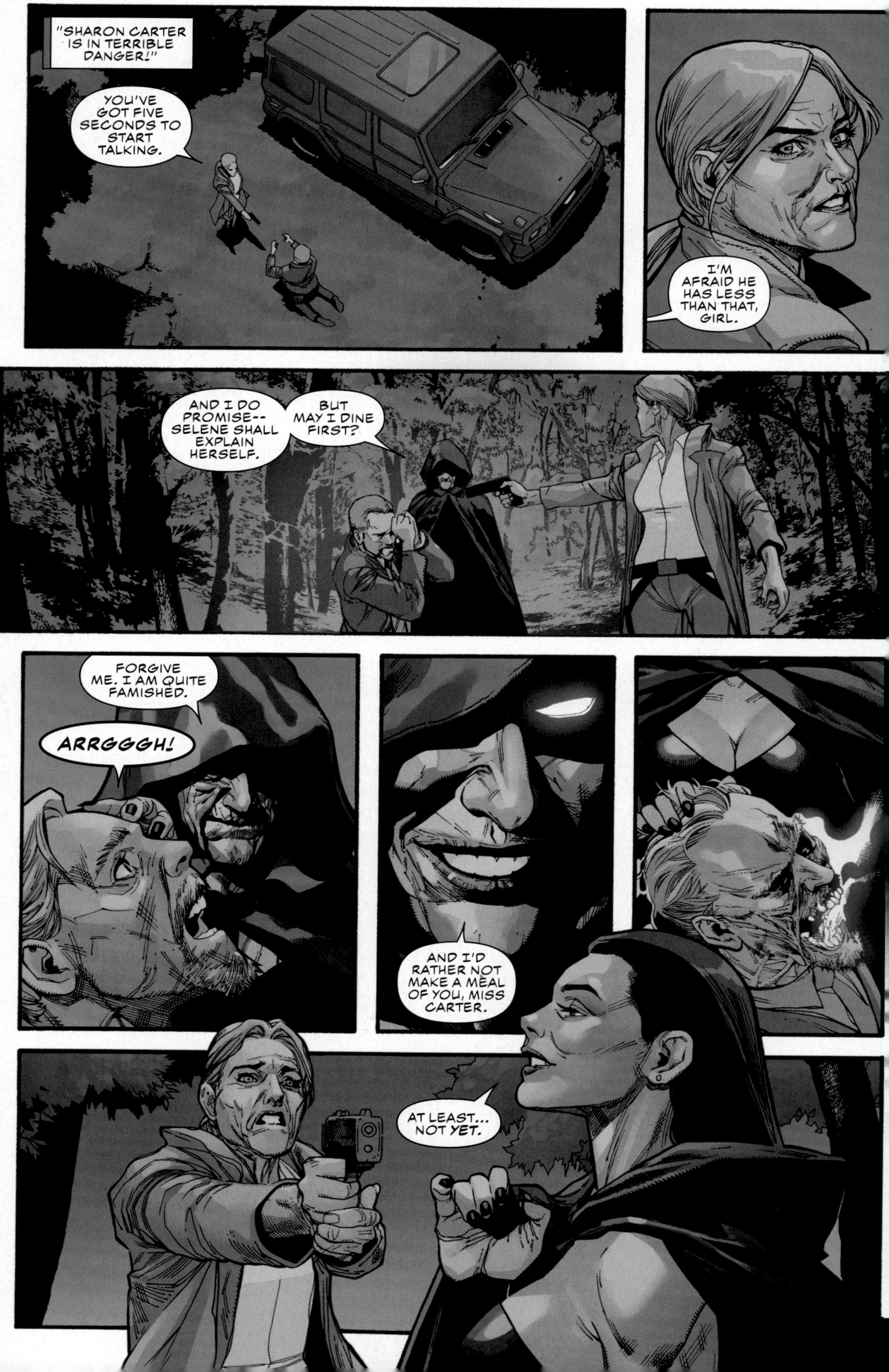
"SHARON CARTER IS IN TERRIBLE DANGER!"
YOU'VE GOT FIVE SECONDS TO START TALKING.
I'M AFRAID HE HAS LESS THAN THAT, GIRL.
AND I DO PROMISE-- SELENE SHALL EXPLAIN HERSELF.
BUT MAY I DINE FIRST?
FORGIVE ME. I AM QUITE FAMISHED.
ARRGGGH!
AND I'D RATHER NOT MAKE A MEAL OF YOU, MISS CARTER.
AT LEAST... NOT YET.

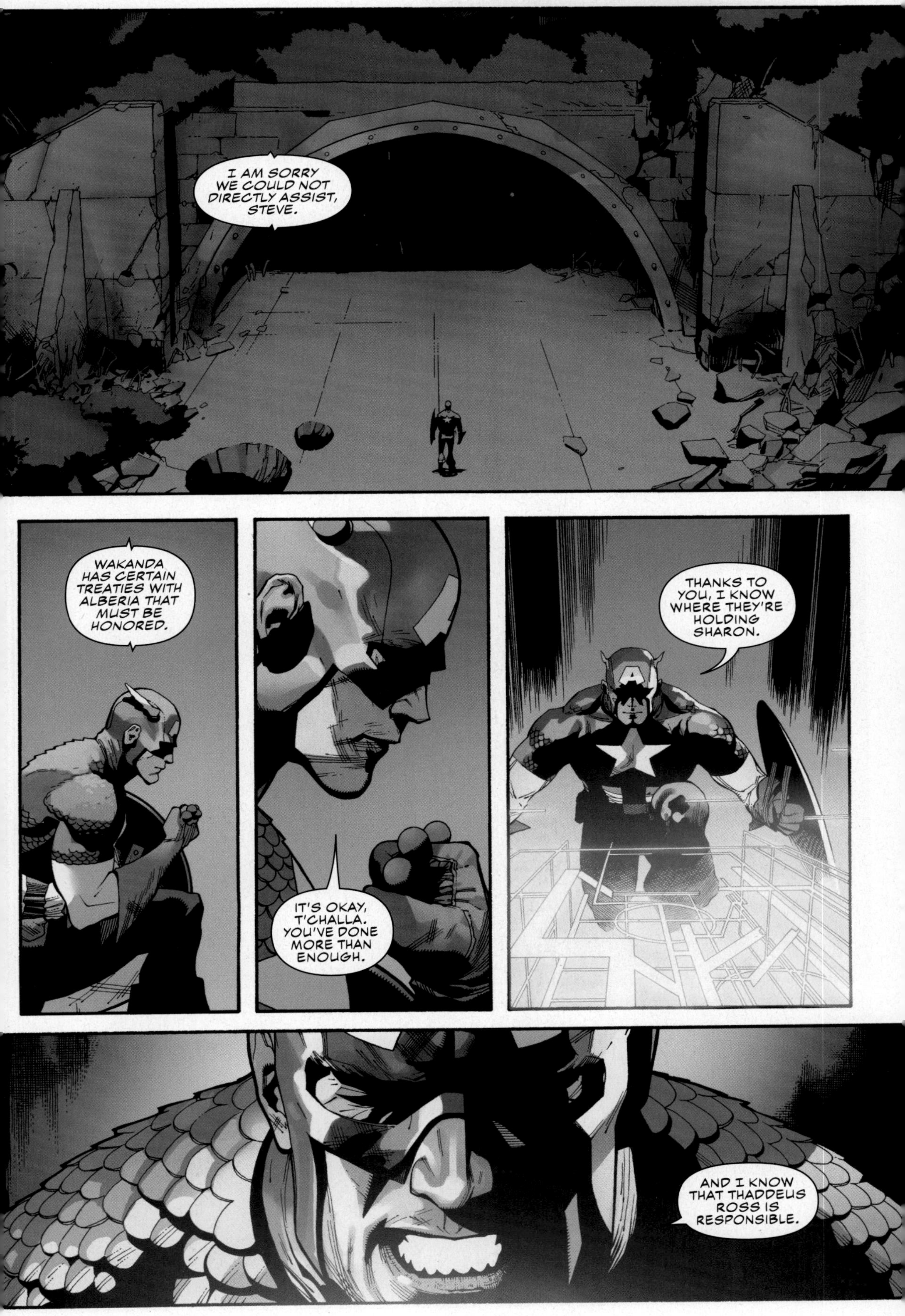
I AM SORRY WE COULD NOT DIRECTLY ASSIST, STEVE.
WAKANDA HAS CERTAIN TREATIES WITH ALBERIA THAT MUST BE HONORED.
IT'S OKAY, T'CHALLA. YOU'VE DONE MORE THAN ENOUGH.
THANKS TO YOU, I KNOW WHERE THEY'RE HOLDING SHARON.
AND I KNOW THAT THADDEUS ROSS IS RESPONSIBLE.

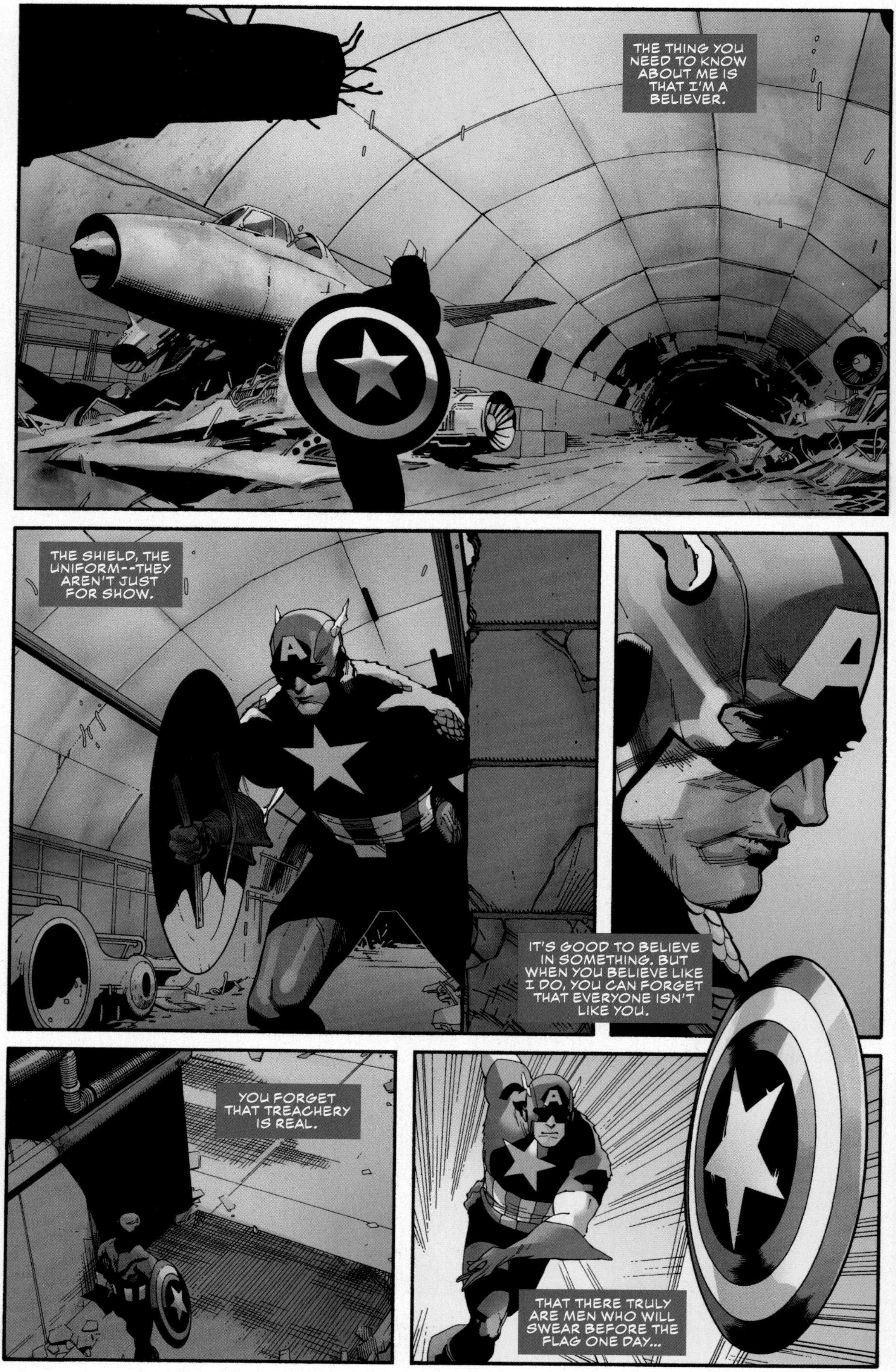
THE THING YOU NEED TO KNOW ABOUT ME IS THAT I'M A BELIEVER.
THE SHIELD, THE UNIFORM--THEY AREN'T JUST FOR SHOW.
IT'S GOOD TO BELIEVE IN SOMETHING. BUT WHEN YOU BELIEVE LIKE I DO, YOU CAN FORGET THAT EVERYONE ISN'T LIKE YOU.
YOU FORGET THAT TREACHERY IS REAL.
THAT THERE TRULY ARE MEN WHO WILL SWEAR BEFORE THE FLAG ONE DAY...

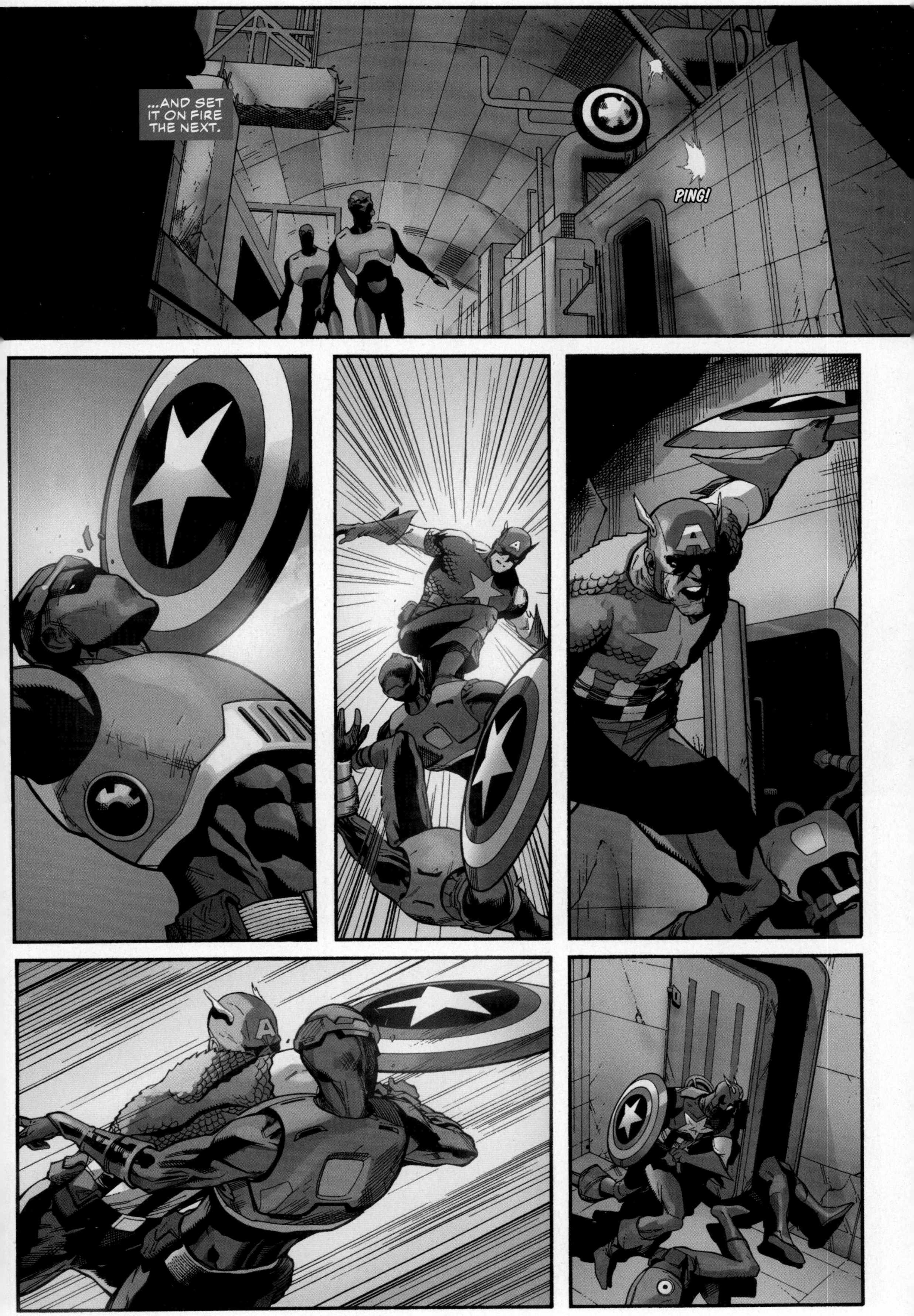
...AND SET IT ON FIRE THE NEXT.
PING!

WHATEVER HIS PAST "ACTIVITIES," I THOUGHT GENERAL ROSS WAS A BELIEVER TOO.

ROSS COMES FROM A LONG LINE OF SOLDIERS. I SERVED WITH HIS AUNT DURING THE WAR.

AND HE KEPT THAT TRADITION ALIVE-- ROSS ISN'T AN ARMCHAIR GENERAL. HE'S A DECORATED AIR FORCE PILOT.

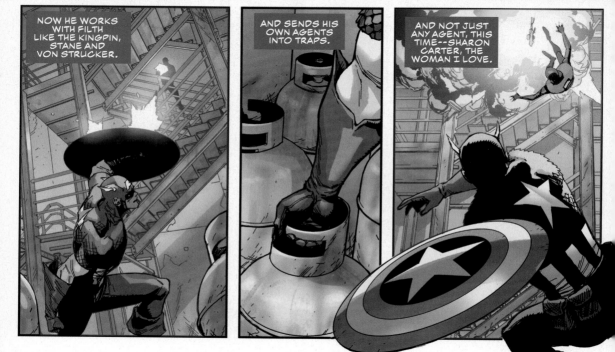

NOW HE WORKS WITH FILTH LIKE THE KINGPIN, STANE AND VON STRUCKER.

AND SENDS HIS OWN AGENTS INTO TRAPS.

AND NOT JUST ANY AGENT, THIS TIME--SHARON CARTER, THE WOMAN I LOVE.

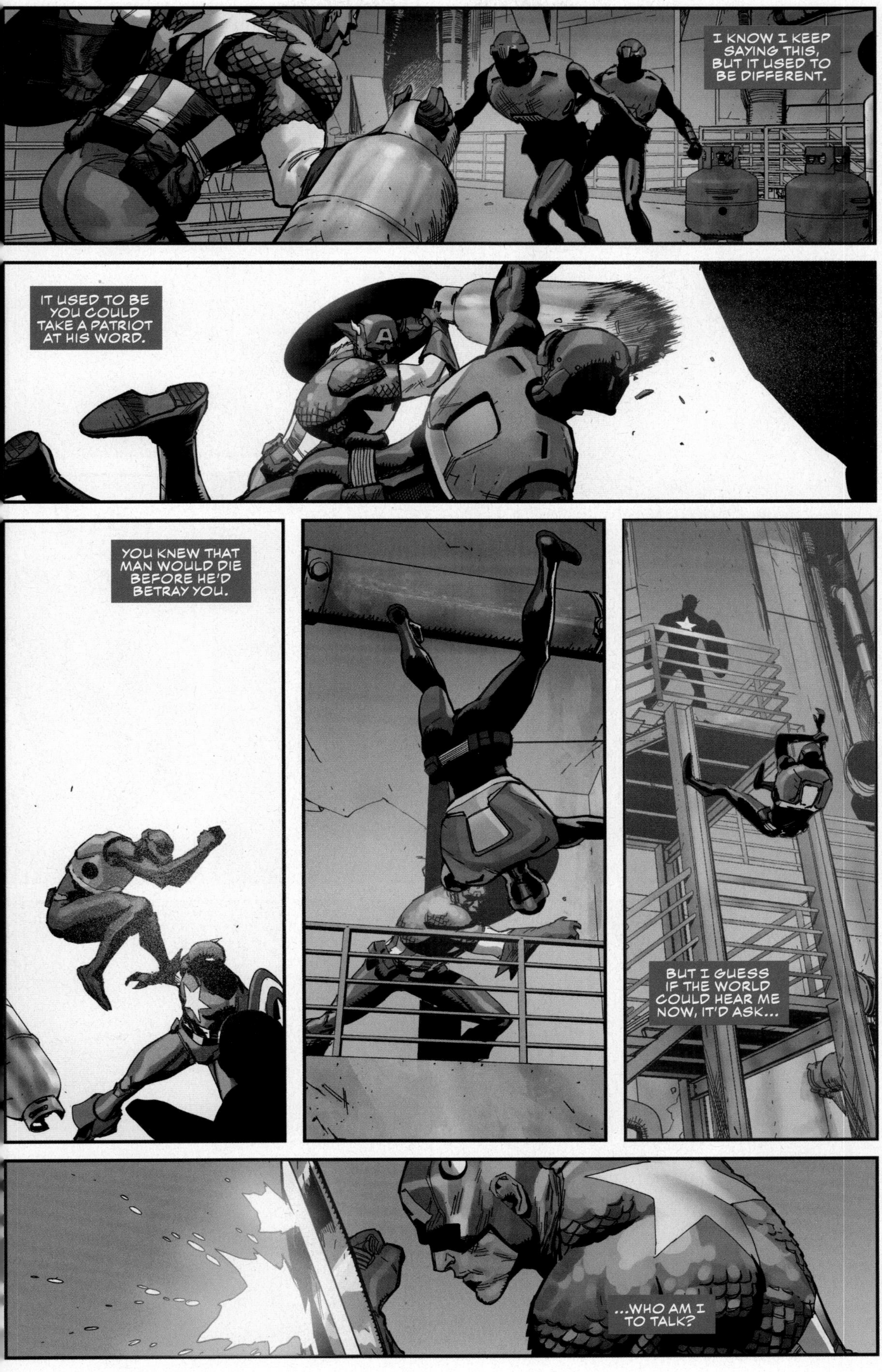
I KNOW I KEEP SAYING THIS, BUT IT USED TO BE DIFFERENT.
IT USED TO BE YOU COULD TAKE A PATRIOT AT HIS WORD.
YOU KNEW THAT MAN WOULD DIE BEFORE HE'D BETRAY YOU.
BUT I GUESS IF THE WORLD COULD HEAR ME NOW, IT'D ASK...
...WHO AM I TO TALK?

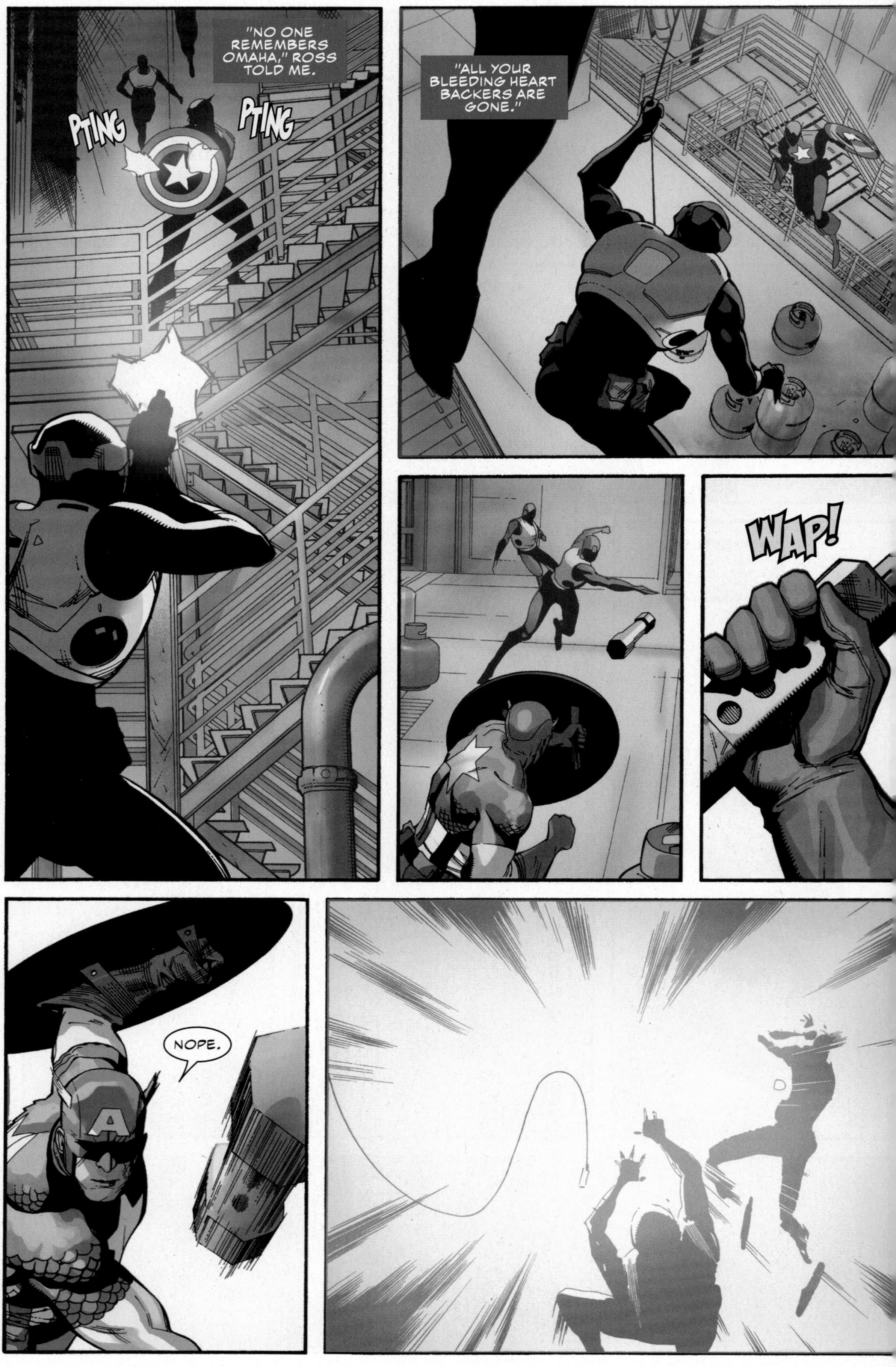
"NO ONE REMEMBERS OMAHA," ROSS TOLD ME.
PTING
PTING
"ALL YOUR BLEEDING HEART BACKERS ARE GONE."
WAP!
NOPE.

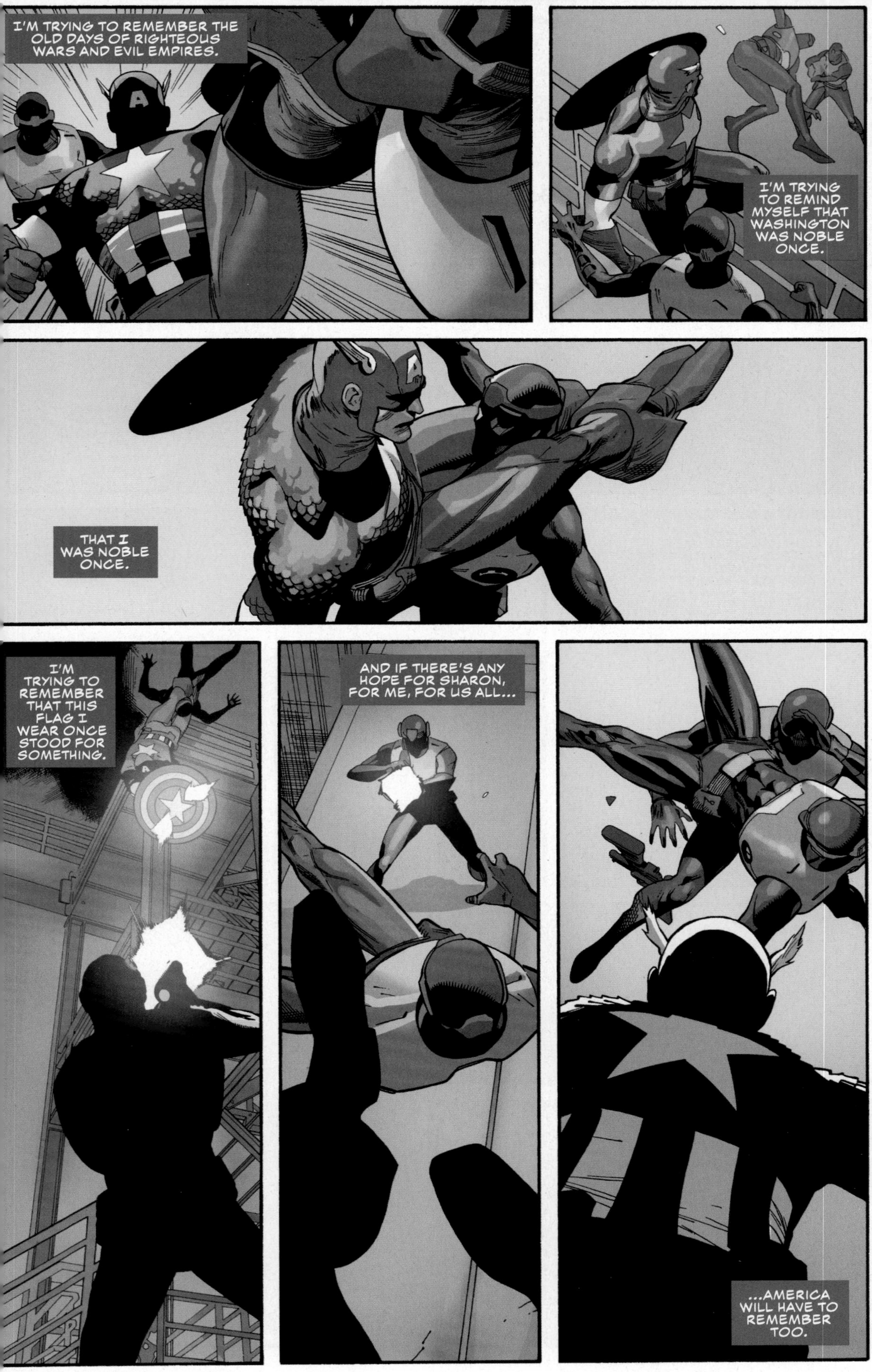
I'M TRYING TO REMEMBER THE OLD DAYS OF RIGHTEOUS WARS AND EVIL EMPIRES.
I'M TRYING TO REMIND MYSELF THAT WASHINGTON WAS NOBLE ONCE.
THAT I WAS NOBLE ONCE.
I'M TRYING TO REMEMBER THAT THIS FLAG I WEAR ONCE STOOD FOR SOMETHING.
AND IF THERE'S ANY HOPE FOR SHARON, FOR ME, FOR US ALL...
...AMERICA WILL HAVE TO REMEMBER TOO.

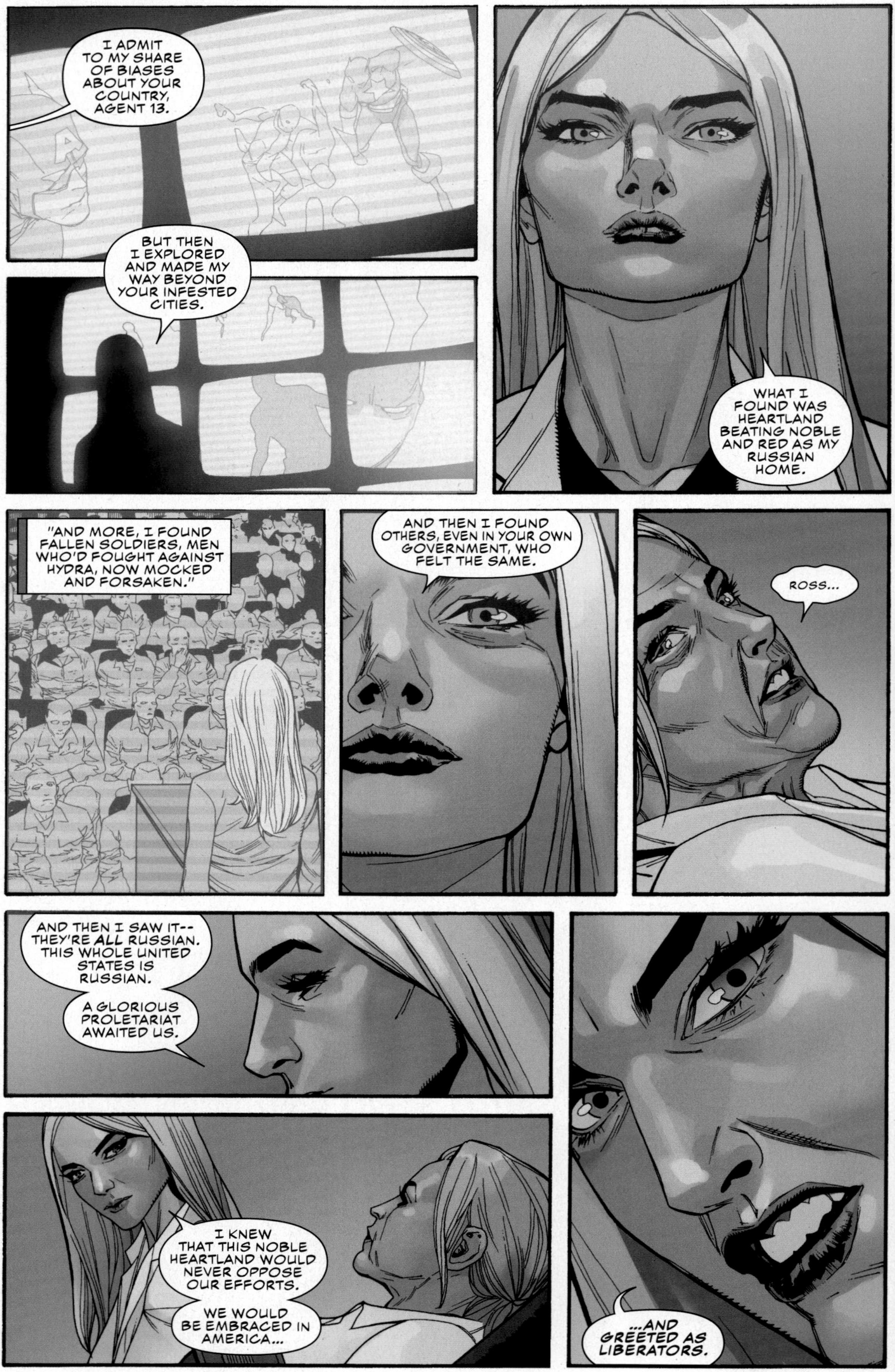

I ADMIT TO MY SHARE OF BIASES ABOUT YOUR COUNTRY, AGENT 13.
BUT THEN I EXPLORED AND MADE MY WAY BEYOND YOUR INFESTED CITIES.
WHAT I FOUND WAS HEARTLAND BEATING NOBLE AND RED AS MY RUSSIAN HOME.
"AND MORE, I FOUND FALLEN SOLDIERS, MEN WHO'D FOUGHT AGAINST HYDRA, NOW MOCKED AND FORSAKEN."
AND THEN I FOUND OTHERS, EVEN IN YOUR OWN GOVERNMENT, WHO FELT THE SAME.
ROSS...
AND THEN I SAW IT-- THEY'RE ALL RUSSIAN. THIS WHOLE UNITED STATES IS RUSSIAN.
A GLORIOUS PROLETARIAT AWAITED US.
I KNEW THAT THIS NOBLE HEARTLAND WOULD NEVER OPPOSE OUR EFFORTS.
WE WOULD BE EMBRACED IN AMERICA...
...AND GREETED AS LIBERATORS.

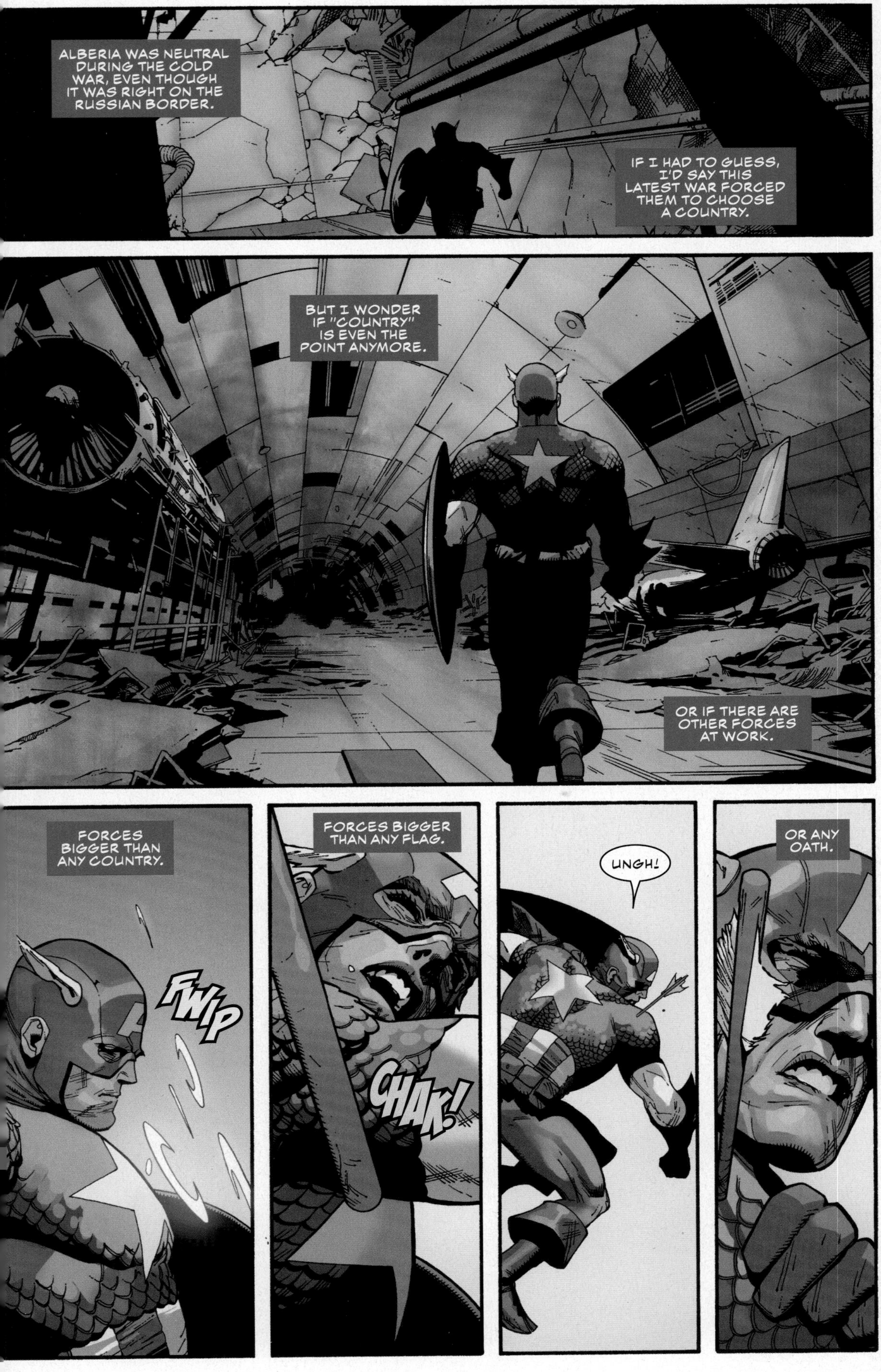
ALBERIA WAS NEUTRAL DURING THE COLD WAR, EVEN THOUGH IT WAS RIGHT ON THE RUSSIAN BORDER.
IF I HAD TO GUESS, I'D SAY THIS LATEST WAR FORCED THEM TO CHOOSE A COUNTRY.
BUT I WONDER IF "COUNTRY" IS EVEN THE POINT ANYMORE.
OR IF THERE ARE OTHER FORCES AT WORK.
FORCES BIGGER THAN ANY COUNTRY.
FWIP
FORCES BIGGER THAN ANY FLAG.
CHAK!
UNGH!
OR ANY OATH.

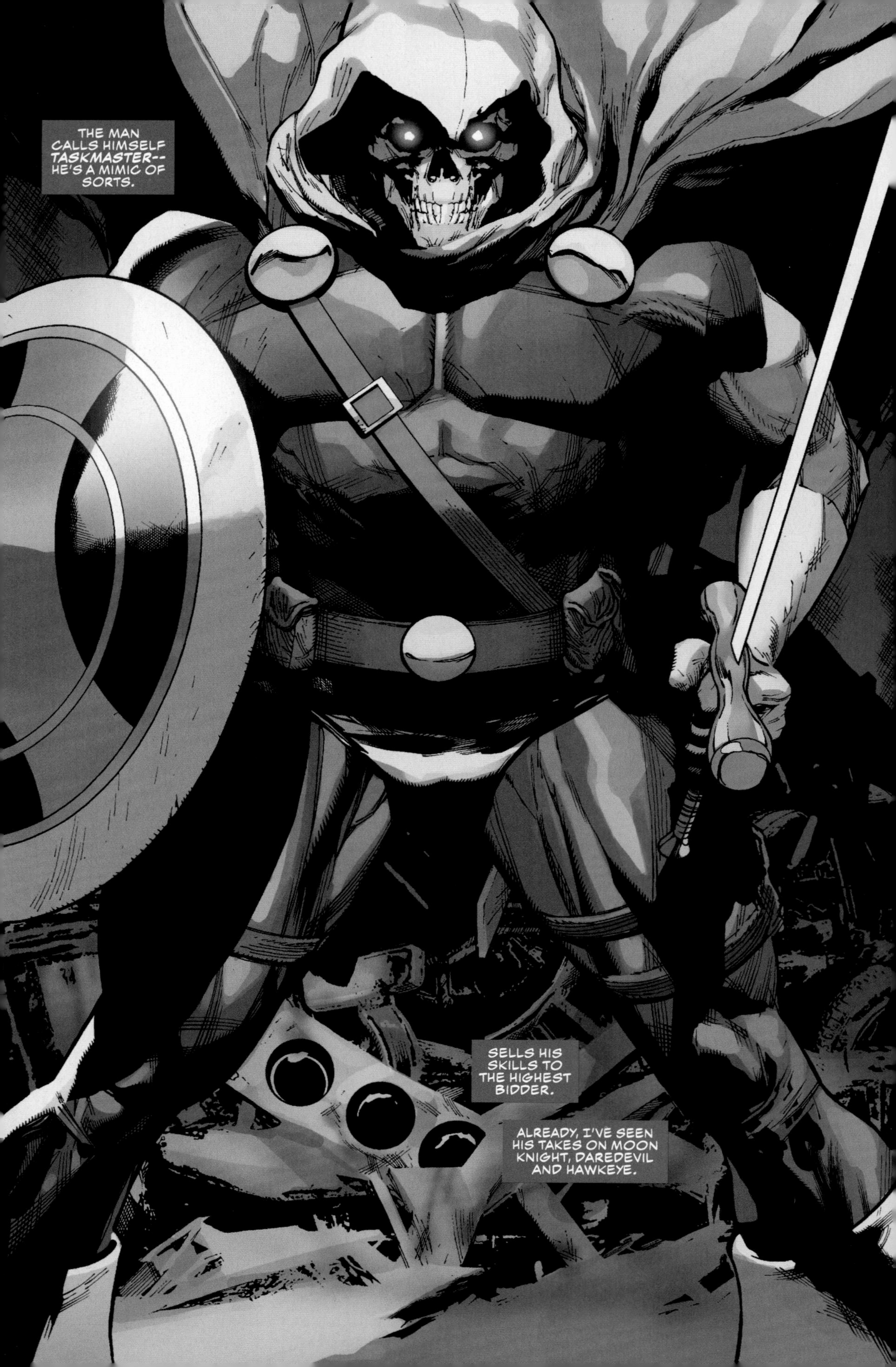
THE MAN CALLS HIMSELF TASKMASTER-- HE'S A MIMIC OF SORTS.
SELLS HIS SKILLS TO THE HIGHEST BIDDER.
ALREADY, I'VE SEEN HIS TAKES ON MOON KNIGHT, DAREDEVIL AND HAWKEYE.

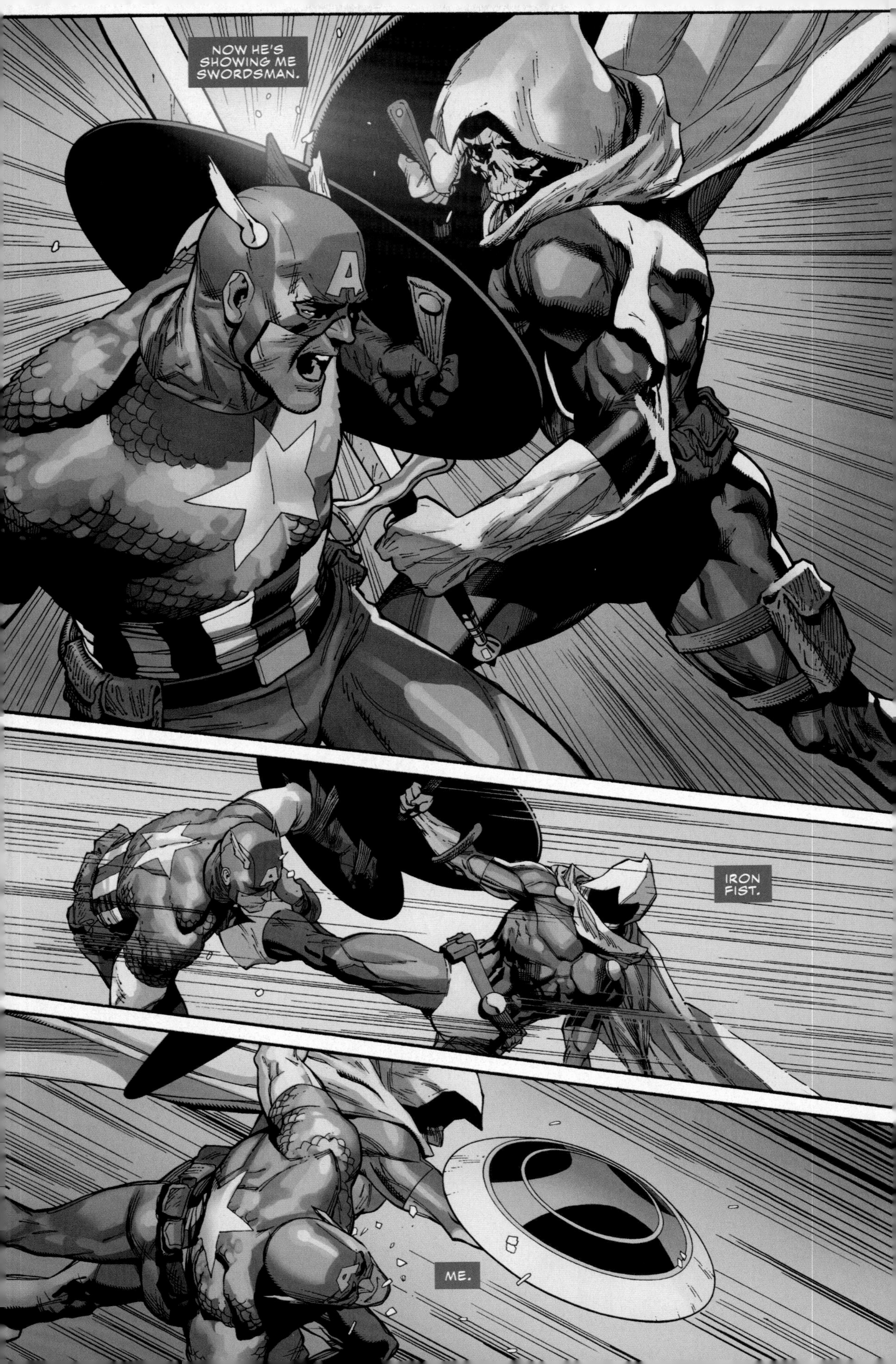
NOW HE'S SHOWING ME SWORDSMAN.
IRON FIST.
ME.

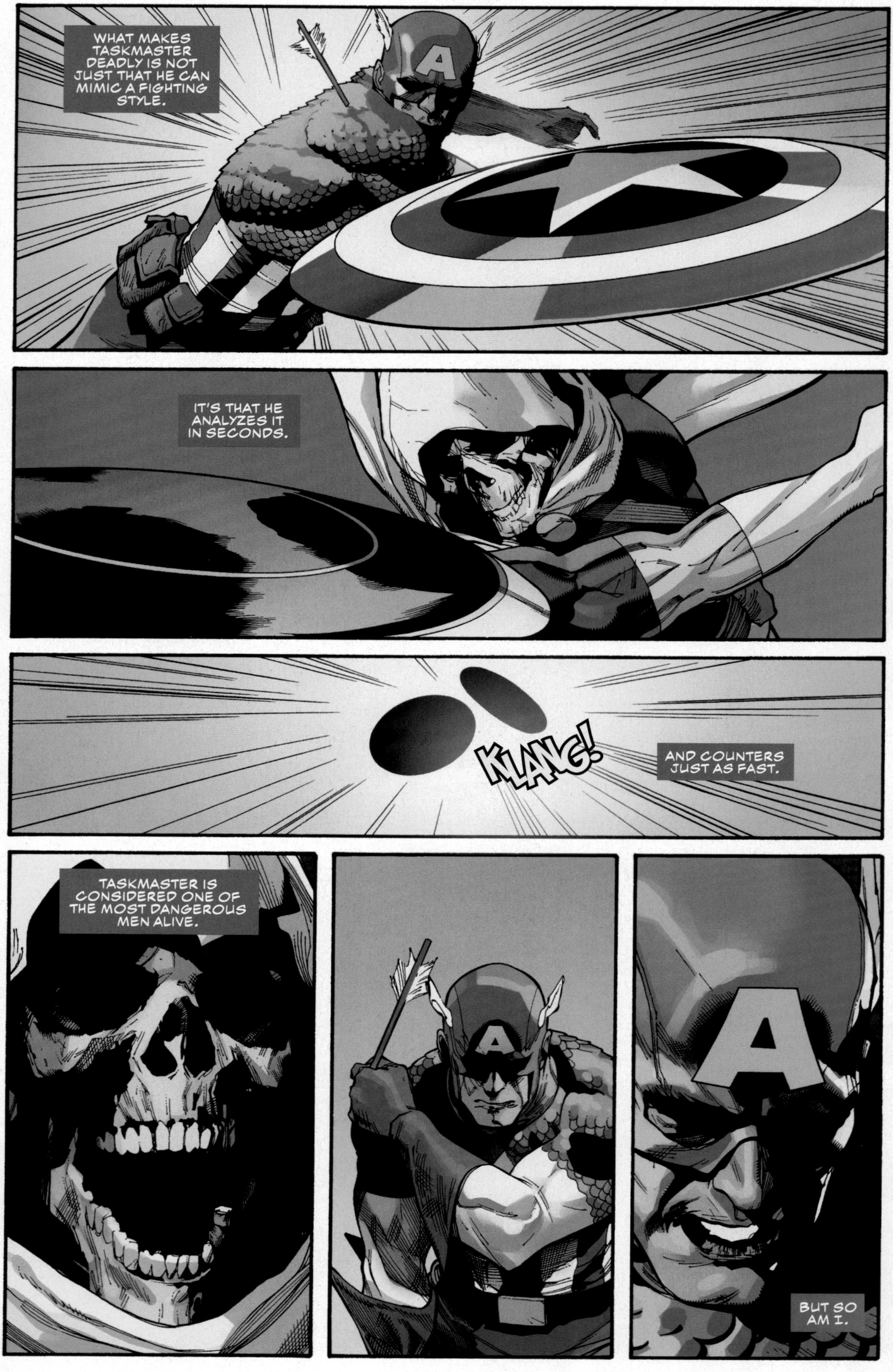
WHAT MAKES TASKMASTER DEADLY IS NOT JUST THAT HE CAN MIMIC A FIGHTING STYLE.
IT'S THAT HE ANALYZES IT IN SECONDS.
KLANG!
AND COUNTERS JUST AS FAST.
TASKMASTER IS CONSIDERED ONE OF THE MOST DANGEROUS MEN ALIVE.
BUT SO AM I.

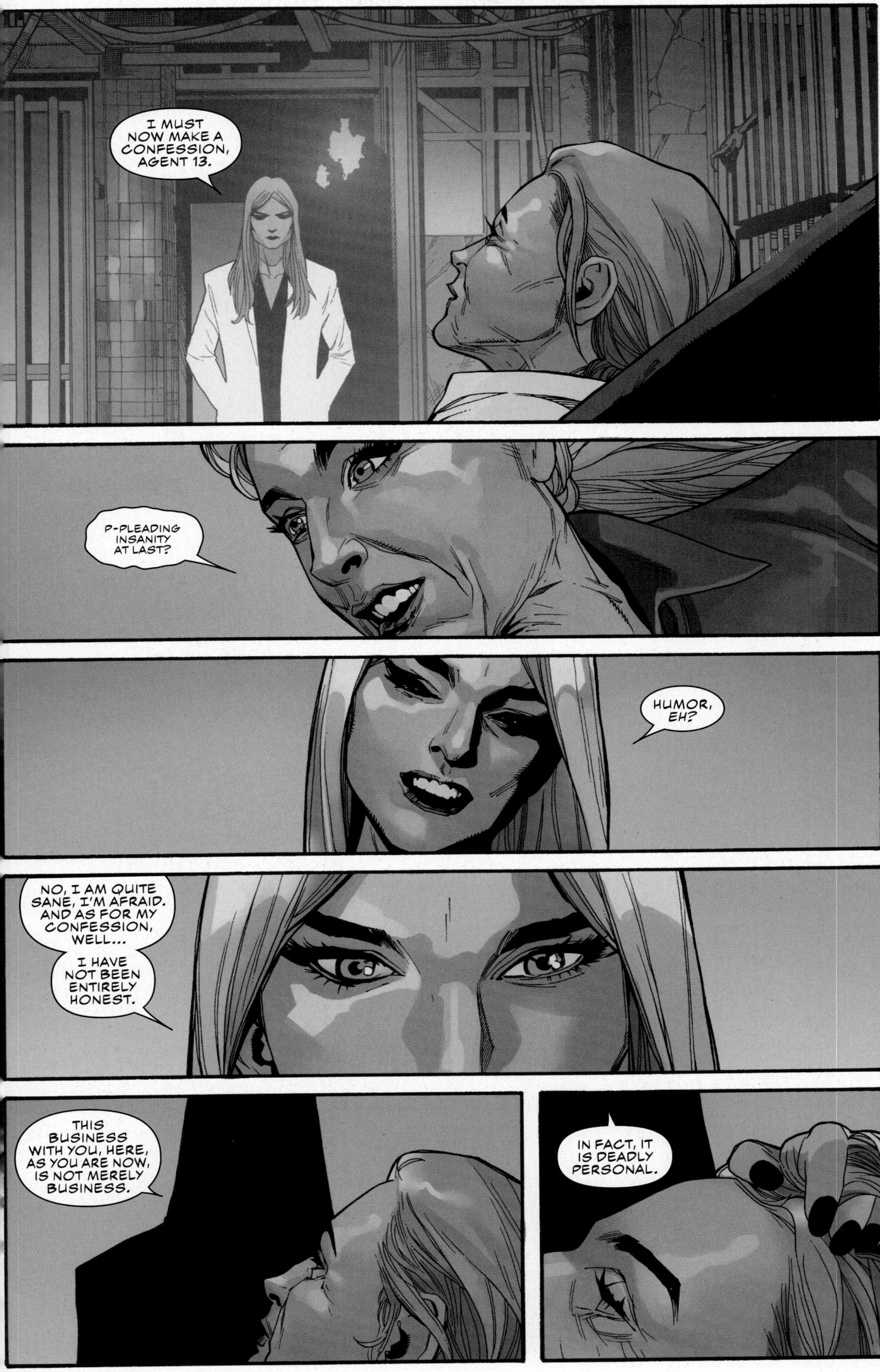
I MUST NOW MAKE A CONFESSION, AGENT 13.
P-PLEADING INSANITY AT LAST?
HUMOR, EH?
NO, I AM QUITE SANE, I'M AFRAID. AND AS FOR MY CONFESSION, WELL...
I HAVE NOT BEEN ENTIRELY HONEST.
THIS BUSINESS WITH YOU, HERE, AS YOU ARE NOW, IS NOT MERELY BUSINESS.
IN FACT, IT IS DEADLY PERSONAL.

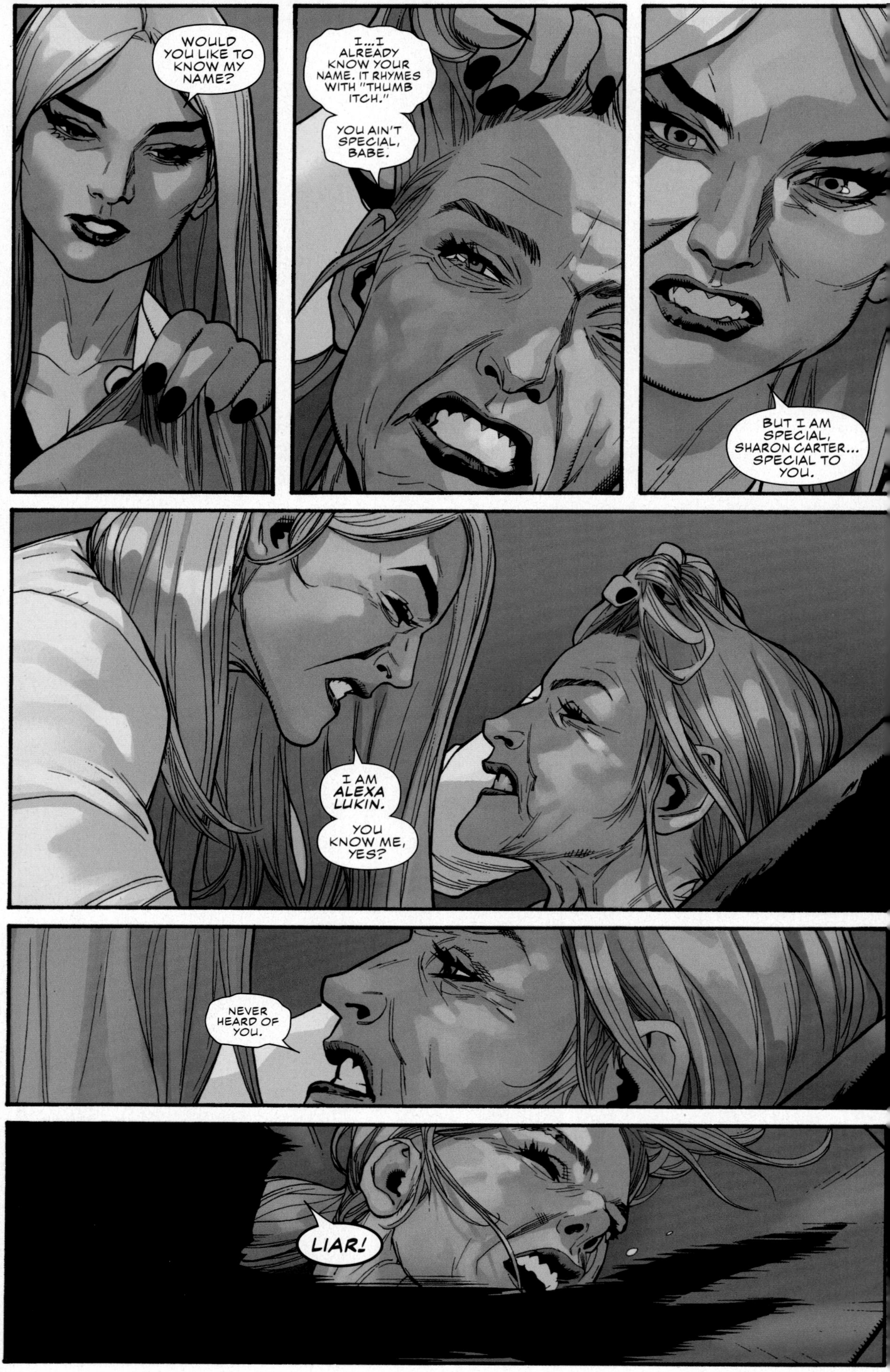
WOULD YOU LIKE TO KNOW MY NAME?
I...I ALREADY KNOW YOUR NAME. IT RHYMES WITH "THUMB ITCH."
YOU AIN'T SPECIAL, BABE.
BUT I AM SPECIAL, SHARON CARTER... SPECIAL TO YOU.
I AM ALEXA LUKIN.
YOU KNOW ME, YES?
NEVER HEARD OF YOU.
LIAR!

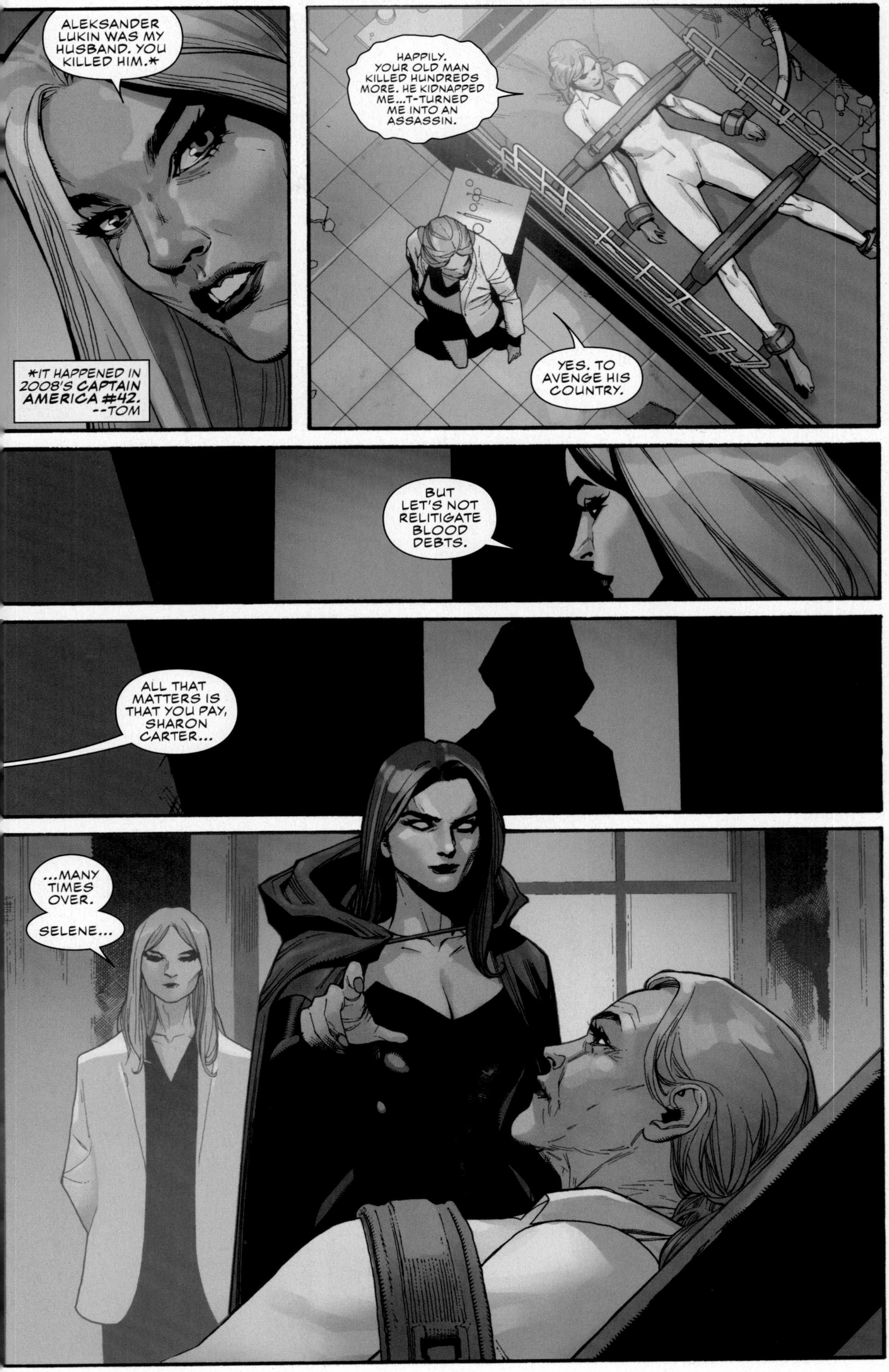
ALEKSANDER LUKIN WAS MY HUSBAND. YOU KILLED HIM.*
*IT HAPPENED IN 2008'S CAPTAIN AMERICA #42. --TOM
HAPPILY. YOUR OLD MAN KILLED HUNDREDS MORE. HE KIDNAPPED ME...T-TURNED ME INTO AN ASSASSIN.
YES. TO AVENGE HIS COUNTRY.
BUT LET'S NOT RELITIGATE BLOOD DEBTS.
ALL THAT MATTERS IS THAT YOU PAY, SHARON CARTER...
...MANY TIMES OVER.
SELENE...

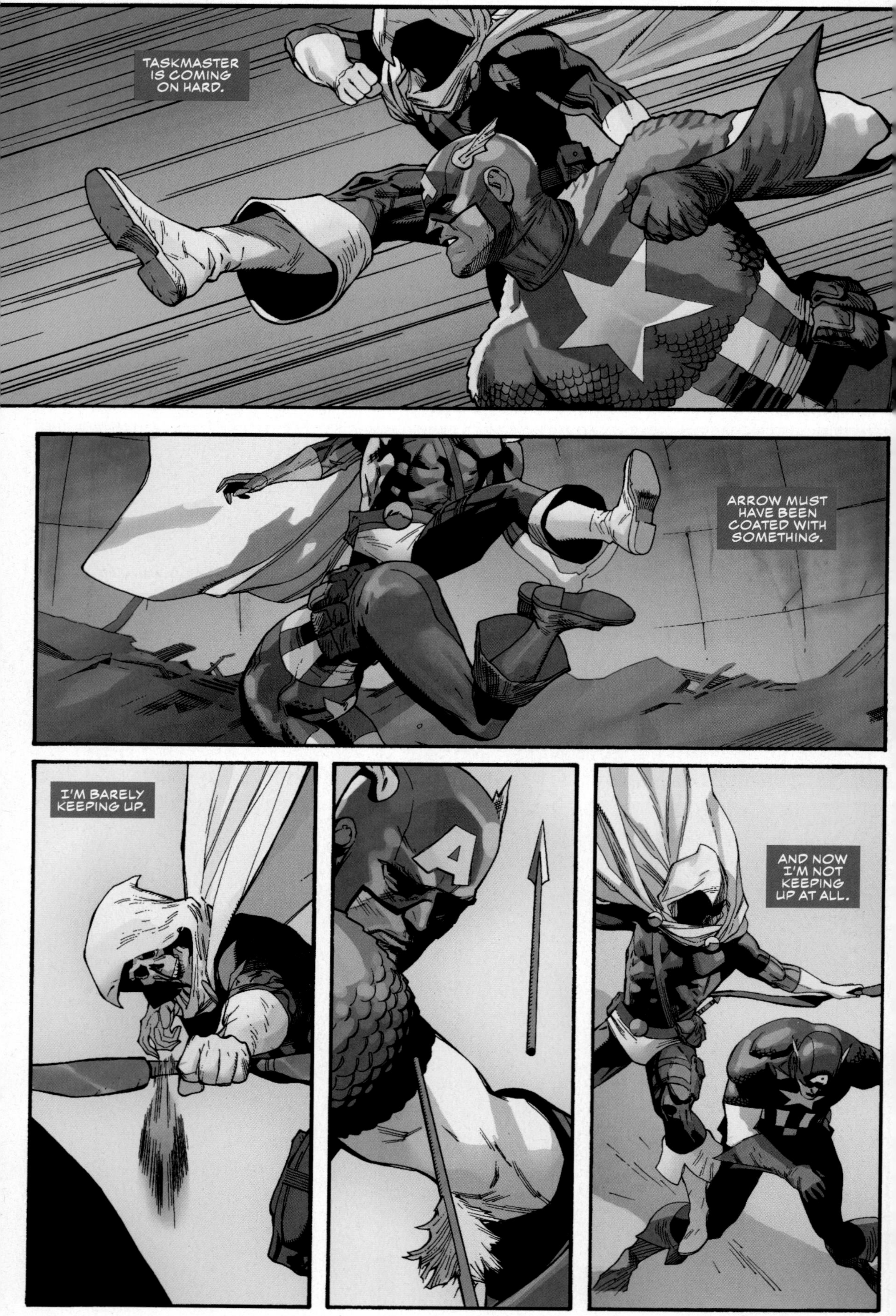
TASKMASTER IS COMING ON HARD.
ARROW MUST HAVE BEEN COATED WITH SOMETHING.
I'M BARELY KEEPING UP.
AND NOW I'M NOT KEEPING UP AT ALL.

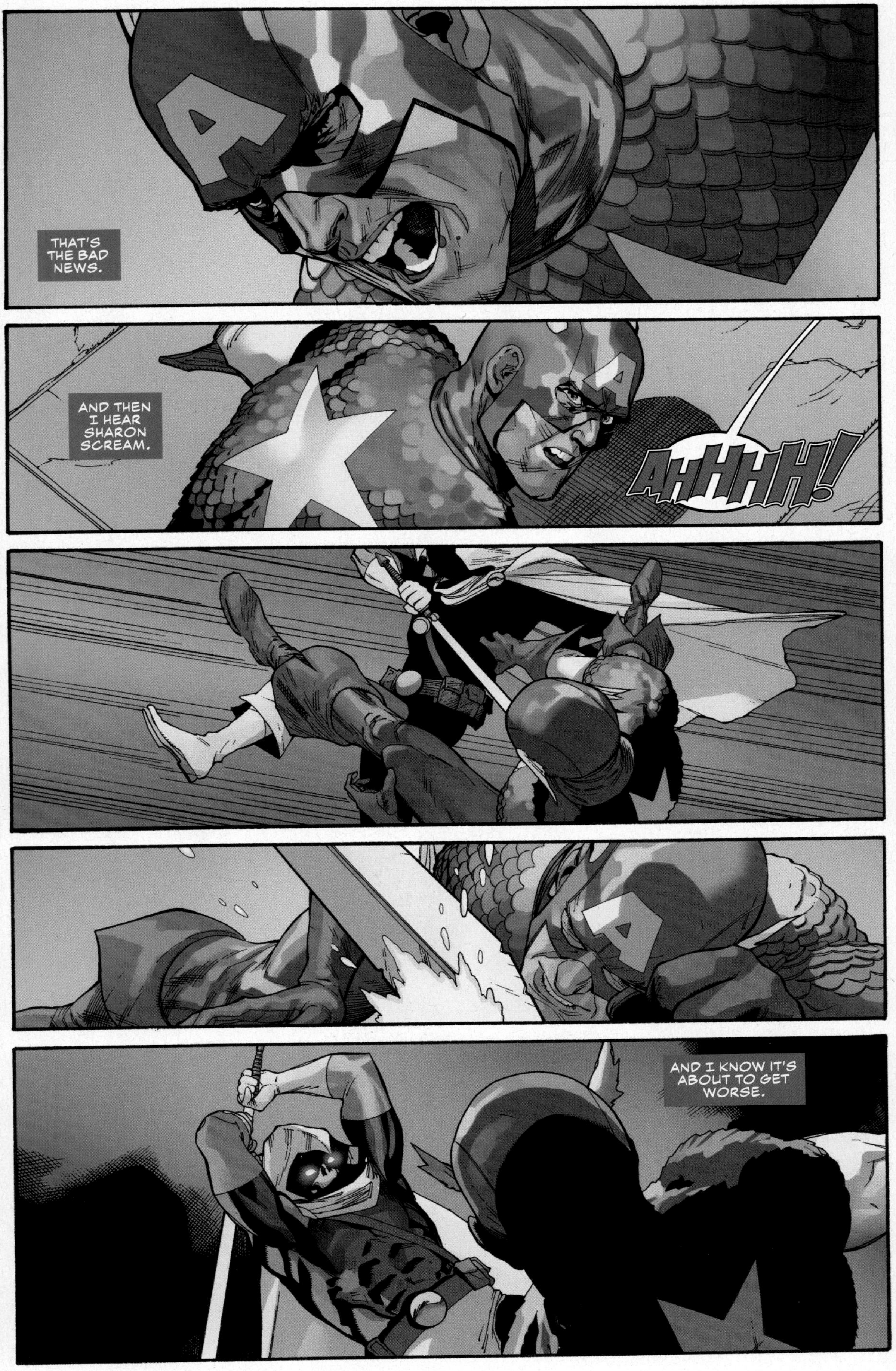
THAT'S THE BAD NEWS.
AND THEN I HEAR SHARON SCREAM.
AHHHH!
AND I KNOW IT'S ABOUT TO GET WORSE.

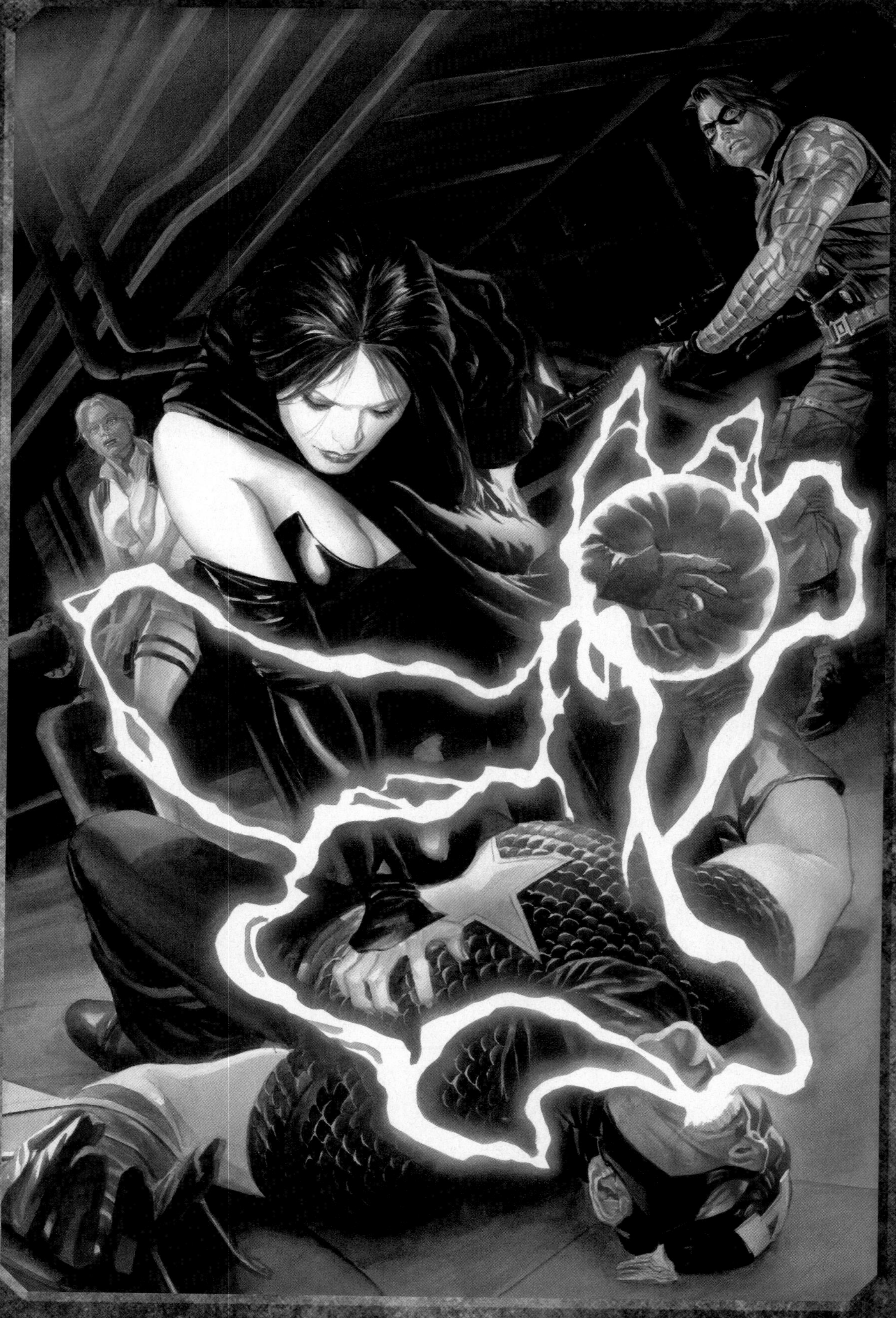

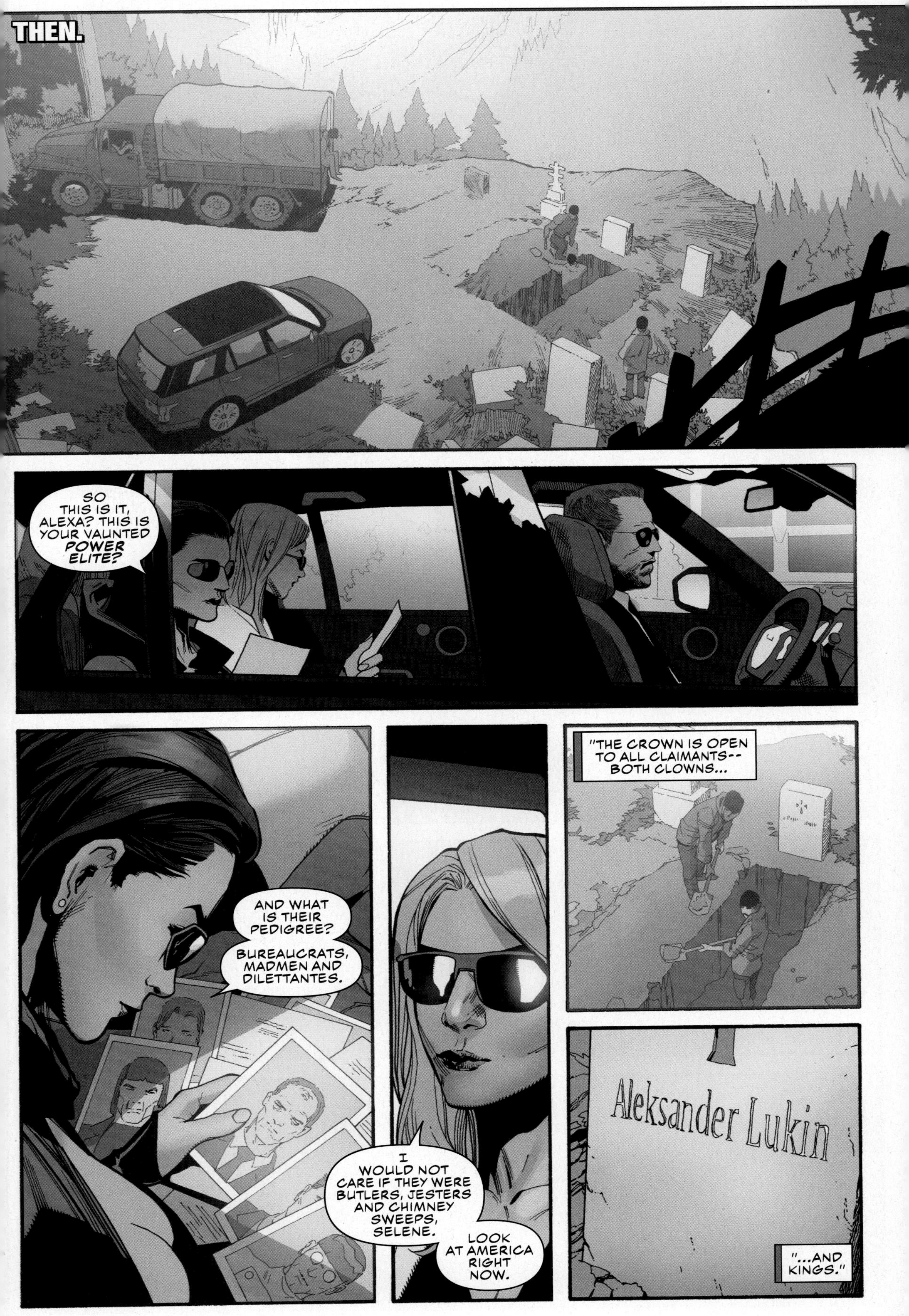
THEN.
SO THIS IS IT, ALEXA? THIS IS YOUR VAUNTED POWER ELITE?
AND WHAT IS THEIR PEDIGREE?
BUREAUCRATS, MADMEN AND DILETTANTES.
I WOULD NOT CARE IF THEY WERE BUTLERS, JESTERS AND CHIMNEY SWEEPS, SELENE.
LOOK AT AMERICA RIGHT NOW.
"THE CROWN IS OPEN TO ALL CLAIMANTS-- BOTH CLOWNS...
Aleksander Lukin
"...AND KINGS."

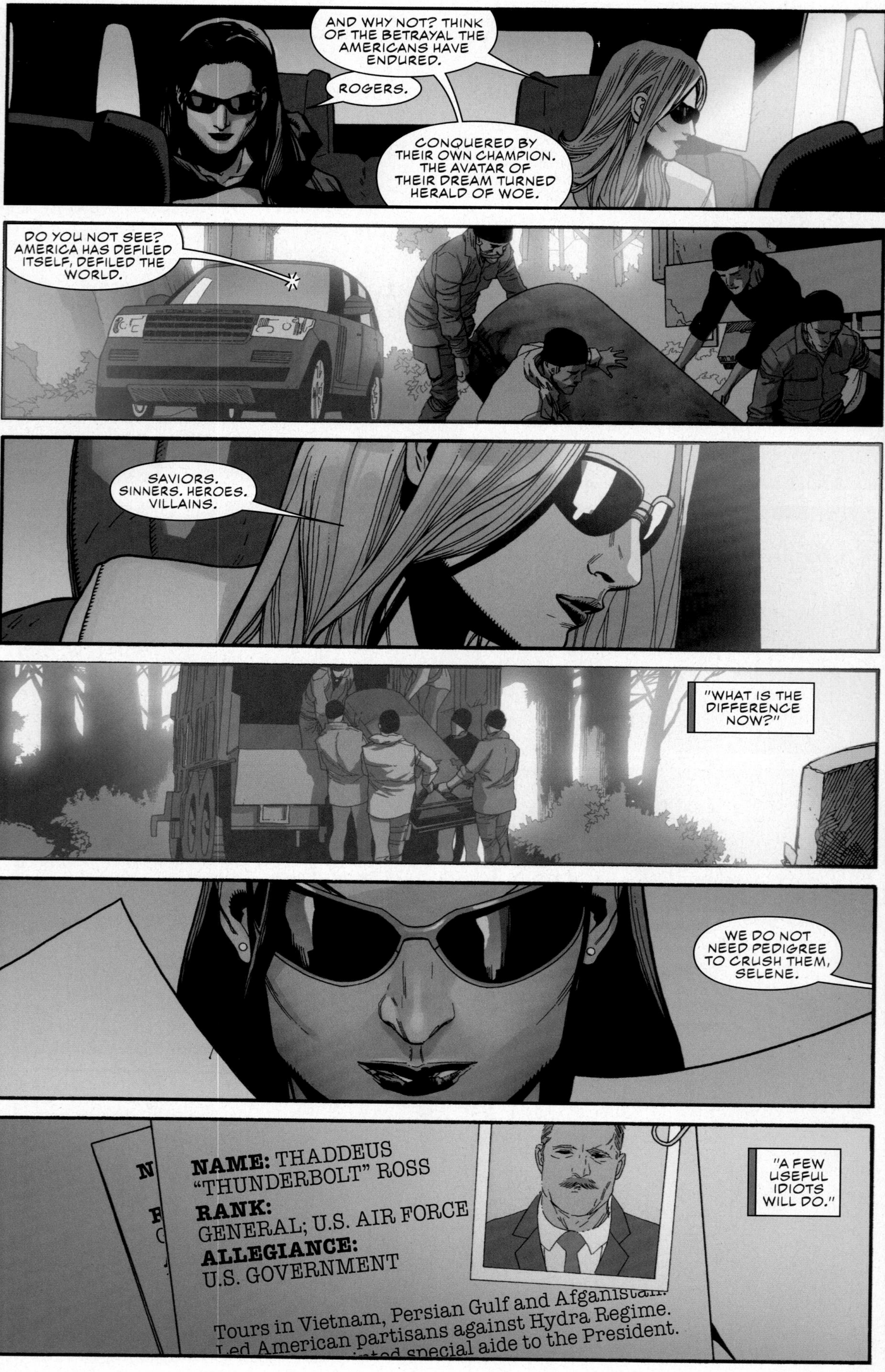
AND WHY NOT? THINK OF THE BETRAYAL THE AMERICANS HAVE ENDURED.
ROGERS.
CONQUERED BY THEIR OWN CHAMPION. THE AVATAR OF THEIR DREAM TURNED HERALD OF WOE.
DO YOU NOT SEE? AMERICA HAS DEFILED ITSELF, DEFILED THE WORLD.
SAVIORS. SINNERS. HEROES. VILLAINS.
"WHAT IS THE DIFFERENCE NOW?"
WE DO NOT NEED PEDIGREE TO CRUSH THEM, SELENE.
NAME: THADDEUS "THUNDERBOLT" ROSS
RANK:
GENERAL; U.S. AIR FORCE
ALLEGIANCE:
U.S. GOVERNMENT
Tours in Vietnam, Persian Gulf and Afganistan.
Led American partisans against Hydra Regime.
"A FEW USEFUL IDIOTS WILL DO."

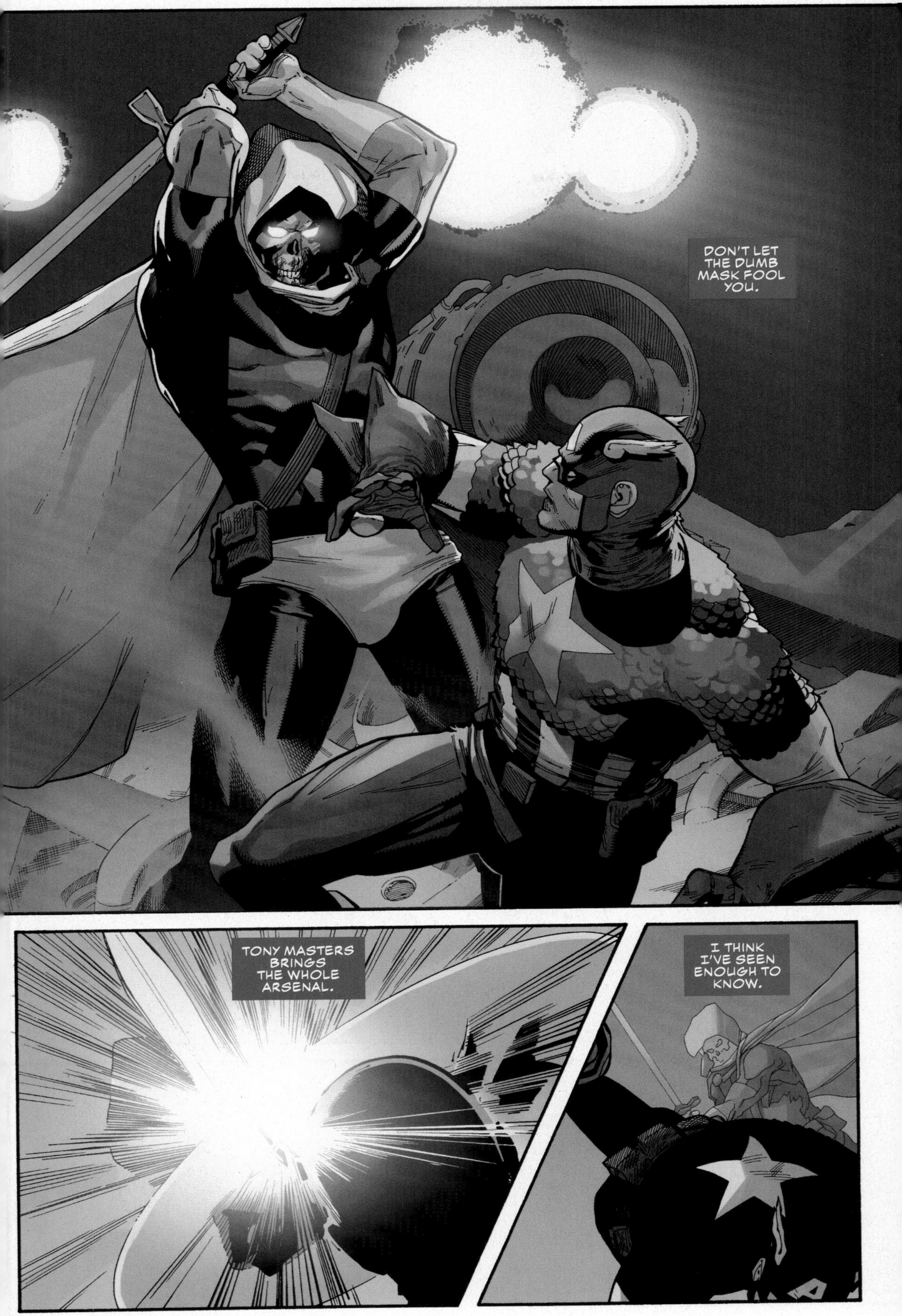
DON'T LET THE DUMB MASK FOOL YOU.
TONY MASTERS BRINGS THE WHOLE ARSENAL.
I THINK I'VE SEEN ENOUGH TO KNOW.

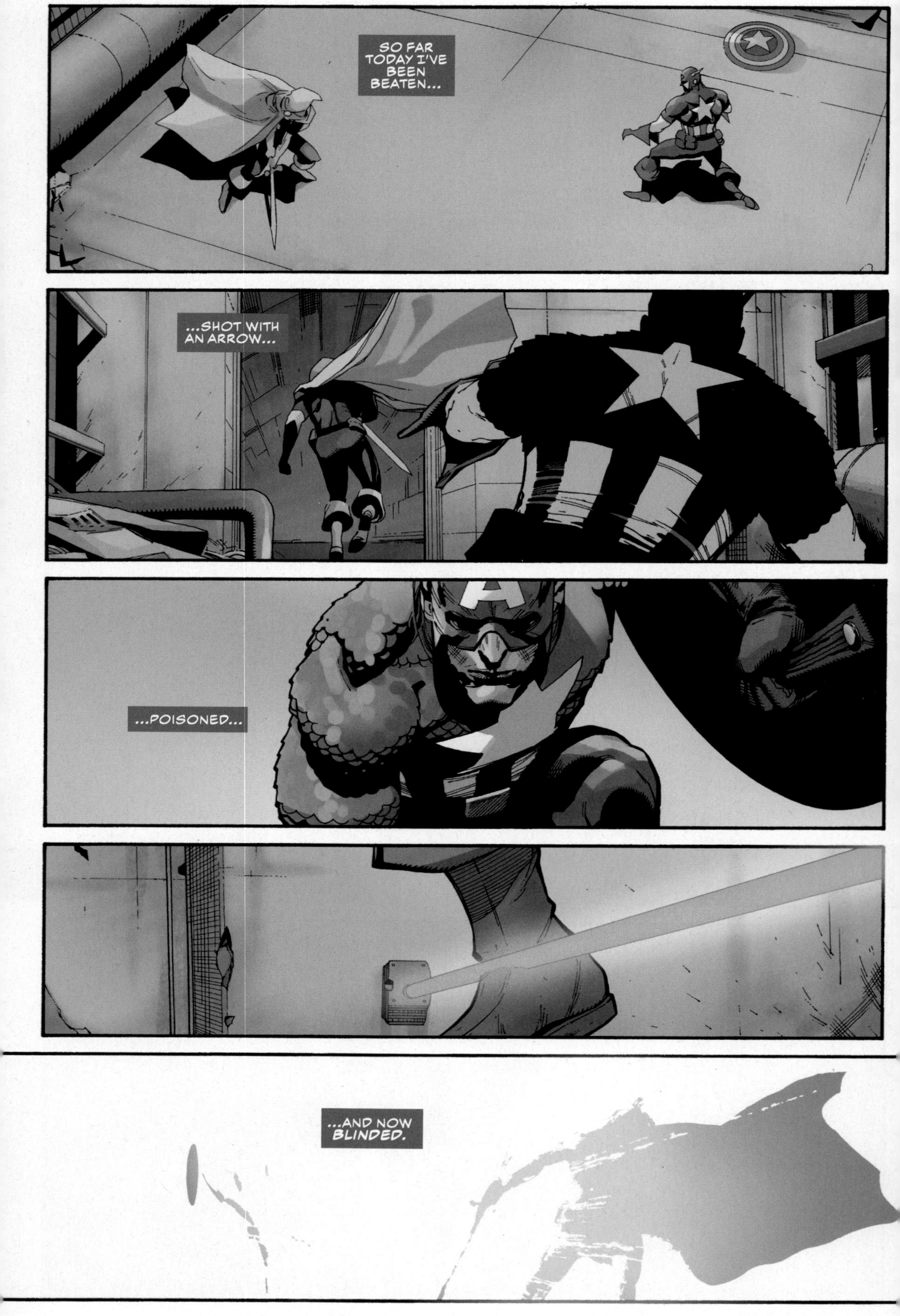
SO FAR TODAY I'VE BEEN BEATEN...
...SHOT WITH AN ARROW...
...POISONED...
...AND NOW BLINDED.

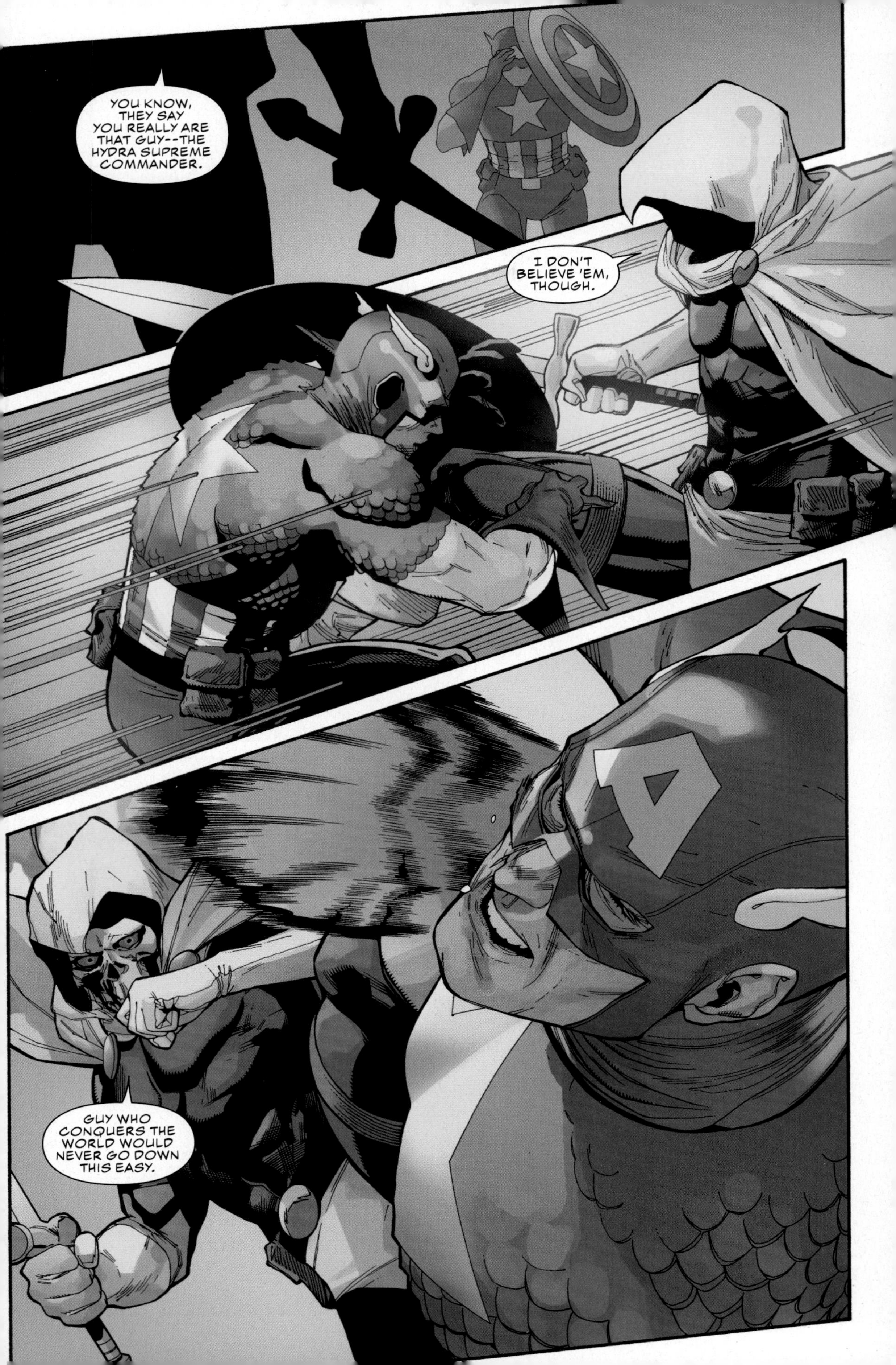
YOU KNOW, THEY SAY YOU REALLY ARE THAT GUY--THE HYDRA SUPREME COMMANDER.
I DON'T BELIEVE 'EM, THOUGH.
GUY WHO CONQUERS THE WORLD WOULD NEVER GO DOWN THIS EASY.

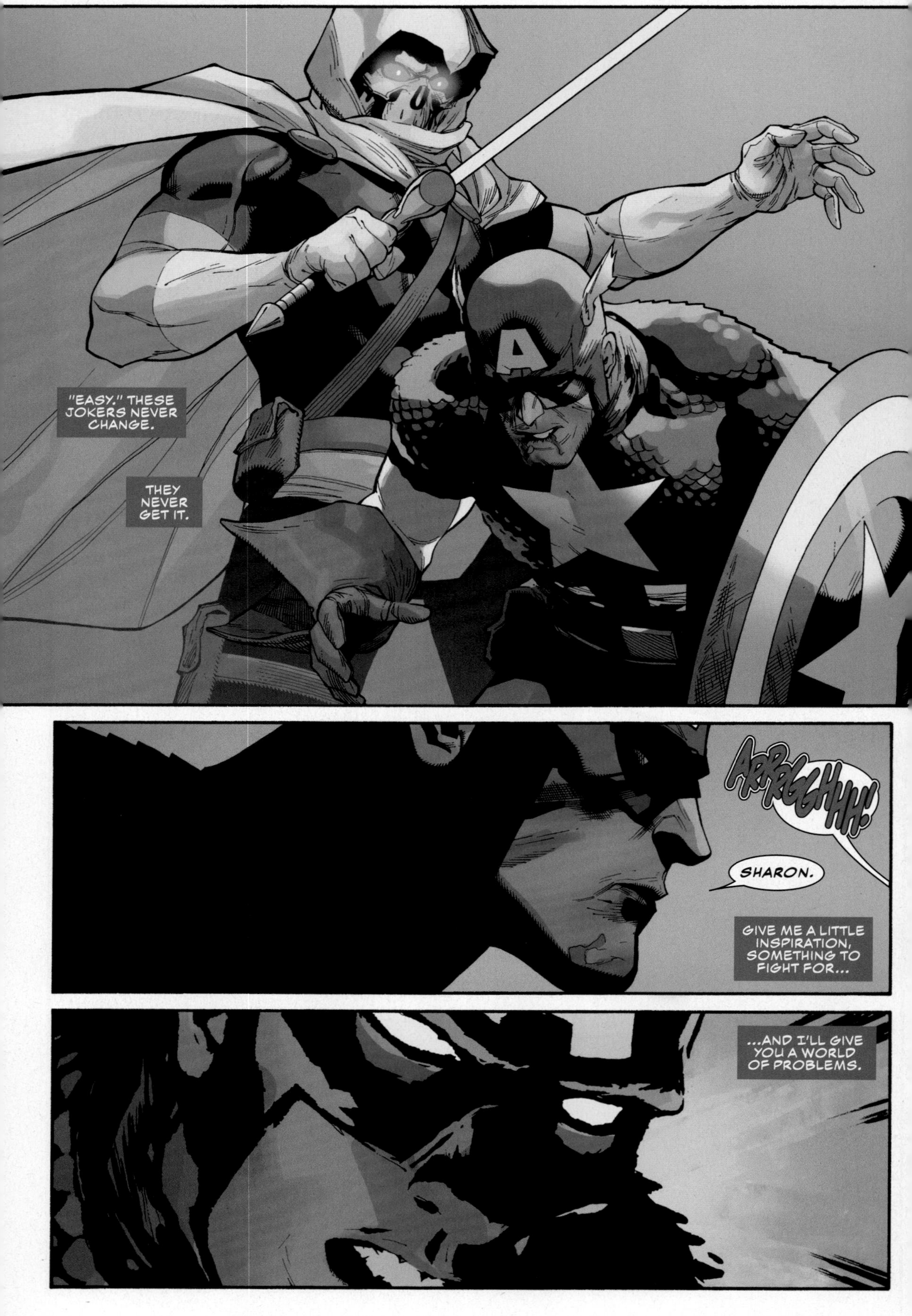
"EASY." THESE JOKERS NEVER CHANGE.
THEY NEVER GET IT.
ARRRGGHHH!
SHARON.
GIVE ME A LITTLE INSPIRATION, SOMETHING TO FIGHT FOR...
...AND I'LL GIVE YOU A WORLD OF PROBLEMS.

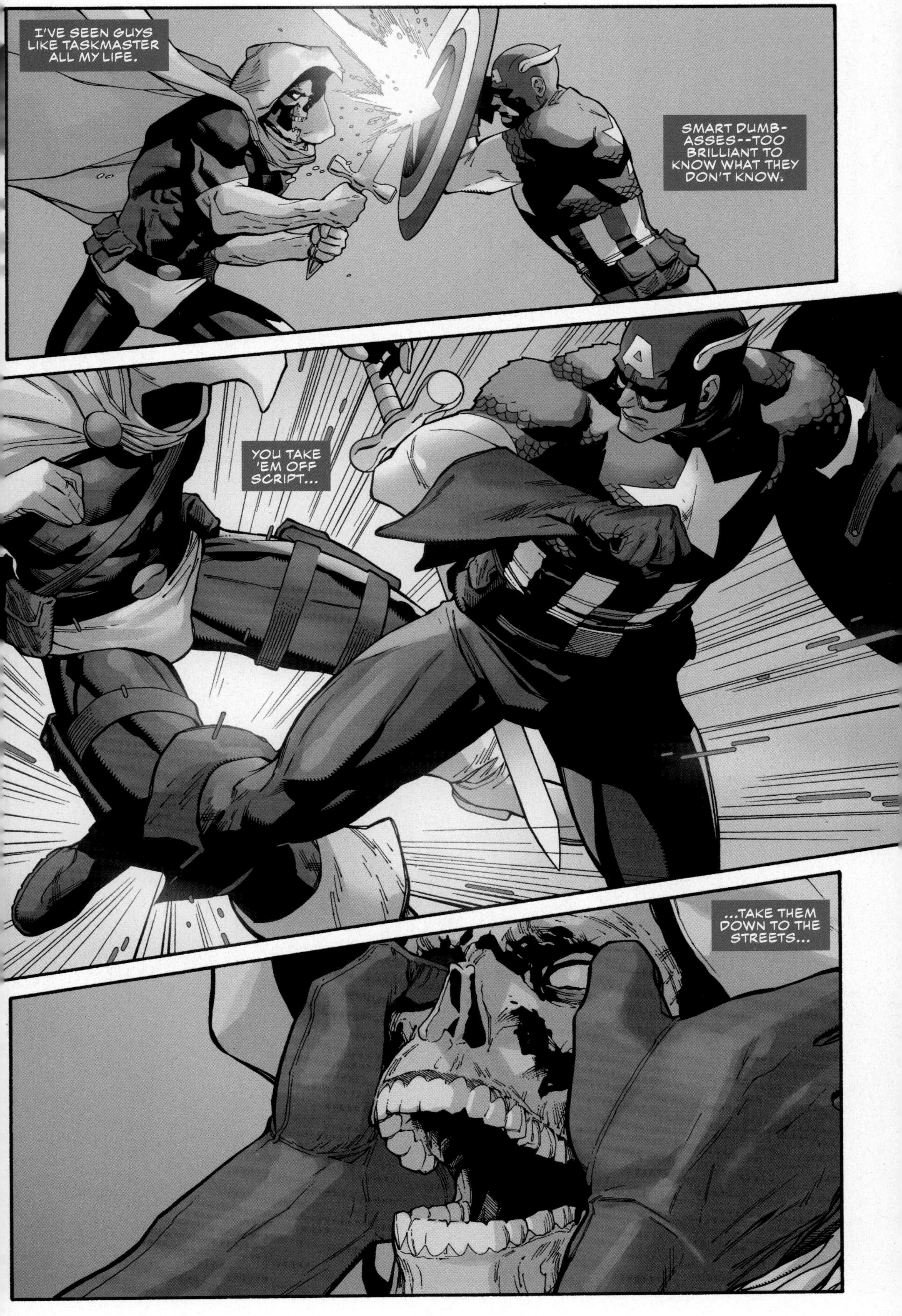
I'VE SEEN GUYS LIKE TASKMASTER ALL MY LIFE.
SMART DUMB-ASSES--TOO BRILLIANT TO KNOW WHAT THEY DON'T KNOW.
YOU TAKE 'EM OFF SCRIPT...
...TAKE THEM DOWN TO THE STREETS...

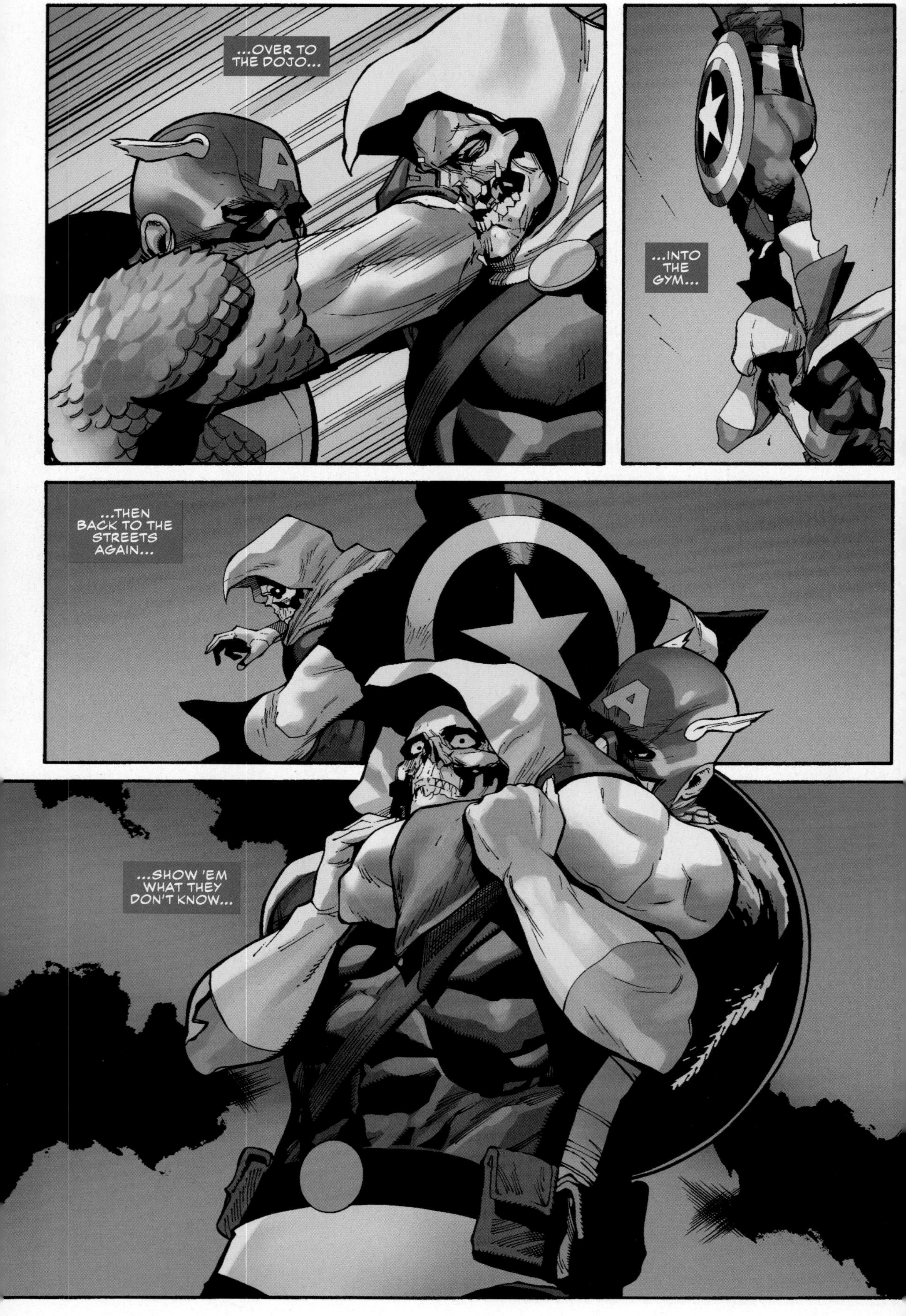
...OVER TO THE DOJO...
...INTO THE GYM...
...THEN BACK TO THE STREETS AGAIN...
...SHOW 'EM WHAT THEY DON'T KNOW...

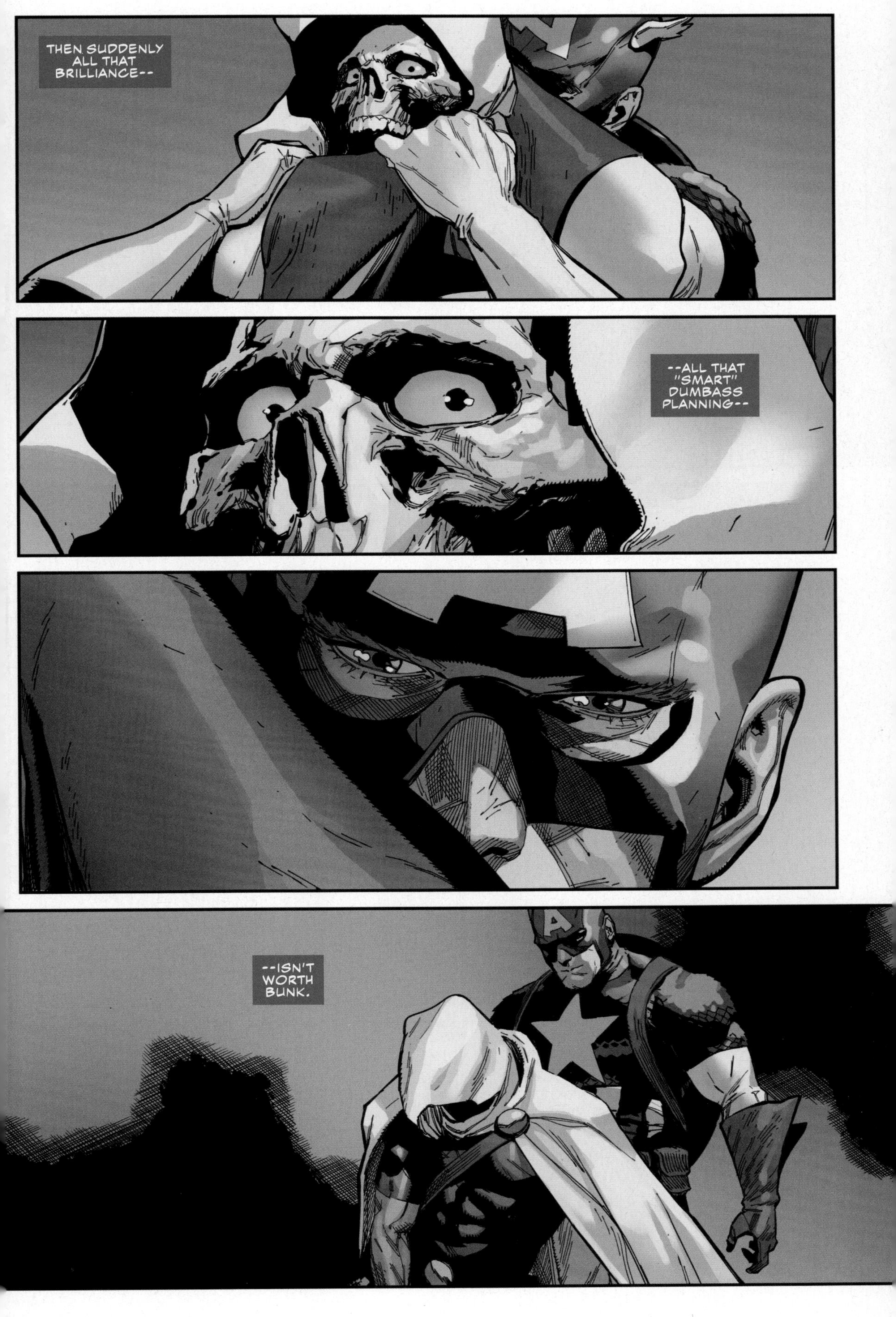
THEN SUDDENLY ALL THAT BRILLIANCE--
--ALL THAT "SMART" DUMBASS PLANNING--
--ISN'T WORTH BUNK.

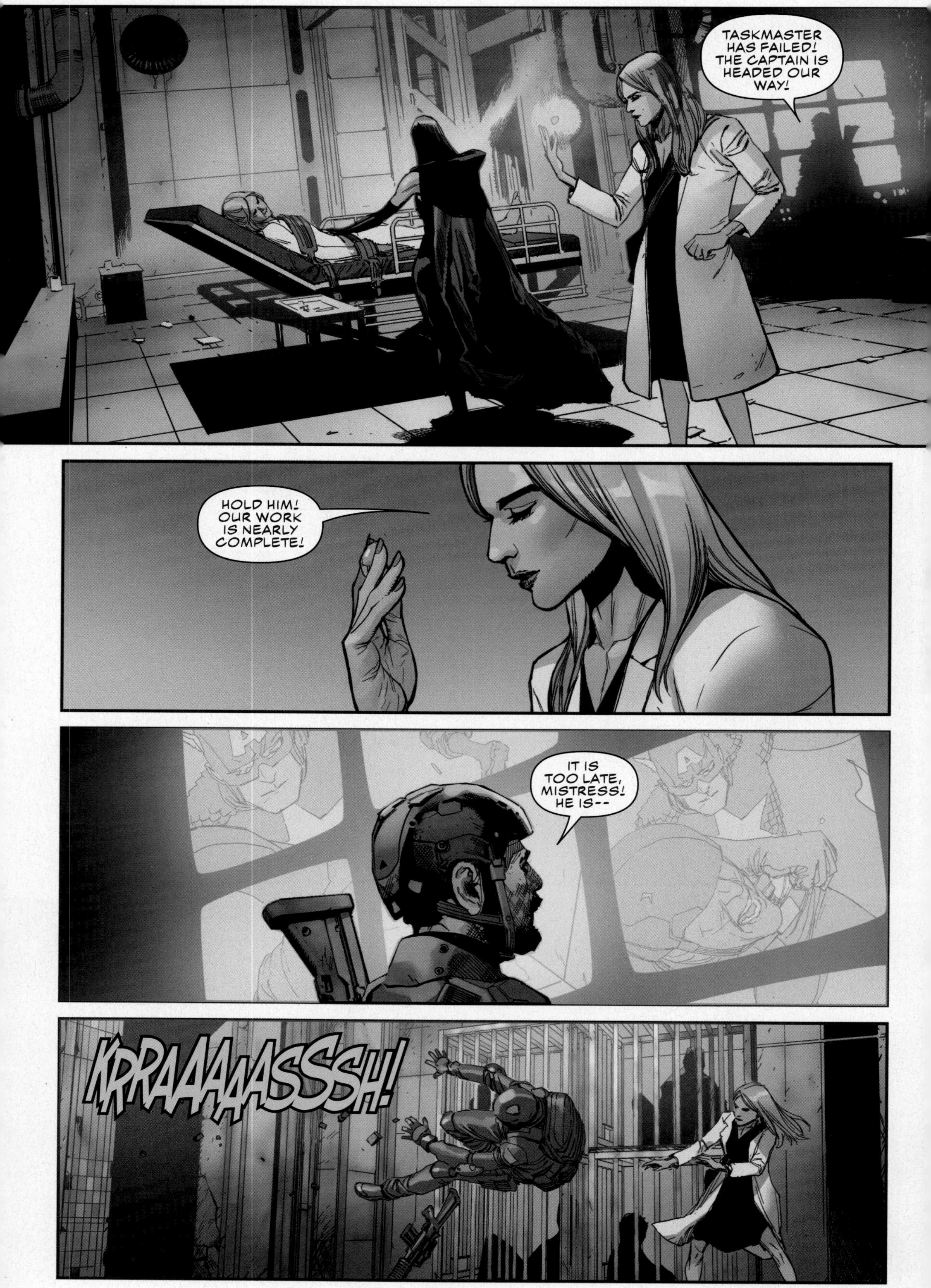
TASKMASTER HAS FAILED! THE CAPTAIN IS HEADED OUR WAY!
HOLD HIM! OUR WORK IS NEARLY COMPLETE!
IT IS TOO LATE, MISTRESS! HE IS--
KRRAAAAASSSSH!

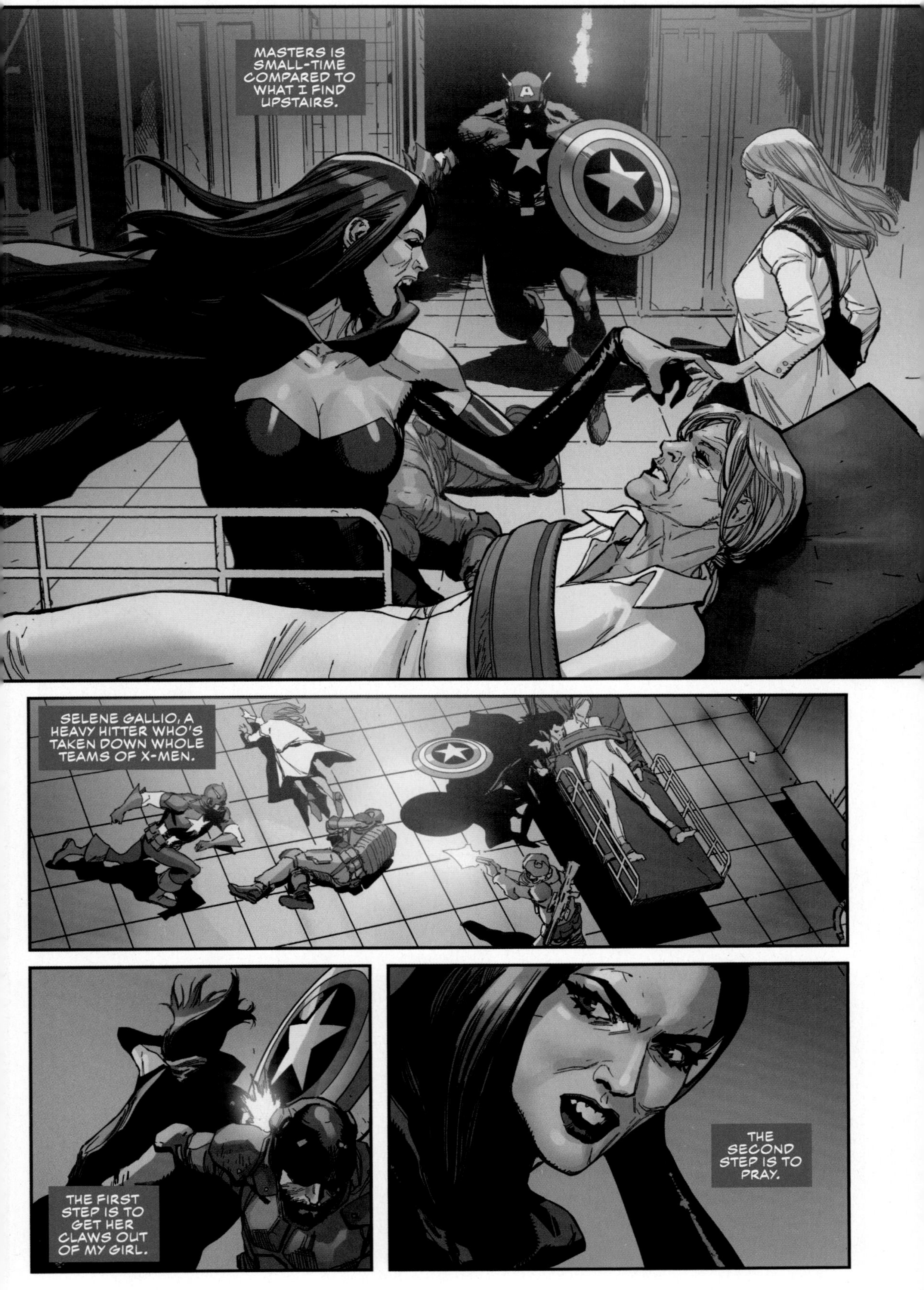
MASTERS IS SMALL-TIME COMPARED TO WHAT I FIND UPSTAIRS.
SELENE GALLIO, A HEAVY HITTER WHO'S TAKEN DOWN WHOLE TEAMS OF X-MEN.
THE FIRST STEP IS TO GET HER CLAWS OUT OF MY GIRL.
THE SECOND STEP IS TO PRAY.

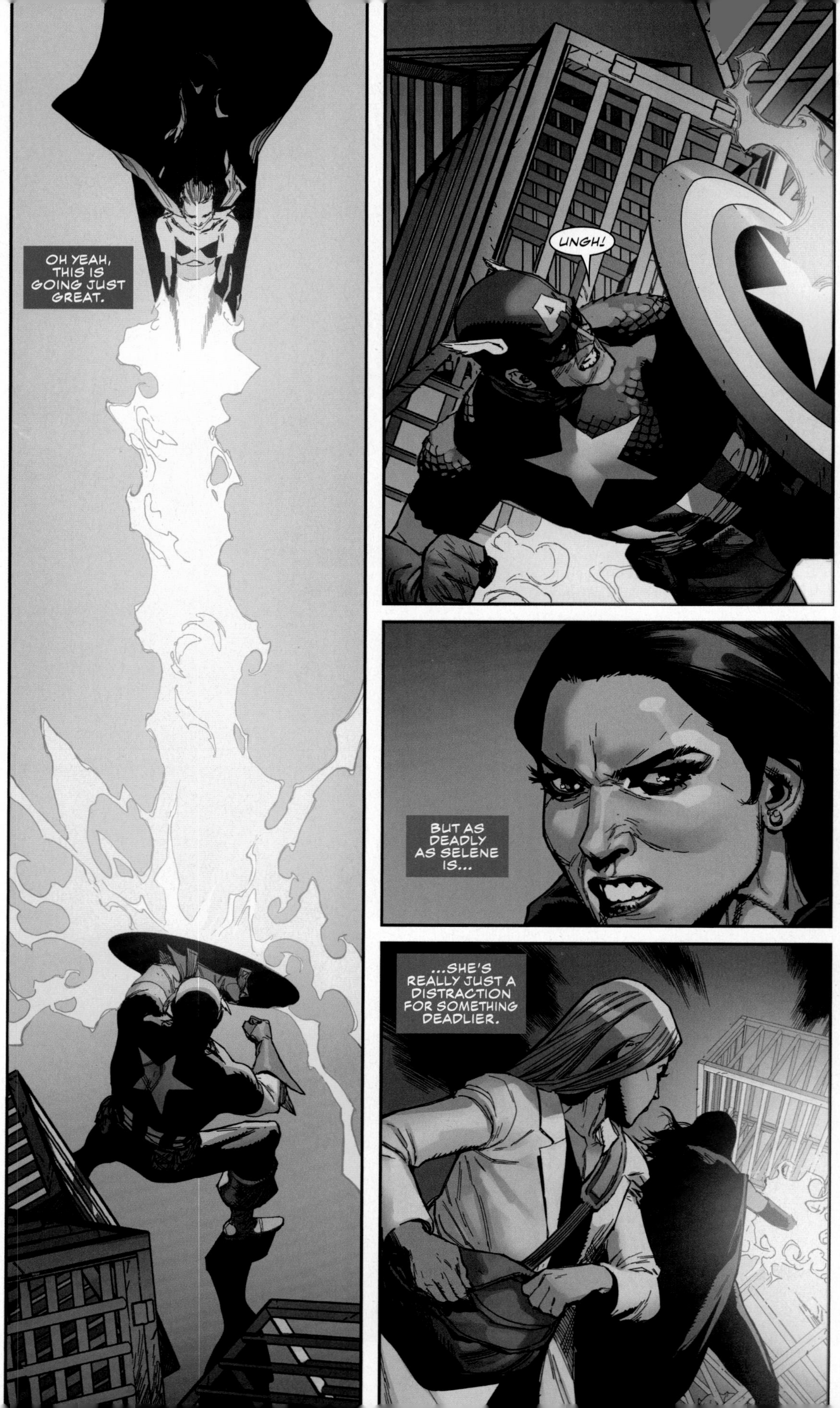
OH YEAH, THIS IS GOING JUST GREAT.
UNGH!
BUT AS DEADLY AS SELENE IS...
...SHE'S REALLY JUST A DISTRACTION FOR SOMETHING DEADLIER.

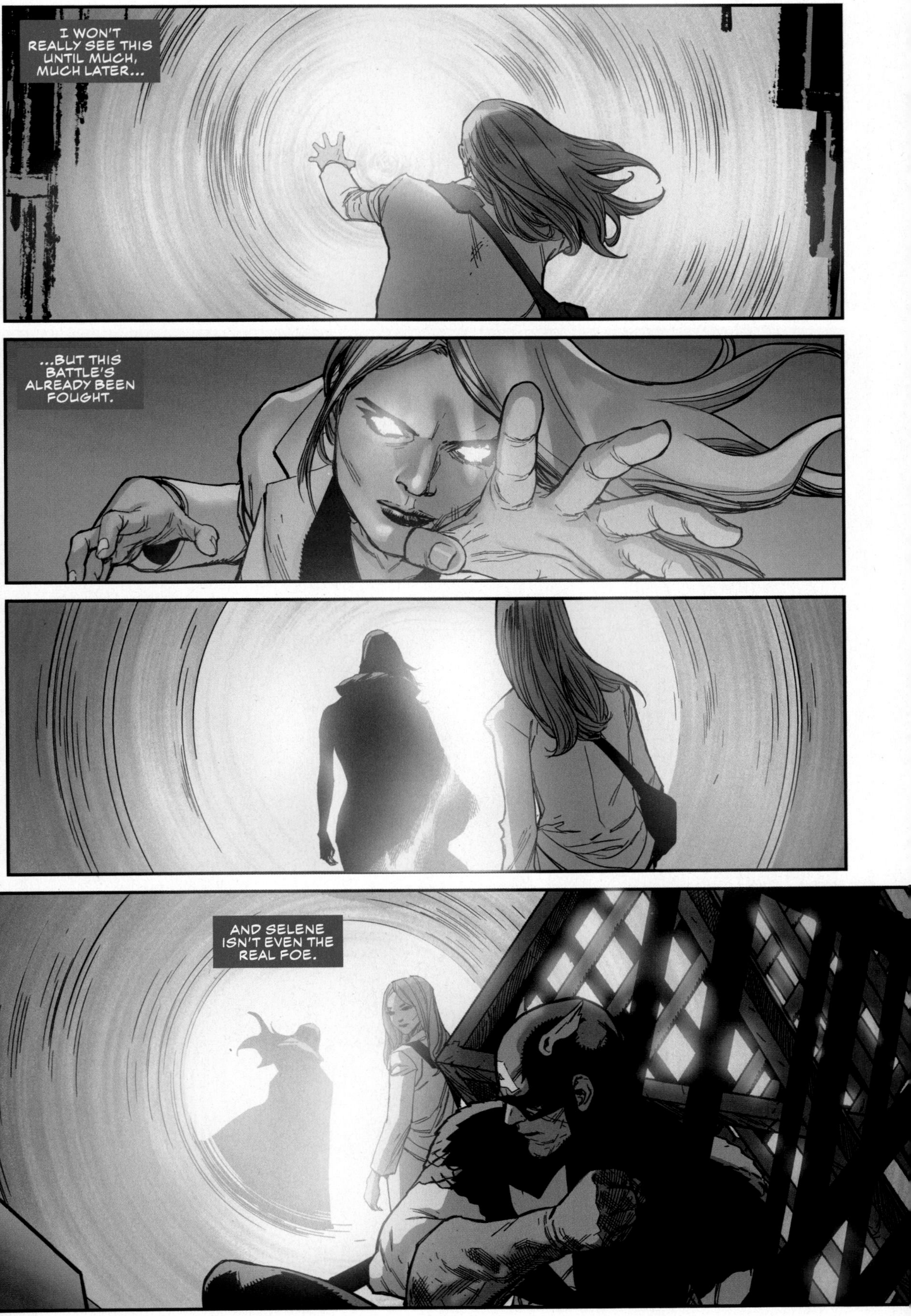
I WON'T REALLY SEE THIS UNTIL MUCH, MUCH LATER...
...BUT THIS BATTLE'S ALREADY BEEN FOUGHT.
AND SELENE ISN'T EVEN THE REAL FOE.

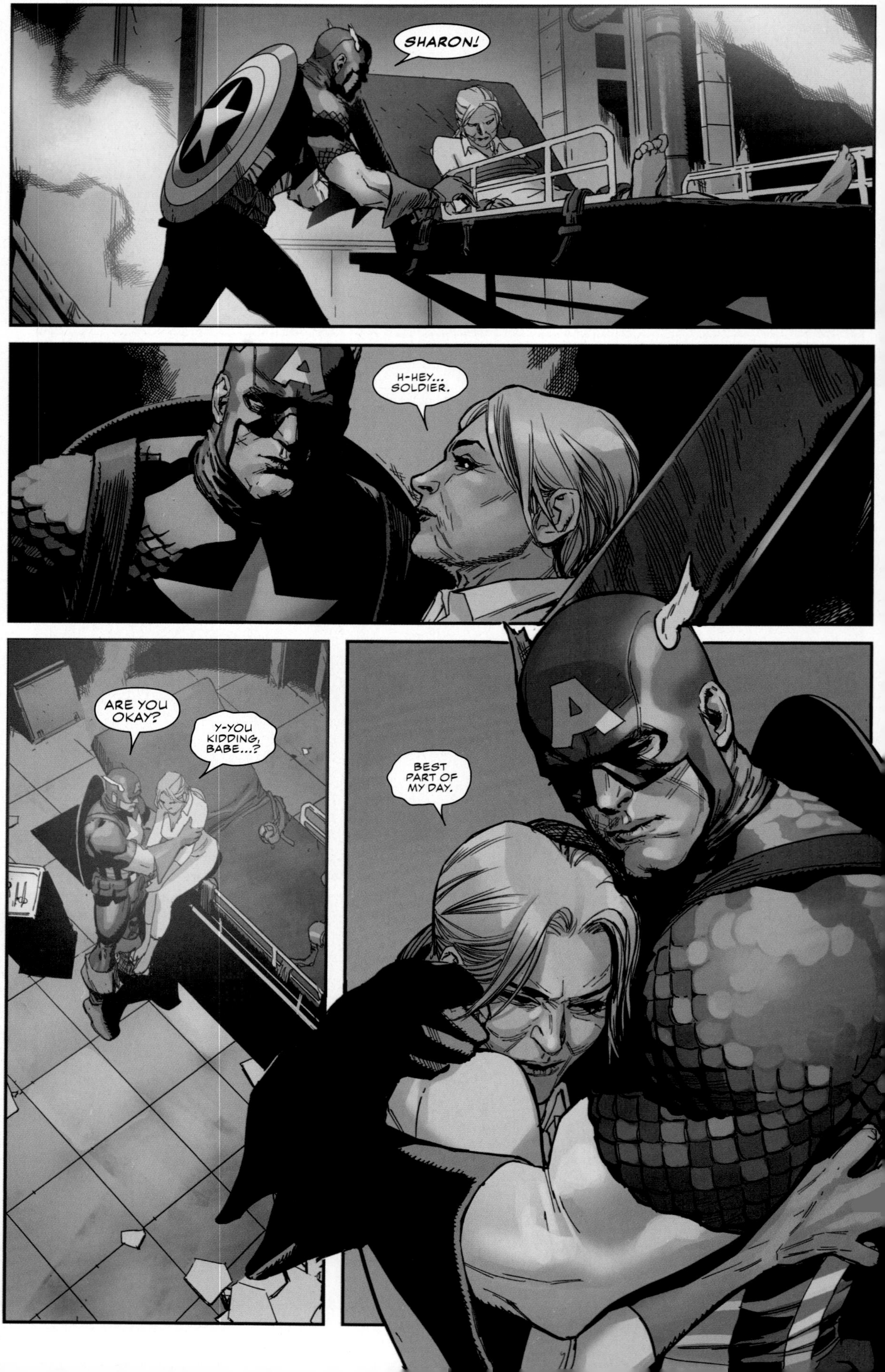
SHARON!
H-HEY... SOLDIER.
ARE YOU OKAY?
Y-YOU KIDDING, BABE...?
BEST PART OF MY DAY.

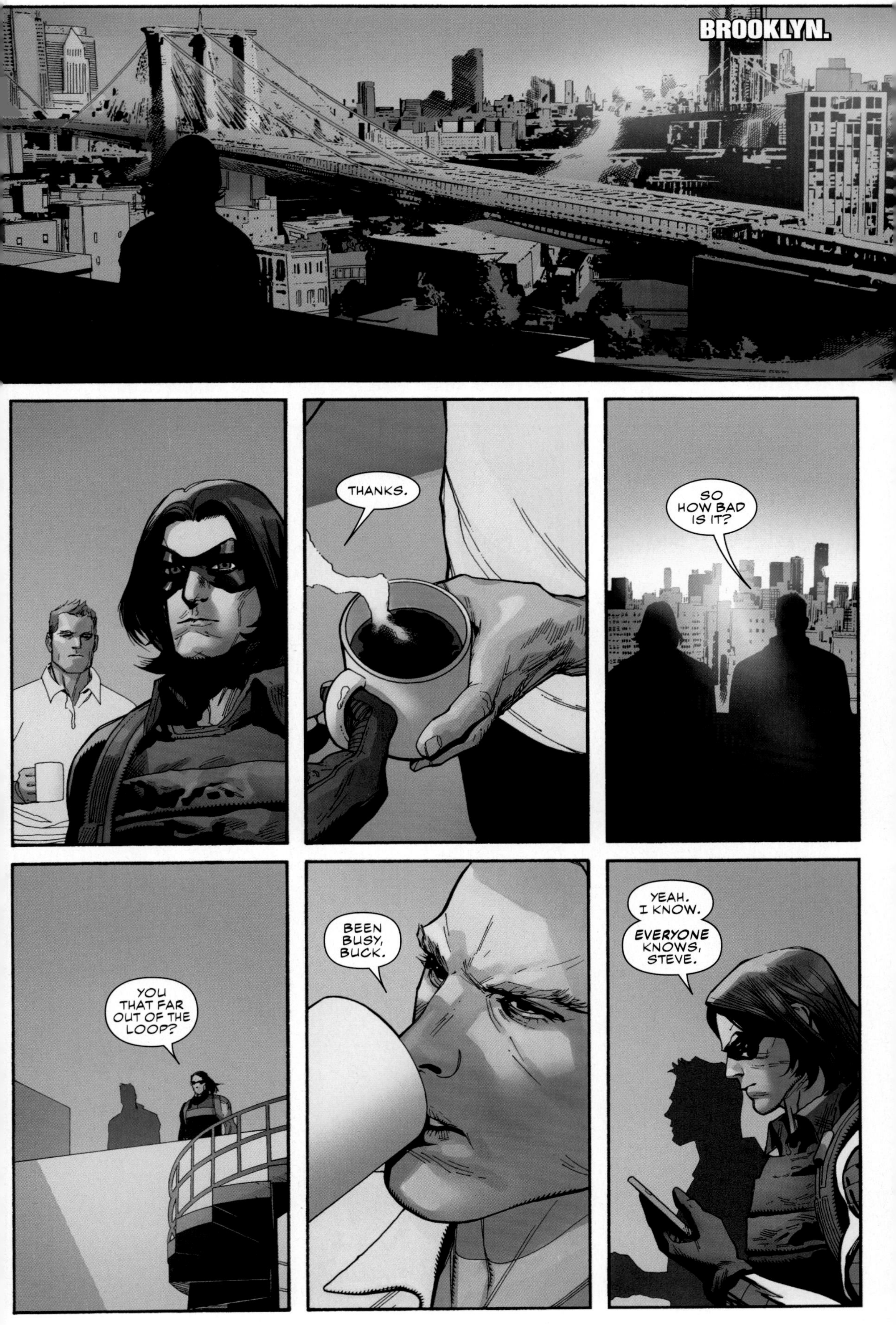
BROOKLYN.
THANKS.
SO HOW BAD IS IT?
YOU THAT FAR OUT OF THE LOOP?
BEEN BUSY, BUCK.
YEAH. I KNOW.
EVERYONE KNOWS, STEVE.

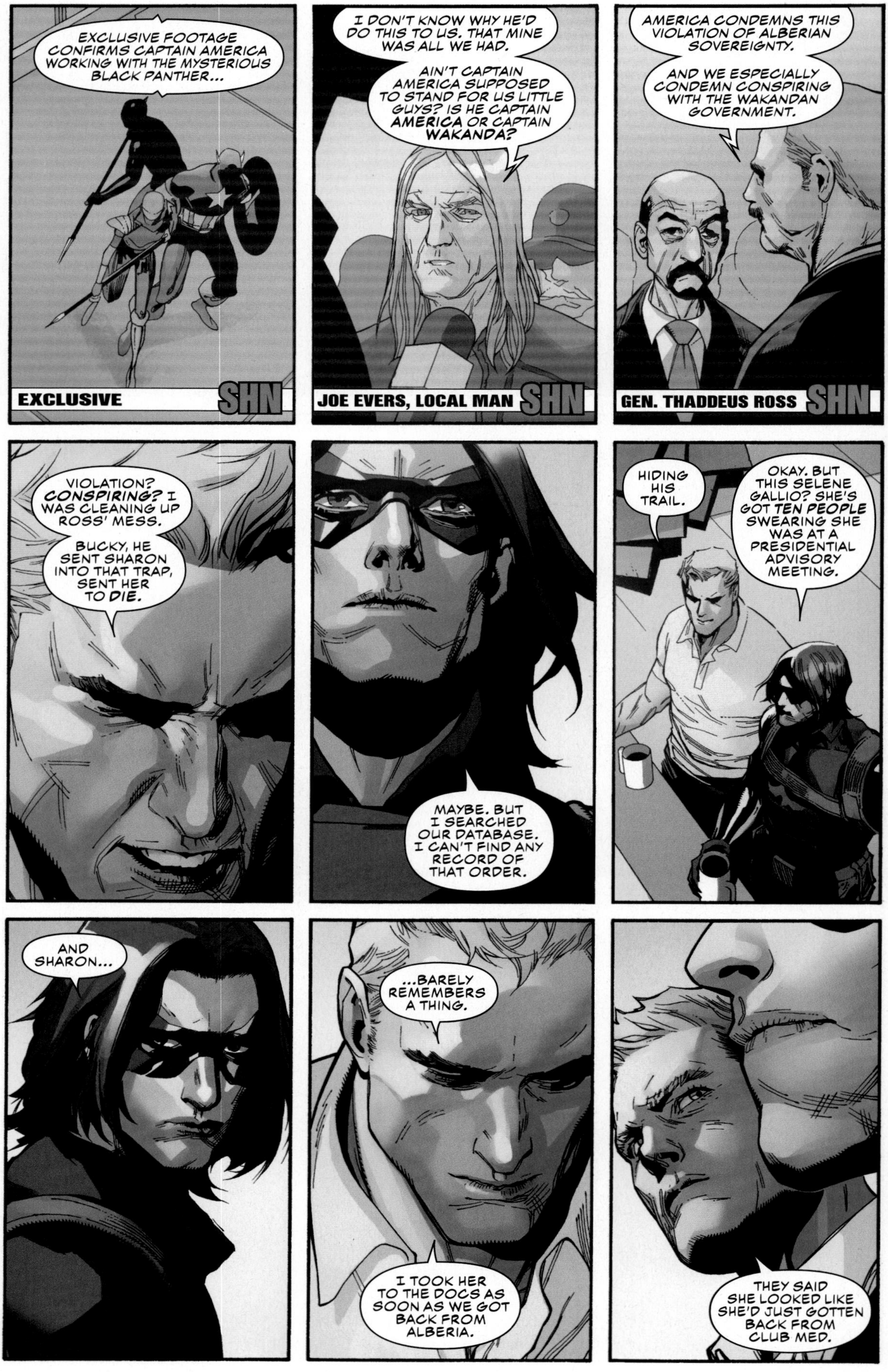

EXCLUSIVE FOOTAGE CONFIRMS CAPTAIN AMERICA WORKING WITH THE MYSTERIOUS BLACK PANTHER...
EXCLUSIVE
SHN
I DON'T KNOW WHY HE'D DO THIS TO US. THAT MINE WAS ALL WE HAD.
AIN'T CAPTAIN AMERICA SUPPOSED TO STAND FOR US LITTLE GUYS? IS HE CAPTAIN AMERICA OR CAPTAIN WAKANDA?
JOE EVERS, LOCAL MAN
SHN
AMERICA CONDEMNS THIS VIOLATION OF ALBERIAN SOVEREIGNTY.
AND WE ESPECIALLY CONDEMN CONSPIRING WITH THE WAKANDAN GOVERNMENT.
GEN. THADDEUS ROSS
SHN
VIOLATION? CONSPIRING? I WAS CLEANING UP ROSS' MESS.
BUCKY, HE SENT SHARON INTO THAT TRAP, SENT HER TO DIE.
MAYBE. BUT I SEARCHED OUR DATABASE. I CAN'T FIND ANY RECORD OF THAT ORDER.
HIDING HIS TRAIL.
OKAY. BUT THIS SELENE GALLIO? SHE'S GOT TEN PEOPLE SWEARING SHE WAS AT A PRESIDENTIAL ADVISORY MEETING.
AND SHARON...
...BARELY REMEMBERS A THING.
I TOOK HER TO THE DOCS AS SOON AS WE GOT BACK FROM ALBERIA.
THEY SAID SHE LOOKED LIKE SHE'D JUST GOTTEN BACK FROM CLUB MED.

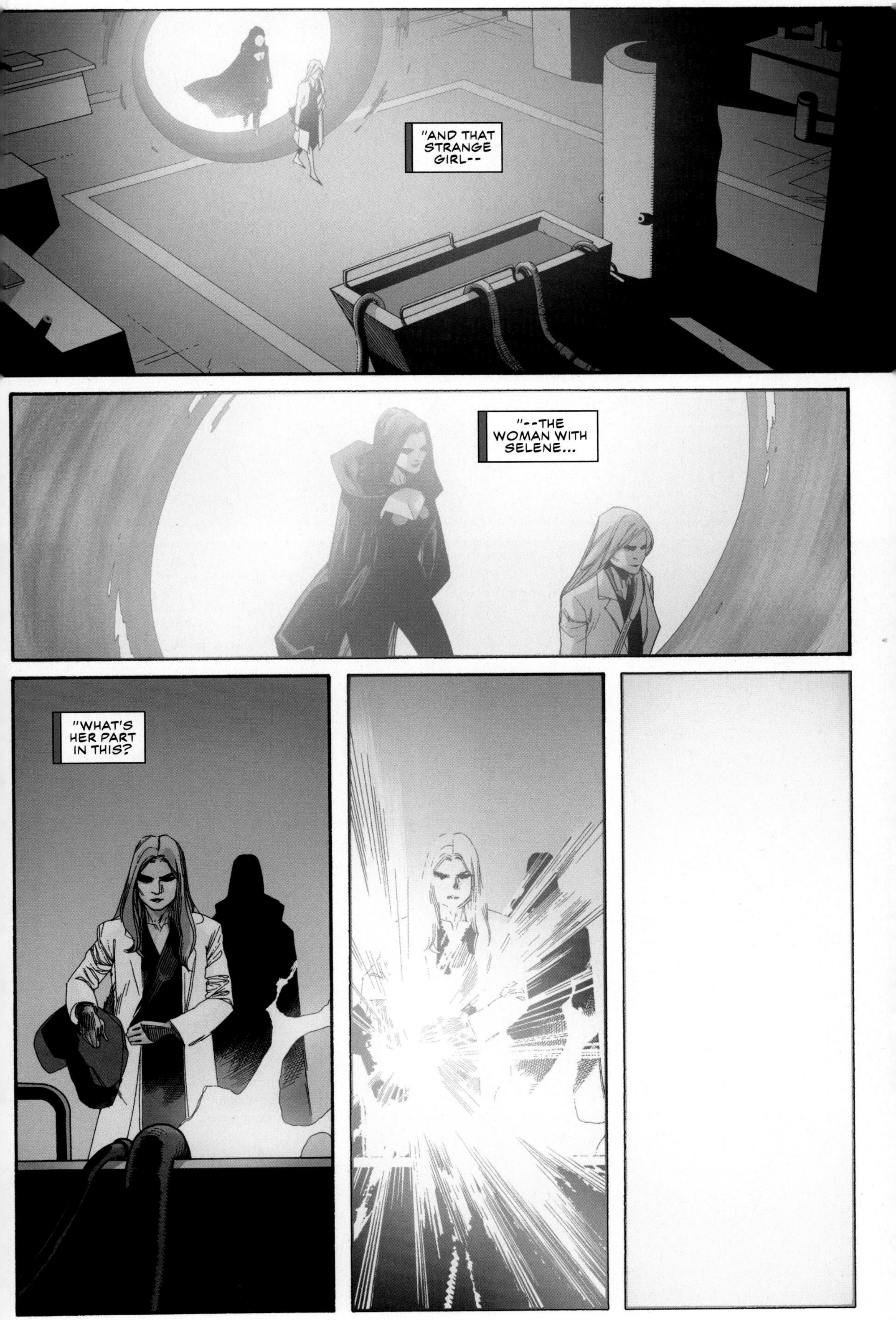
"AND THAT STRANGE GIRL--
"--THE WOMAN WITH SELENE...
"WHAT'S HER PART IN THIS?

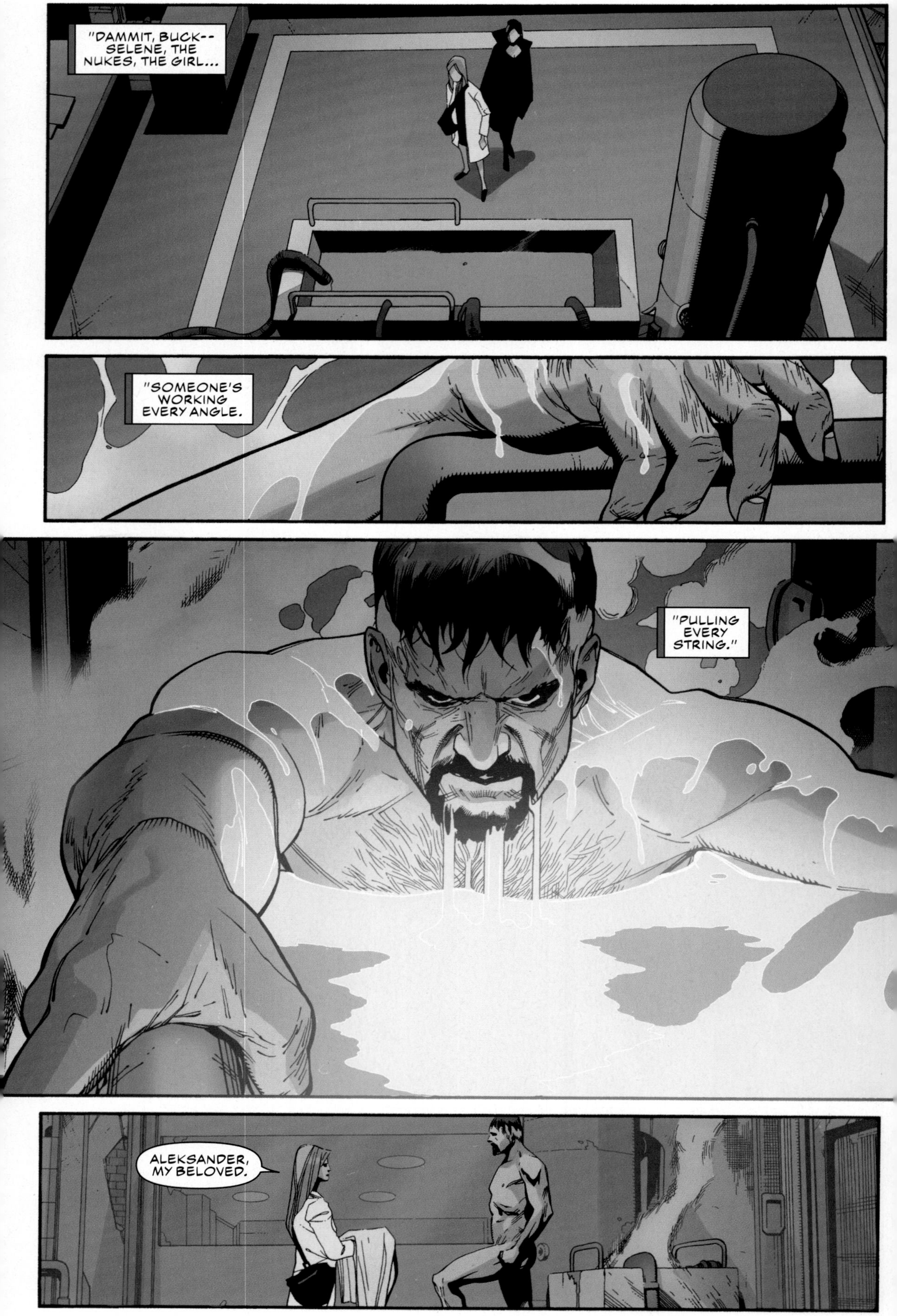
"DAMMIT, BUCK--
SELENE, THE NUKES, THE GIRL...
"SOMEONE'S WORKING EVERY ANGLE.
"PULLING EVERY STRING."
ALEKSANDER, MY BELOVED.

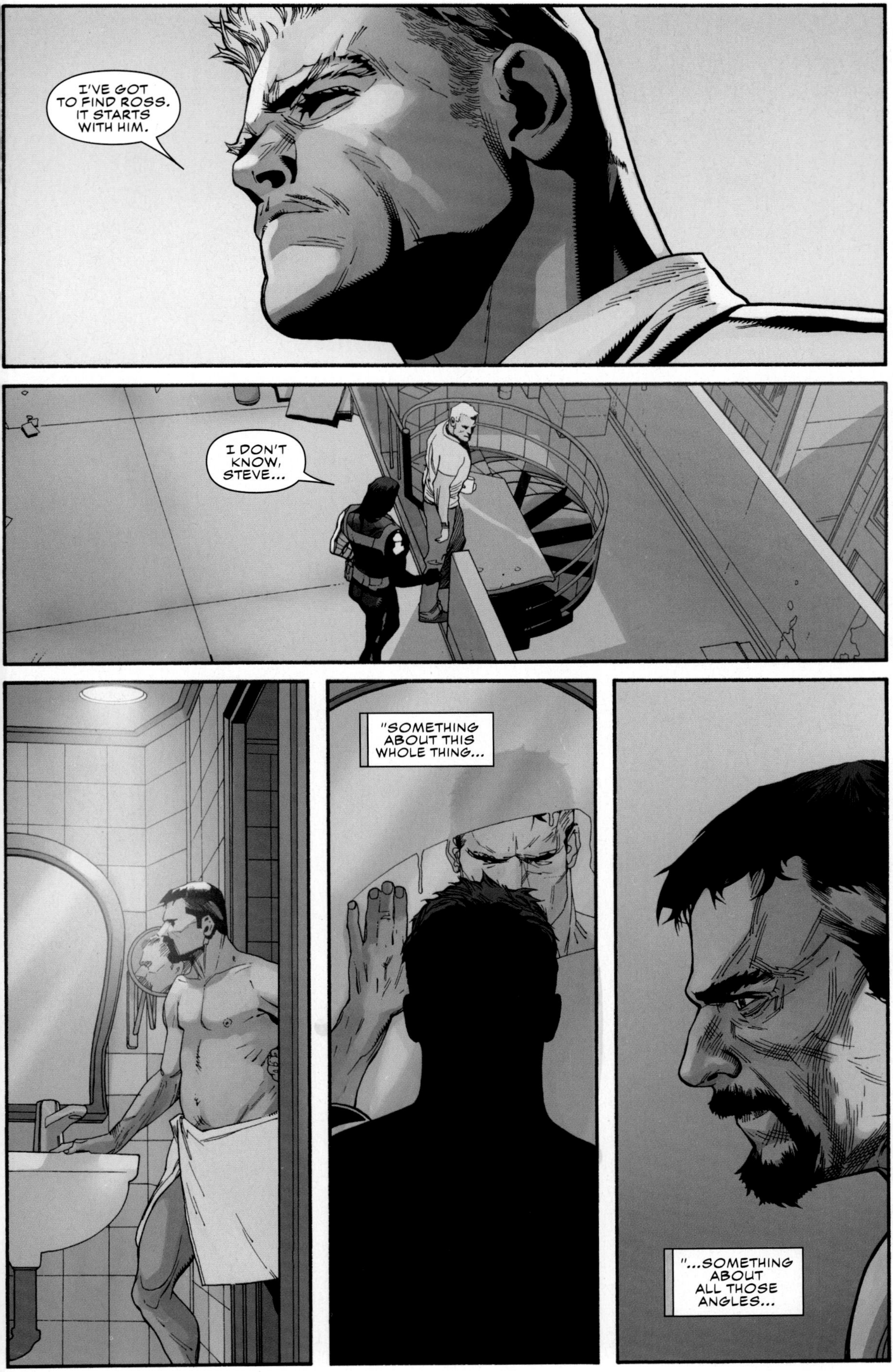
I'VE GOT TO FIND ROSS. IT STARTS WITH HIM.
I DON'T KNOW, STEVE...
"SOMETHING ABOUT THIS WHOLE THING...
"...SOMETHING ABOUT ALL THOSE ANGLES...

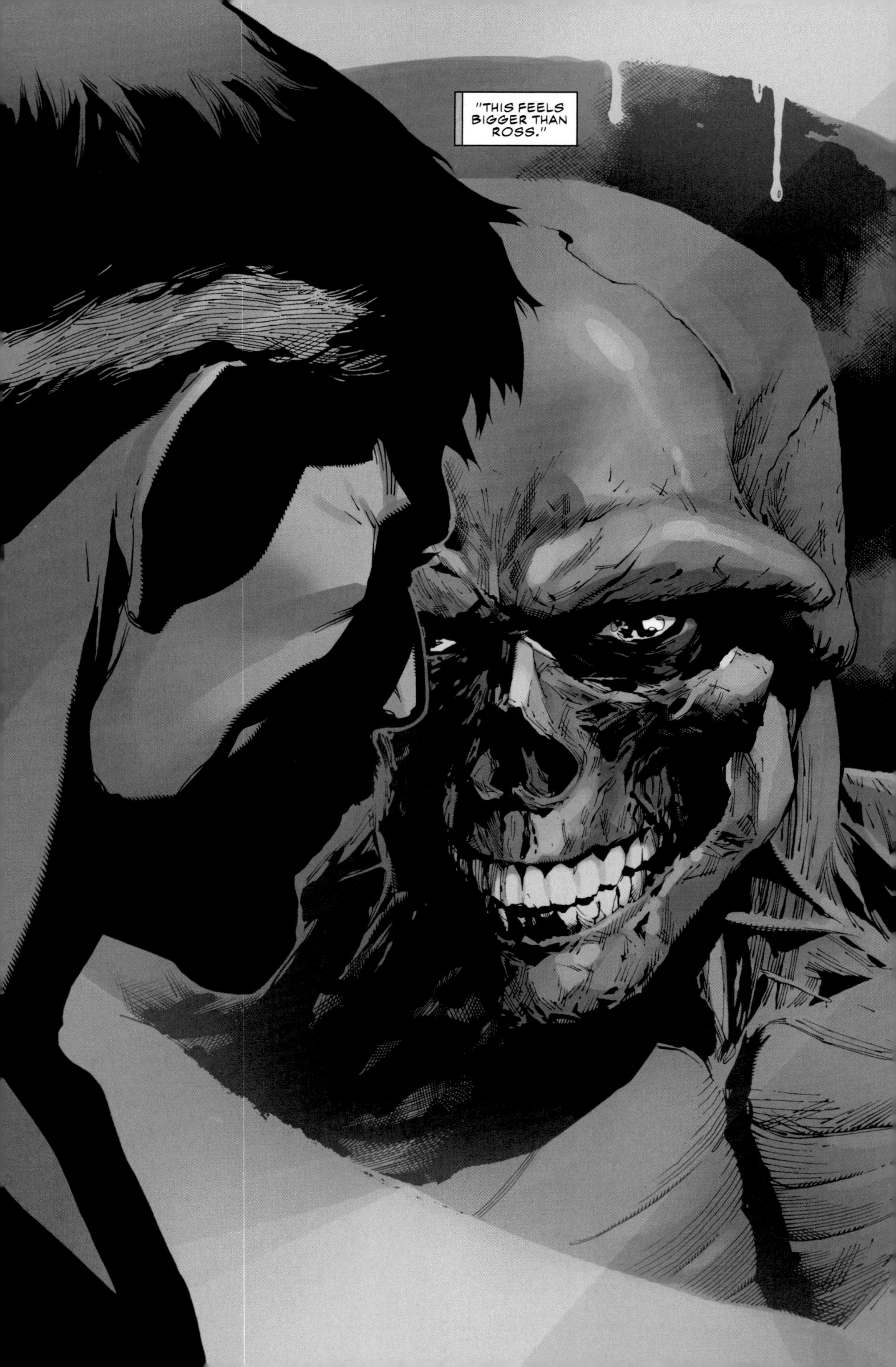
"THIS FEELS BIGGER THAN ROSS."

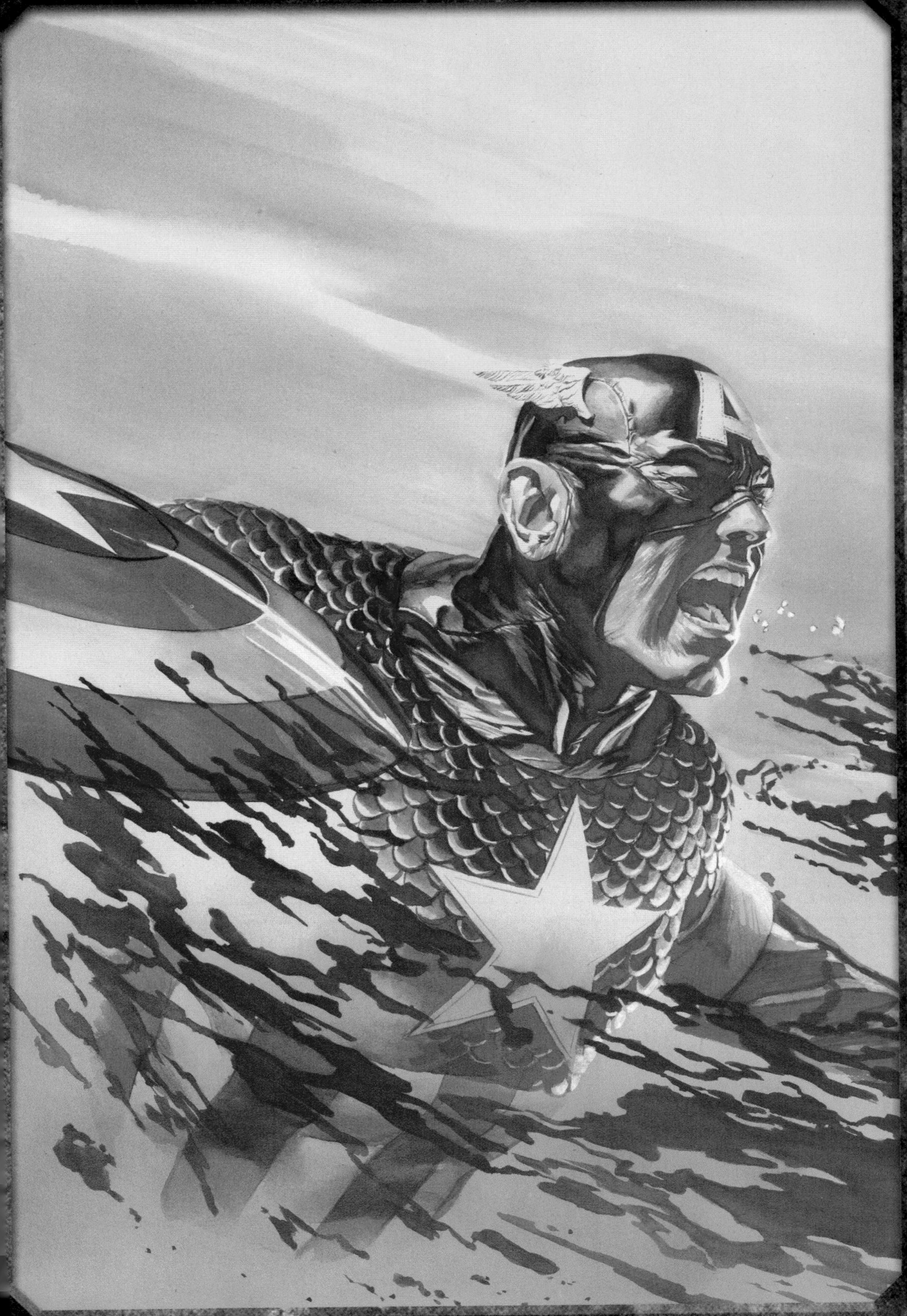

6

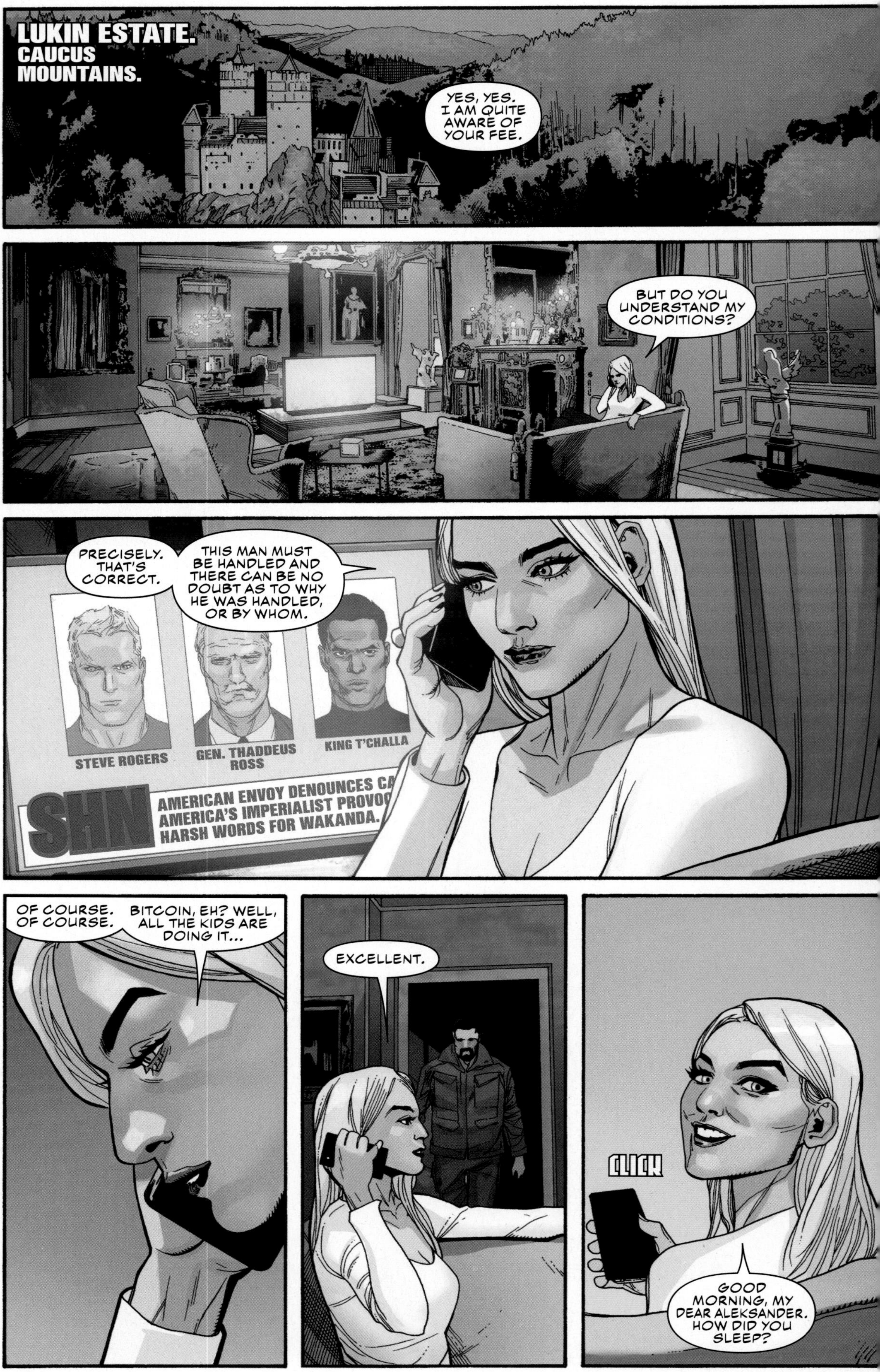
LUKIN ESTATE.
CAUCUS MOUNTAINS.
YES, YES. I AM QUITE AWARE OF YOUR FEE.
BUT DO YOU UNDERSTAND MY CONDITIONS?
PRECISELY. THAT'S CORRECT.
THIS MAN MUST BE HANDLED AND THERE CAN BE NO DOUBT AS TO WHY HE WAS HANDLED, OR BY WHOM.
STEVE ROGERS
GEN. THADDEUS ROSS
KING T'CHALLA
SHN
AMERICAN ENVOY DENOUNCES CA
AMERICA'S IMPERIALIST PROVOC
HARSH WORDS FOR WAKANDA.
OF COURSE. OF COURSE.
BITCOIN, EH? WELL, ALL THE KIDS ARE DOING IT...
EXCELLENT.
CLICK
GOOD MORNING, MY DEAR ALEKSANDER. HOW DID YOU SLEEP?

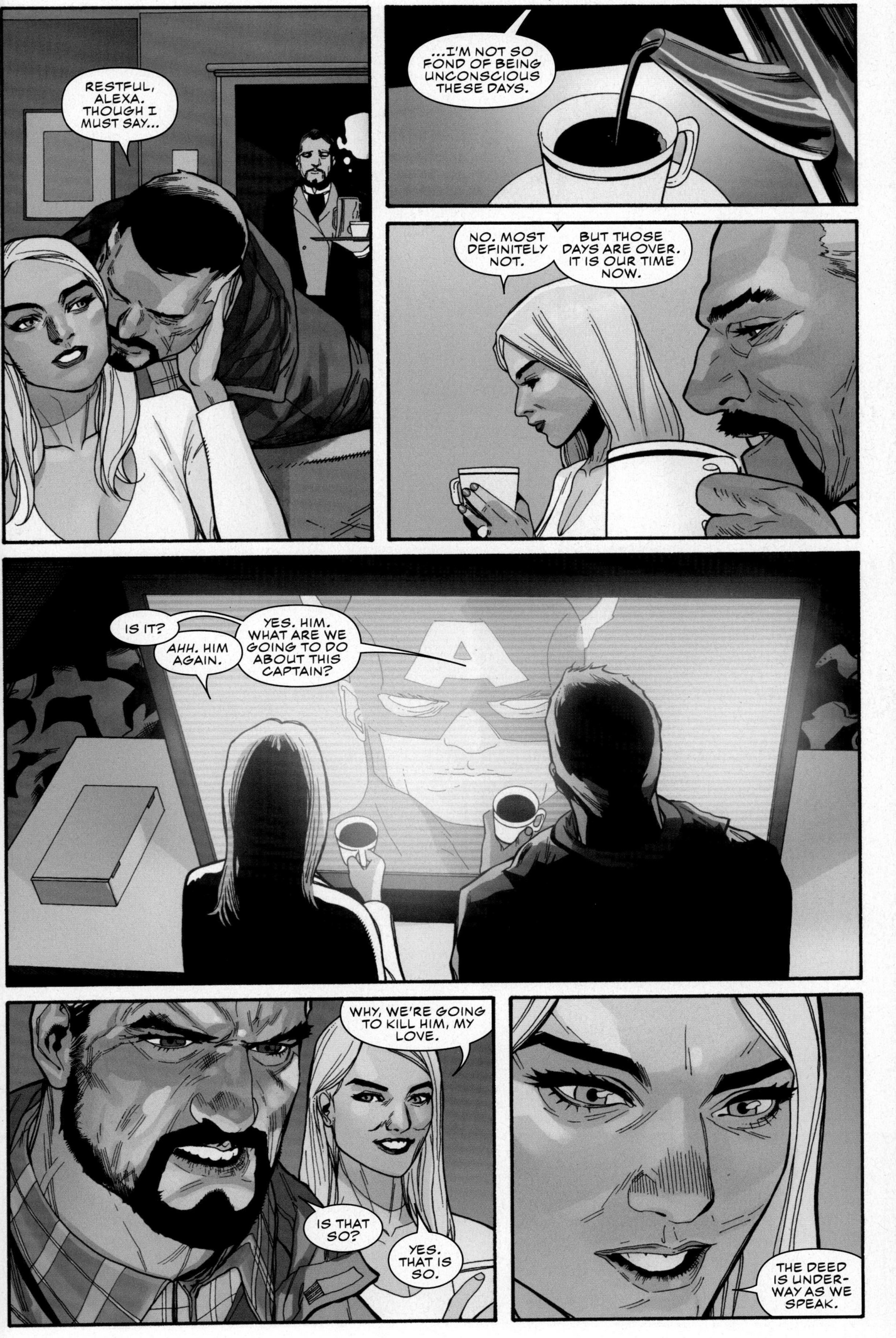
RESTFUL, ALEXA. THOUGH I MUST SAY...
...I'M NOT SO FOND OF BEING UNCONSCIOUS THESE DAYS.
NO. MOST DEFINITELY NOT.
BUT THOSE DAYS ARE OVER. IT IS OUR TIME NOW.
IS IT?
YES. HIM. WHAT ARE WE GOING TO DO ABOUT THIS CAPTAIN?
AHH. HIM AGAIN.
WHY, WE'RE GOING TO KILL HIM, MY LOVE.
IS THAT SO?
YES. THAT IS SO.
THE DEED IS UNDER-WAY AS WE SPEAK.

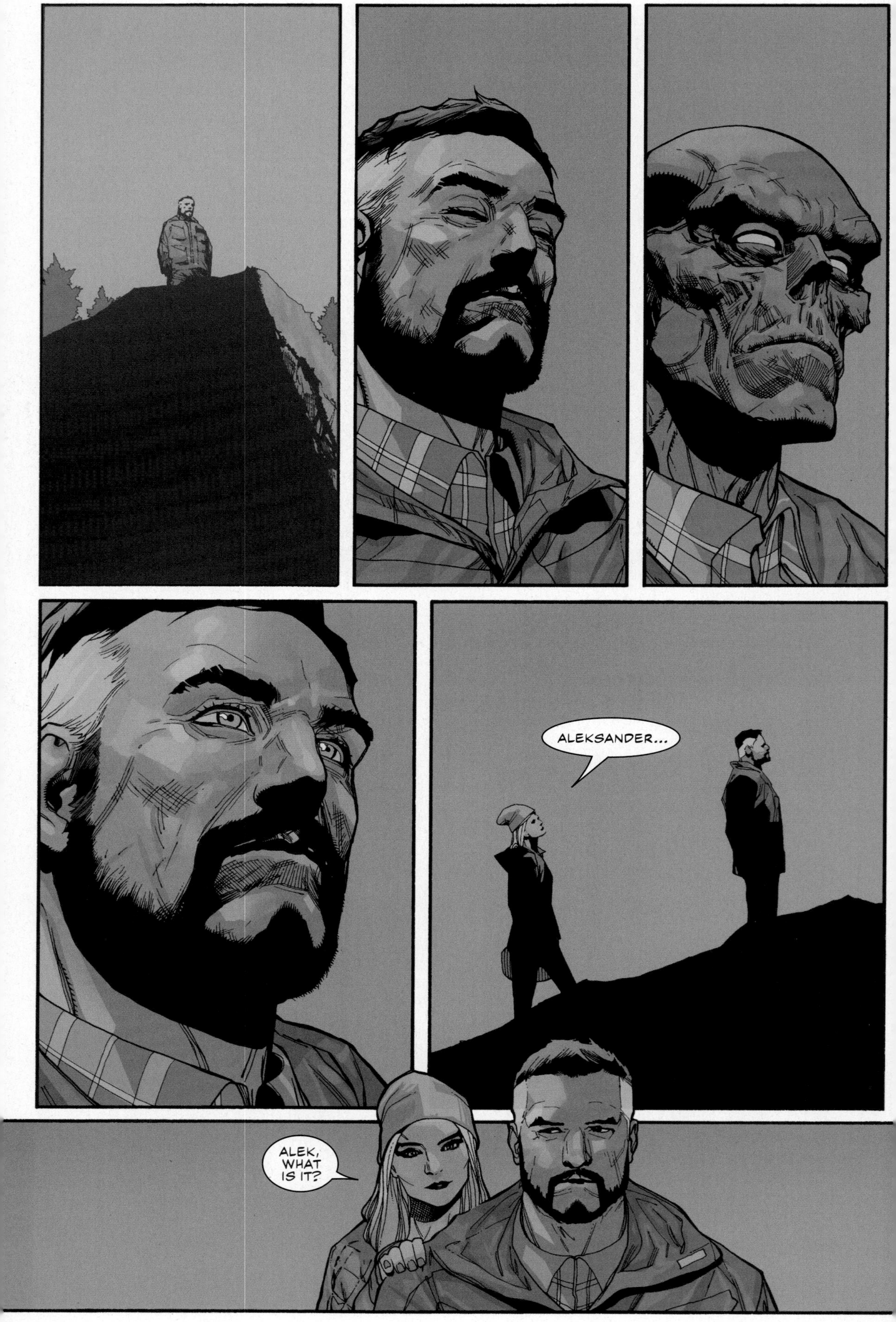
ALEKSANDER...
ALEK, WHAT IS IT?

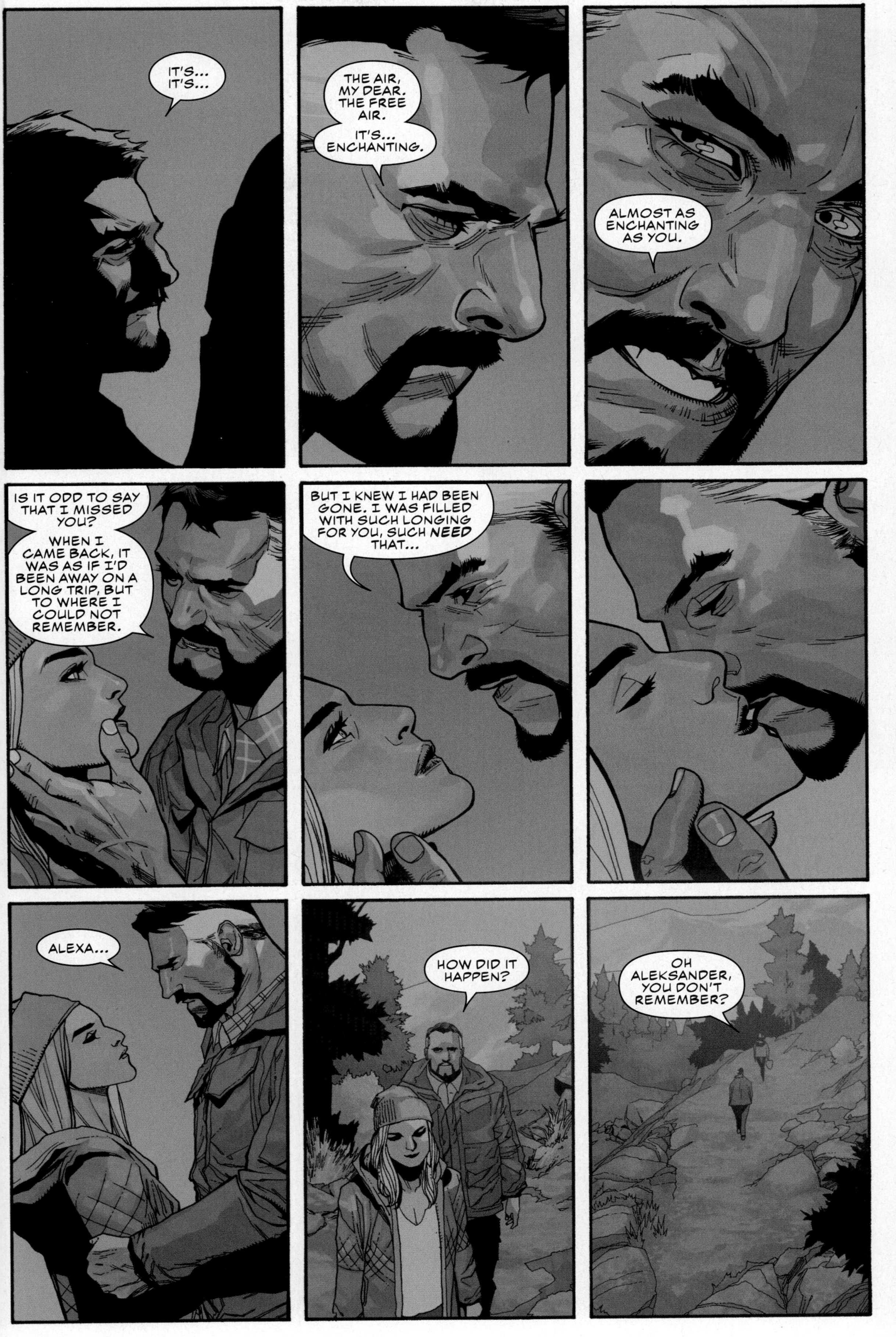
IT'S... IT'S...
THE AIR, MY DEAR. THE FREE AIR.
IT'S... ENCHANTING.
ALMOST AS ENCHANTING AS YOU.
IS IT ODD TO SAY THAT I MISSED YOU?
WHEN I CAME BACK, IT WAS AS IF I'D BEEN AWAY ON A LONG TRIP, BUT TO WHERE I COULD NOT REMEMBER.
BUT I KNEW I HAD BEEN GONE. I WAS FILLED WITH SUCH LONGING FOR YOU, SUCH NEED THAT...
ALEXA...
HOW DID IT HAPPEN?
OH ALEKSANDER, YOU DON'T REMEMBER?

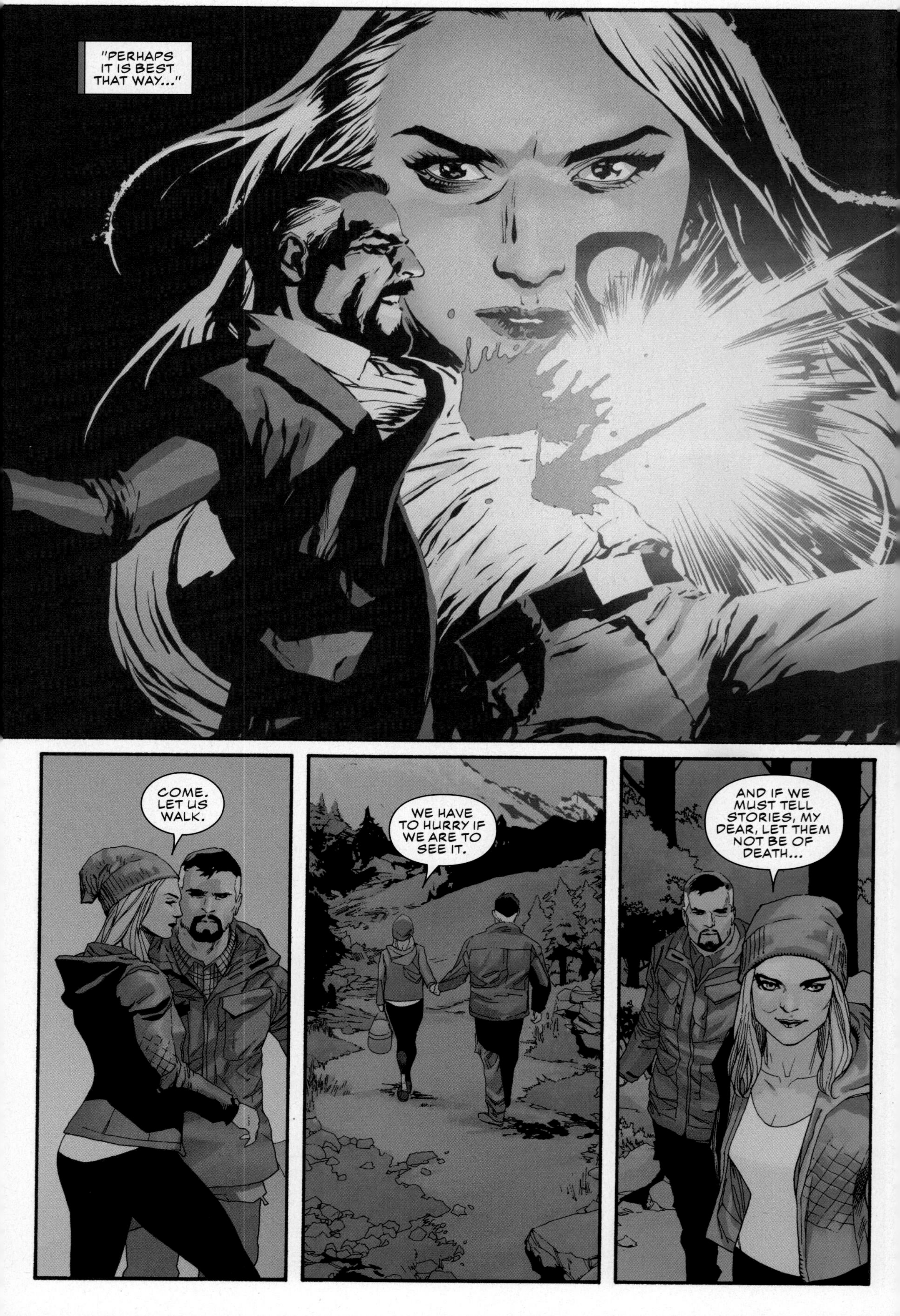
"PERHAPS IT IS BEST THAT WAY..."
COME. LET US WALK.
WE HAVE TO HURRY IF WE ARE TO SEE IT.
AND IF WE MUST TELL STORIES, MY DEAR, LET THEM NOT BE OF DEATH...

"...BUT OF LIFE."

MOSCOW.
YEARS AGO.

WALK AWAY. WALK AWAY *NOW.*

NO.

FHBHY DYYYF.

MHRR$ HYM$FX.

YEEARGGGH!

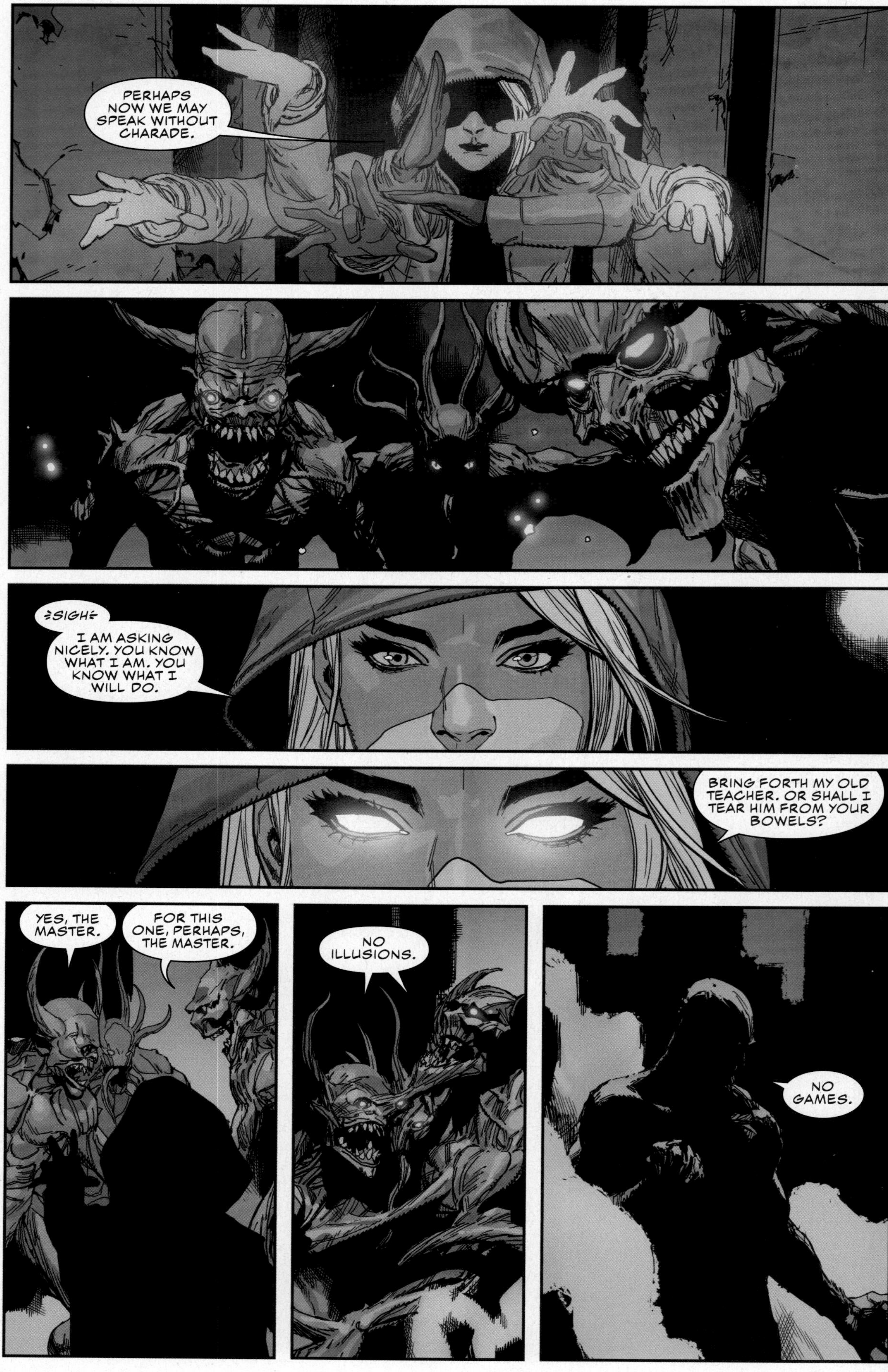
PERHAPS NOW WE MAY SPEAK WITHOUT CHARADE.
SIGH
I AM ASKING NICELY. YOU KNOW WHAT I AM. YOU KNOW WHAT I WILL DO.
BRING FORTH MY OLD TEACHER. OR SHALL I TEAR HIM FROM YOUR BOWELS?
YES, THE MASTER.
FOR THIS ONE, PERHAPS, THE MASTER.
NO ILLUSIONS.
NO GAMES.

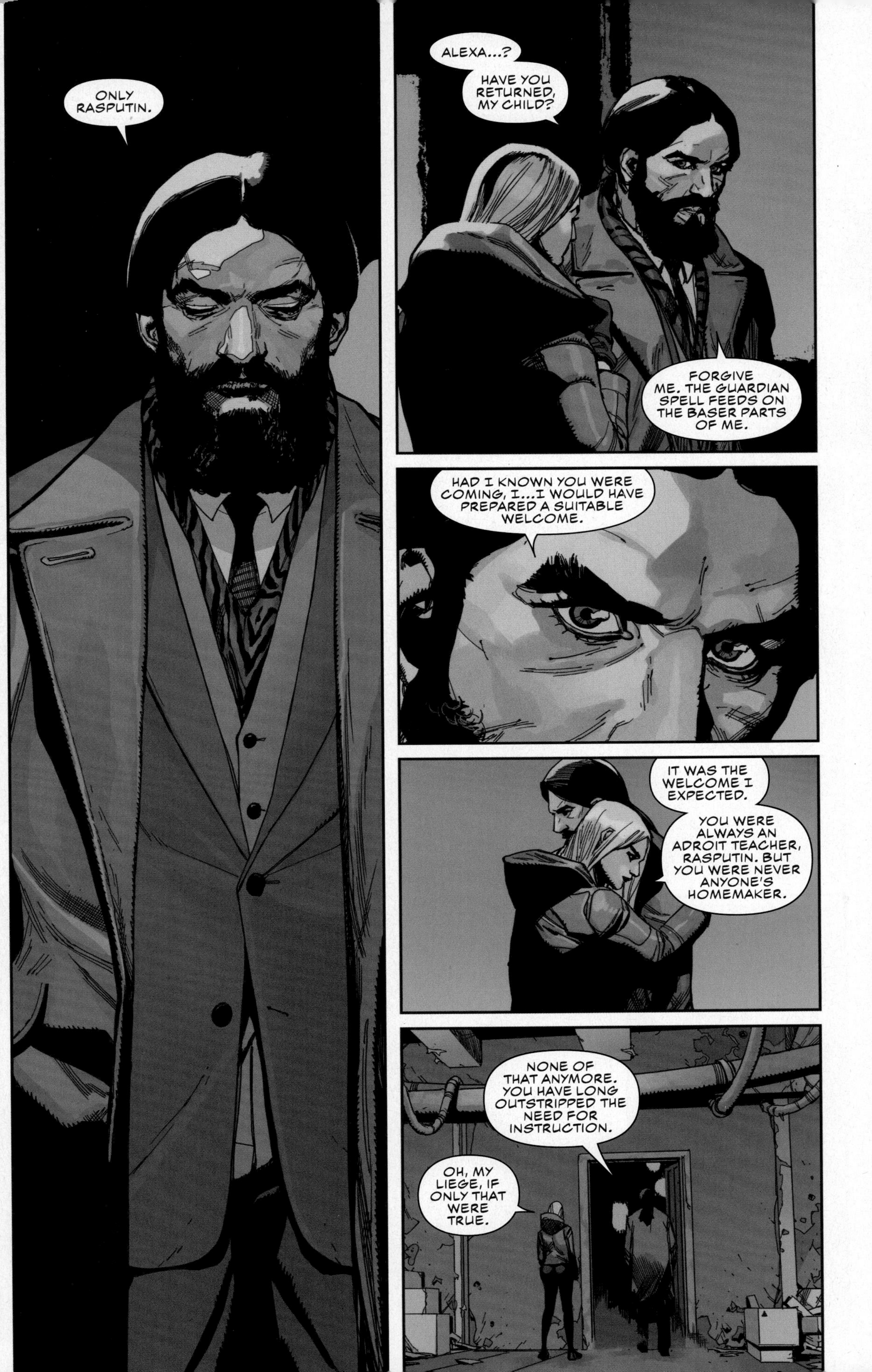
ONLY RASPUTIN.
ALEXA...?
HAVE YOU RETURNED, MY CHILD?
FORGIVE ME. THE GUARDIAN SPELL FEEDS ON THE BASER PARTS OF ME.
HAD I KNOWN YOU WERE COMING, I...I WOULD HAVE PREPARED A SUITABLE WELCOME.
IT WAS THE WELCOME I EXPECTED.
YOU WERE ALWAYS AN ADROIT TEACHER, RASPUTIN. BUT YOU WERE NEVER ANYONE'S HOMEMAKER.
NONE OF THAT ANYMORE. YOU HAVE LONG OUTSTRIPPED THE NEED FOR INSTRUCTION.
OH, MY LIEGE, IF ONLY THAT WERE TRUE.

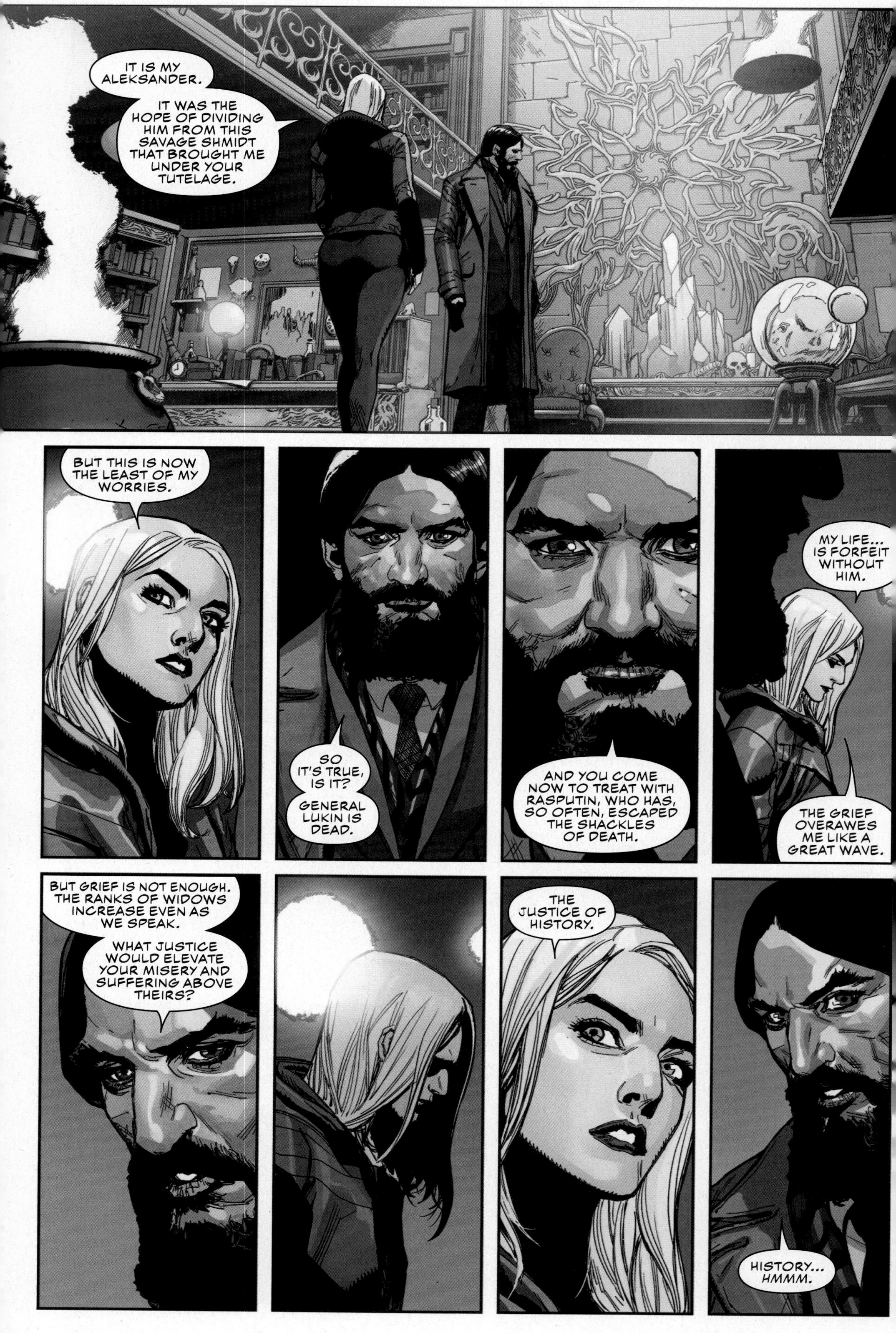

IT IS MY ALEKSANDER.
IT WAS THE HOPE OF DIVIDING HIM FROM THIS SAVAGE SHMIDT THAT BROUGHT ME UNDER YOUR TUTELAGE.
BUT THIS IS NOW THE LEAST OF MY WORRIES.
SO IT'S TRUE, IS IT?
GENERAL LUKIN IS DEAD.
AND YOU COME NOW TO TREAT WITH RASPUTIN, WHO HAS, SO OFTEN, ESCAPED THE SHACKLES OF DEATH.
MY LIFE... IS FORFEIT WITHOUT HIM.
THE GRIEF OVERAWES ME LIKE A GREAT WAVE.
BUT GRIEF IS NOT ENOUGH. THE RANKS OF WIDOWS INCREASE EVEN AS WE SPEAK.
WHAT JUSTICE WOULD ELEVATE YOUR MISERY AND SUFFERING ABOVE THEIRS?
THE JUSTICE OF HISTORY.
HISTORY... HMMM.

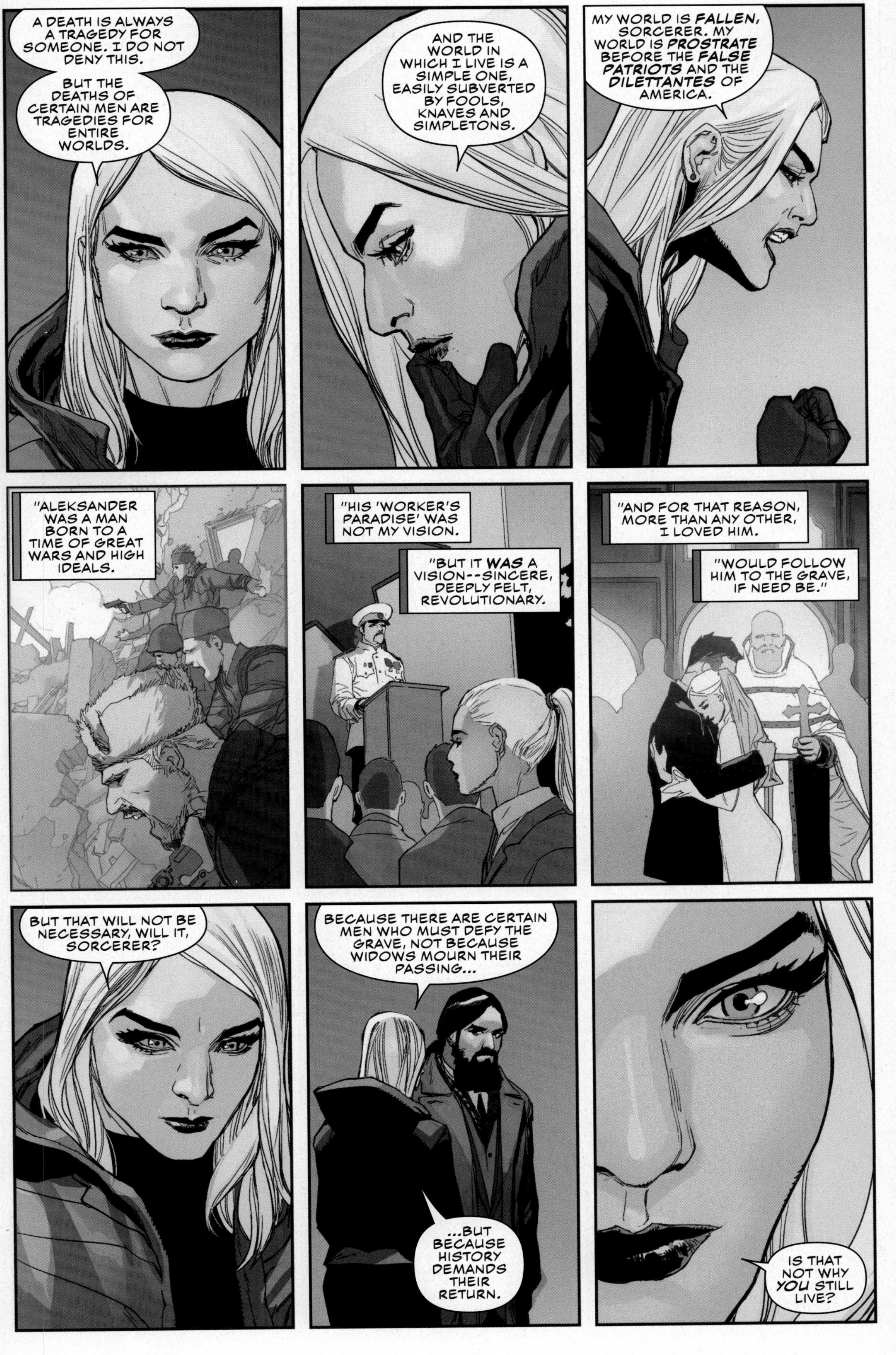

A DEATH IS ALWAYS A TRAGEDY FOR SOMEONE. I DO NOT DENY THIS.
BUT THE DEATHS OF CERTAIN MEN ARE TRAGEDIES FOR ENTIRE WORLDS.
AND THE WORLD IN WHICH I LIVE IS A SIMPLE ONE, EASILY SUBVERTED BY FOOLS, KNAVES AND SIMPLETONS.
MY WORLD IS FALLEN, SORCERER. MY WORLD IS PROSTRATE BEFORE THE FALSE PATRIOTS AND THE DILETTANTES OF AMERICA.
"ALEKSANDER WAS A MAN BORN TO A TIME OF GREAT WARS AND HIGH IDEALS.
"HIS 'WORKER'S PARADISE' WAS NOT MY VISION.
"BUT IT WAS A VISION--SINCERE, DEEPLY FELT, REVOLUTIONARY.
"AND FOR THAT REASON, MORE THAN ANY OTHER, I LOVED HIM.
"WOULD FOLLOW HIM TO THE GRAVE, IF NEED BE."
BUT THAT WILL NOT BE NECESSARY, WILL IT, SORCERER?
BECAUSE THERE ARE CERTAIN MEN WHO MUST DEFY THE GRAVE, NOT BECAUSE WIDOWS MOURN THEIR PASSING...
...BUT BECAUSE HISTORY DEMANDS THEIR RETURN.
IS THAT NOT WHY YOU STILL LIVE?

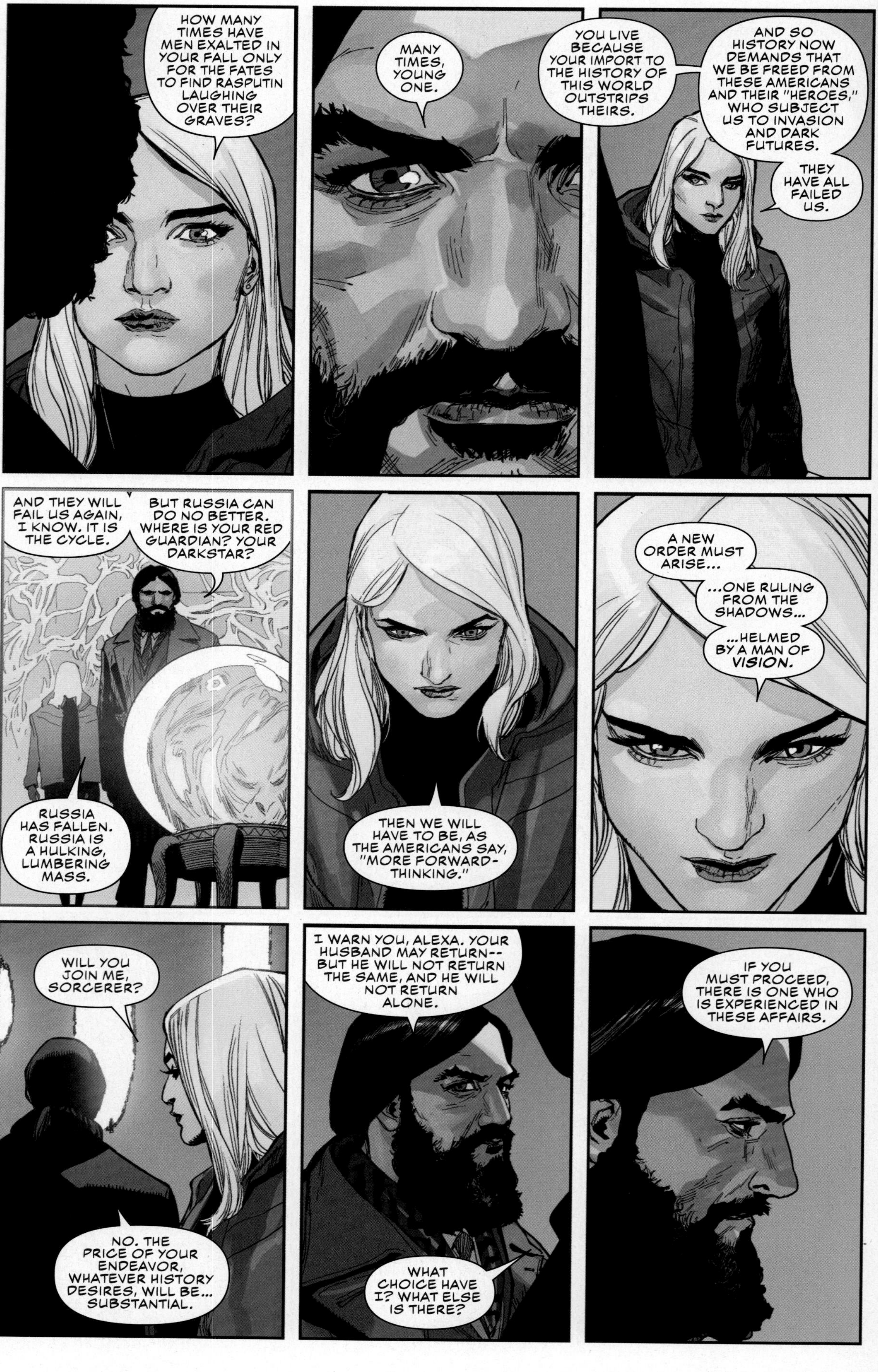

HOW MANY TIMES HAVE MEN EXALTED IN YOUR FALL ONLY FOR THE FATES TO FIND RASPUTIN LAUGHING OVER THEIR GRAVES?
MANY TIMES, YOUNG ONE.
YOU LIVE BECAUSE YOUR IMPORT TO THE HISTORY OF THIS WORLD OUTSTRIPS THEIRS.
AND SO HISTORY NOW DEMANDS THAT WE BE FREED FROM THESE AMERICANS AND THEIR "HEROES," WHO SUBJECT US TO INVASION AND DARK FUTURES.
THEY HAVE ALL FAILED US.
AND THEY WILL FAIL US AGAIN, I KNOW. IT IS THE CYCLE.
BUT RUSSIA CAN DO NO BETTER. WHERE IS YOUR RED GUARDIAN? YOUR DARKSTAR?
RUSSIA HAS FALLEN. RUSSIA IS A HULKING, LUMBERING MASS.
THEN WE WILL HAVE TO BE, AS THE AMERICANS SAY, "MORE FORWARD-THINKING."
A NEW ORDER MUST ARISE...
...ONE RULING FROM THE SHADOWS...
...HELMED BY A MAN OF VISION.
WILL YOU JOIN ME, SORCERER?
NO. THE PRICE OF YOUR ENDEAVOR, WHATEVER HISTORY DESIRES, WILL BE... SUBSTANTIAL.
I WARN YOU, ALEXA. YOUR HUSBAND MAY RETURN-- BUT HE WILL NOT RETURN THE SAME, AND HE WILL NOT RETURN ALONE.
WHAT CHOICE HAVE I? WHAT ELSE IS THERE?
IF YOU MUST PROCEED, THERE IS ONE WHO IS EXPERIENCED IN THESE AFFAIRS.

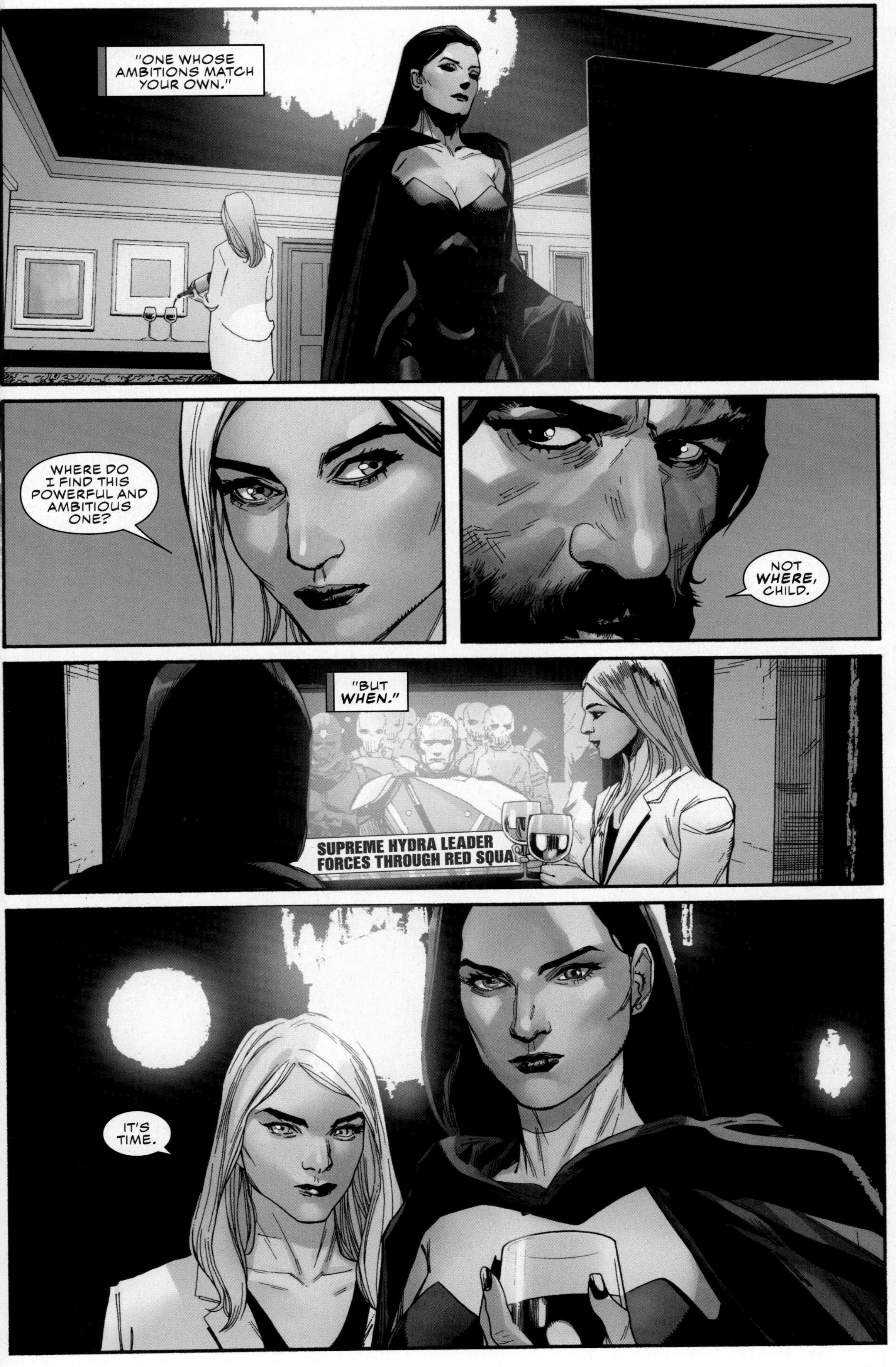
"ONE WHOSE AMBITIONS MATCH YOUR OWN."
WHERE DO I FIND THIS POWERFUL AND AMBITIOUS ONE?
NOT WHERE, CHILD.
"BUT WHEN."
SUPREME HYDRA LEADER FORCES THROUGH RED SQUA
IT'S TIME.

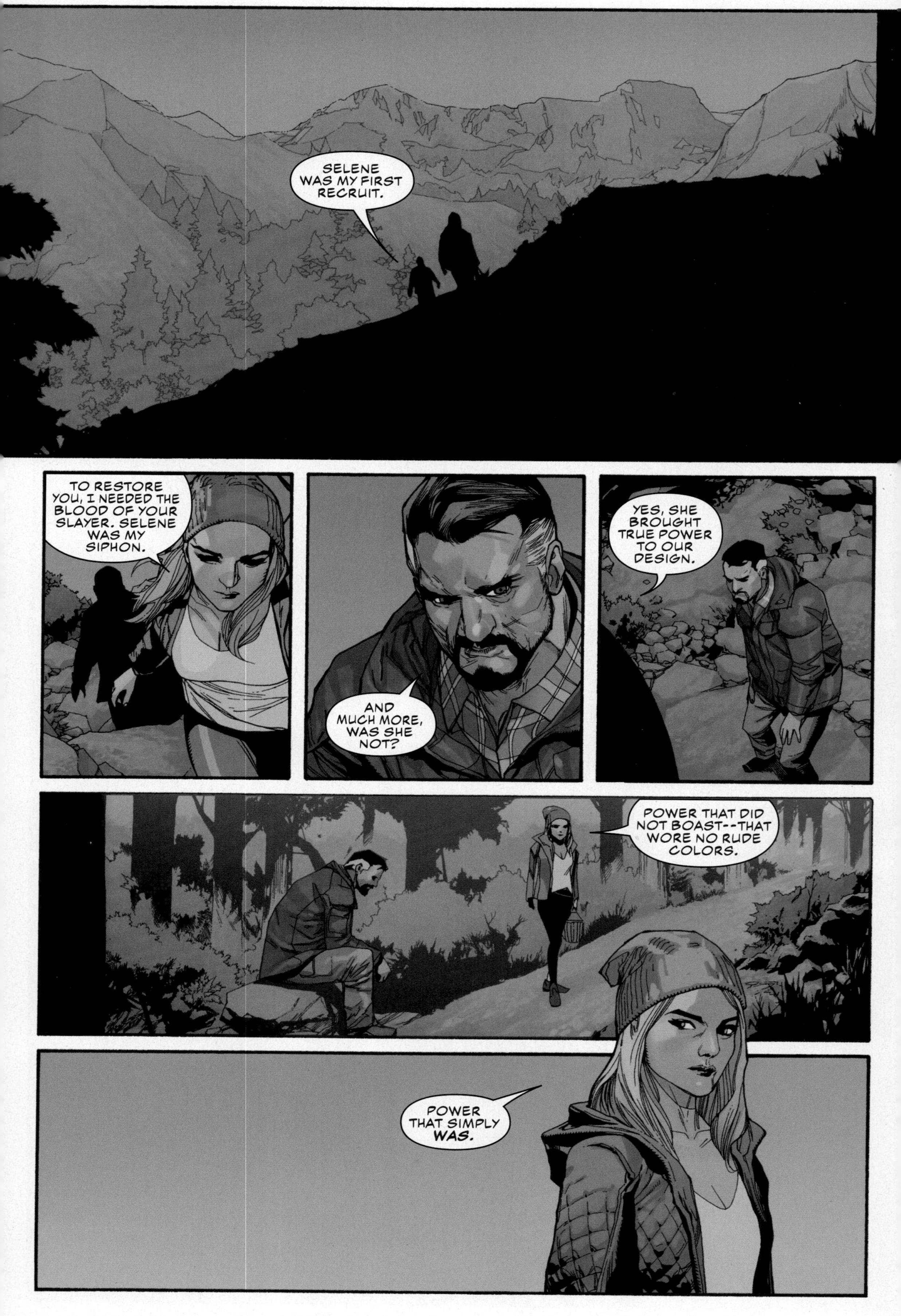
SELENE WAS MY FIRST RECRUIT.
TO RESTORE YOU, I NEEDED THE BLOOD OF YOUR SLAYER. SELENE WAS MY SIPHON.
AND MUCH MORE, WAS SHE NOT?
YES, SHE BROUGHT TRUE POWER TO OUR DESIGN.
POWER THAT DID NOT BOAST--THAT WORE NO RUDE COLORS.
POWER THAT SIMPLY WAS.

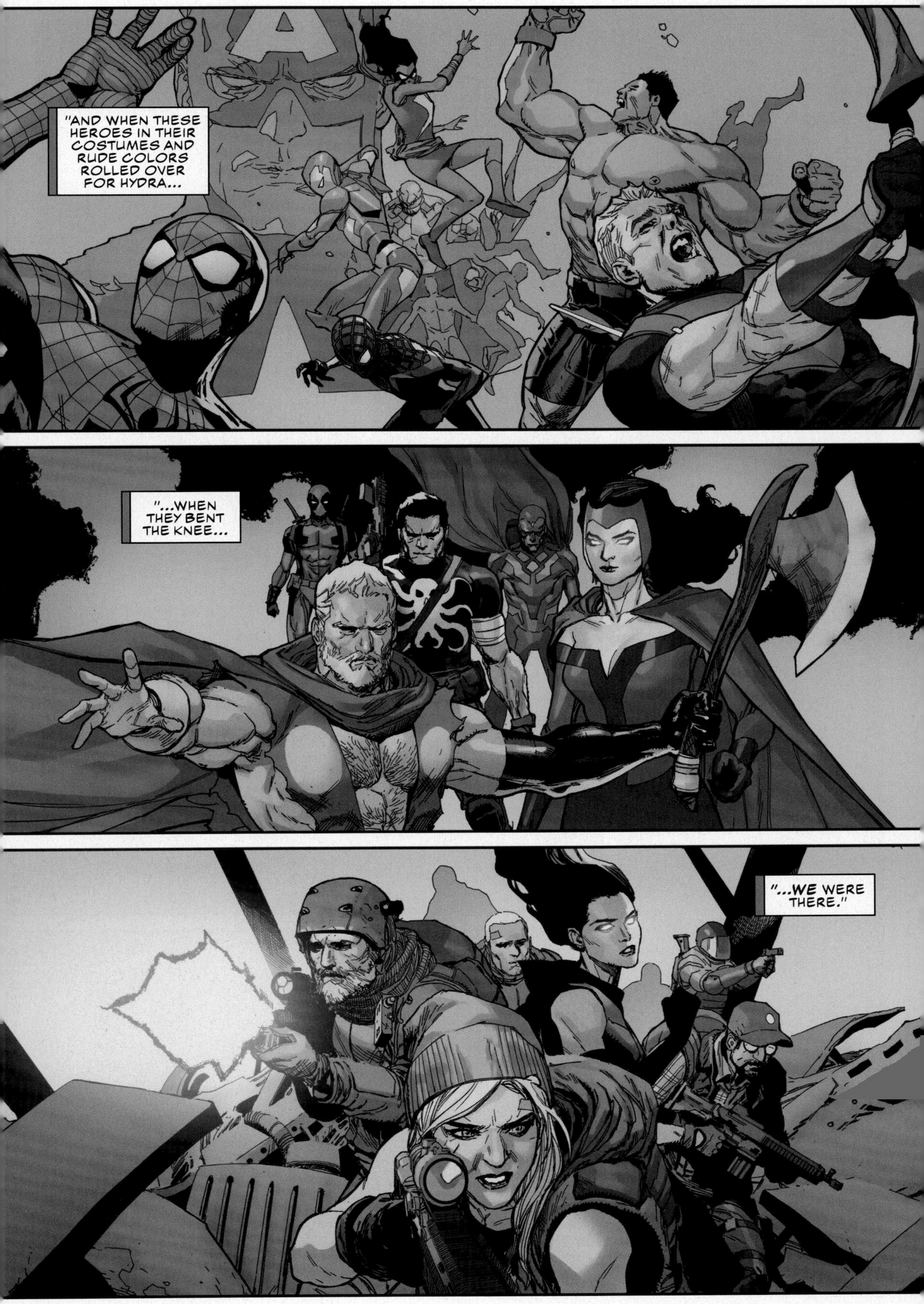
"AND WHEN THESE HEROES IN THEIR COSTUMES AND RUDE COLORS ROLLED OVER FOR HYDRA...
"...WHEN THEY BENT THE KNEE...
"...WE WERE THERE."

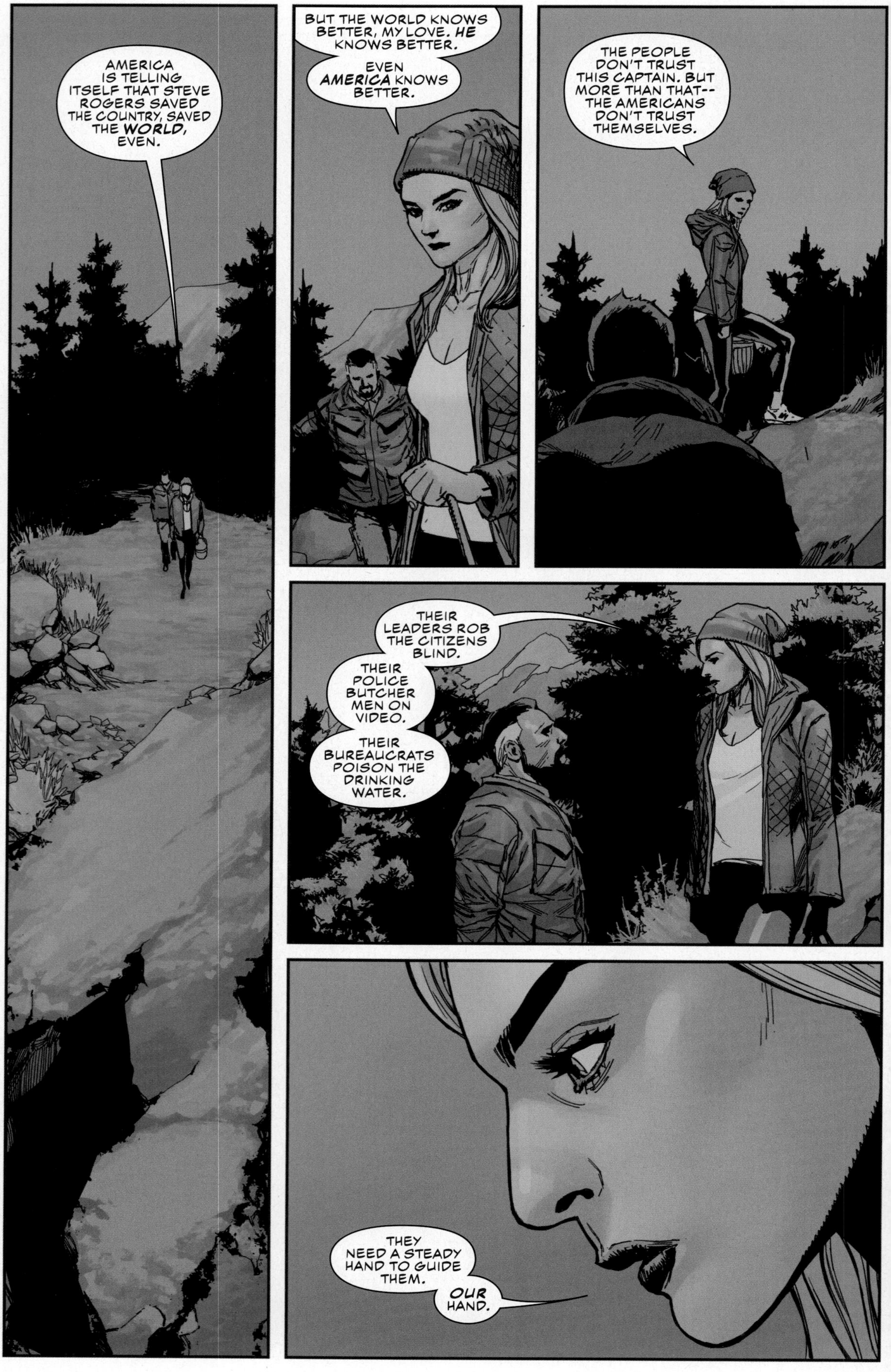
AMERICA IS TELLING ITSELF THAT STEVE ROGERS SAVED THE COUNTRY, SAVED THE **WORLD**, EVEN.
BUT THE WORLD KNOWS BETTER, MY LOVE. ***HE*** KNOWS BETTER.
EVEN ***AMERICA*** KNOWS BETTER.
THE PEOPLE DON'T TRUST THIS CAPTAIN. BUT MORE THAN THAT-- THE AMERICANS DON'T TRUST THEMSELVES.
THEIR LEADERS ROB THE CITIZENS BLIND.
THEIR POLICE BUTCHER MEN ON VIDEO.
THEIR BUREAUCRATS POISON THE DRINKING WATER.
THEY NEED A STEADY HAND TO GUIDE THEM.
OUR HAND.

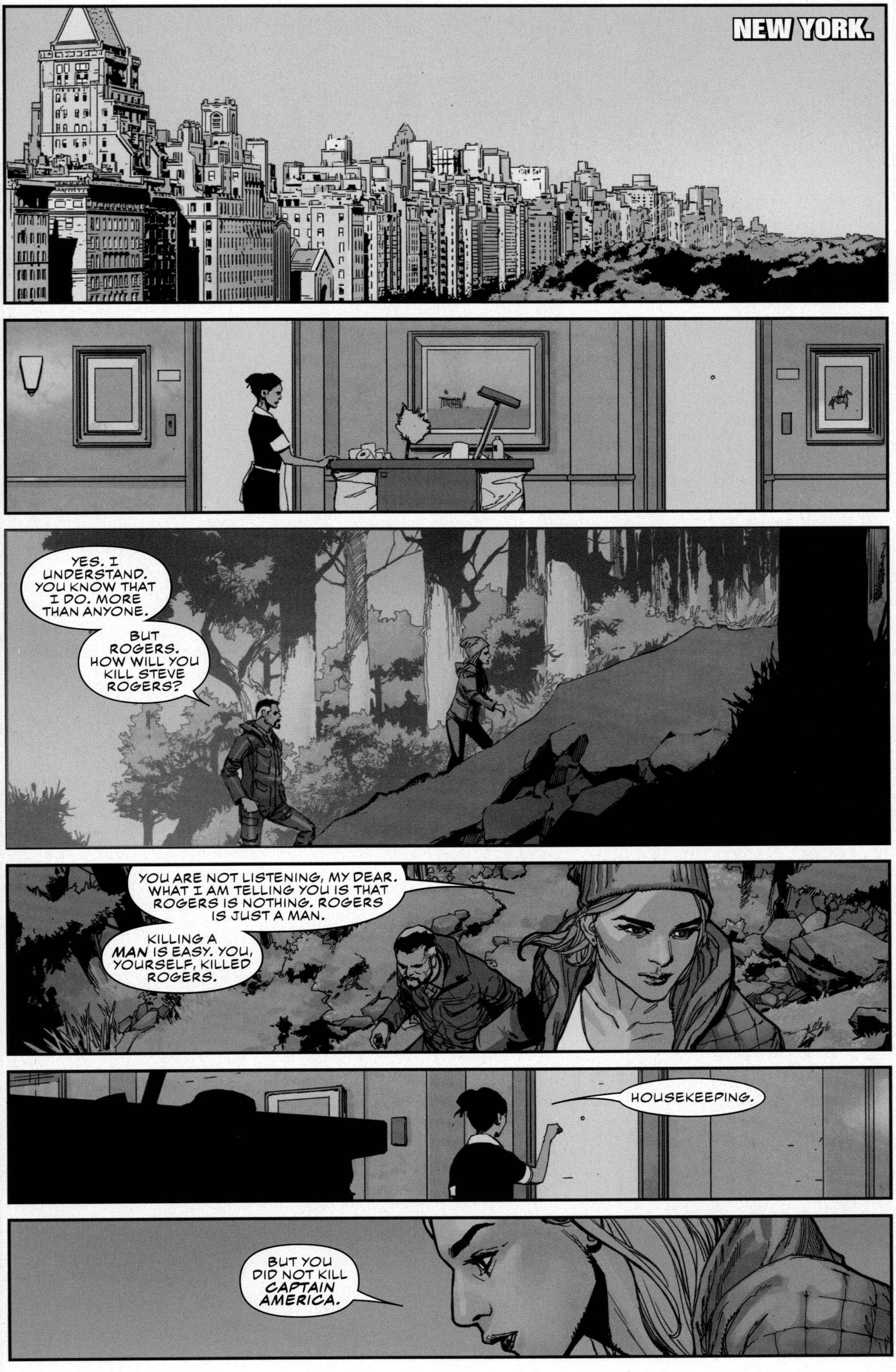
NEW YORK.
YES. I UNDERSTAND. YOU KNOW THAT I DO. MORE THAN ANYONE.
BUT ROGERS. HOW WILL YOU KILL STEVE ROGERS?
YOU ARE NOT LISTENING, MY DEAR. WHAT I AM TELLING YOU IS THAT ROGERS IS NOTHING. ROGERS IS JUST A MAN.
KILLING A MAN IS EASY. YOU, YOURSELF, KILLED ROGERS.
HOUSEKEEPING.
BUT YOU DID NOT KILL CAPTAIN AMERICA.

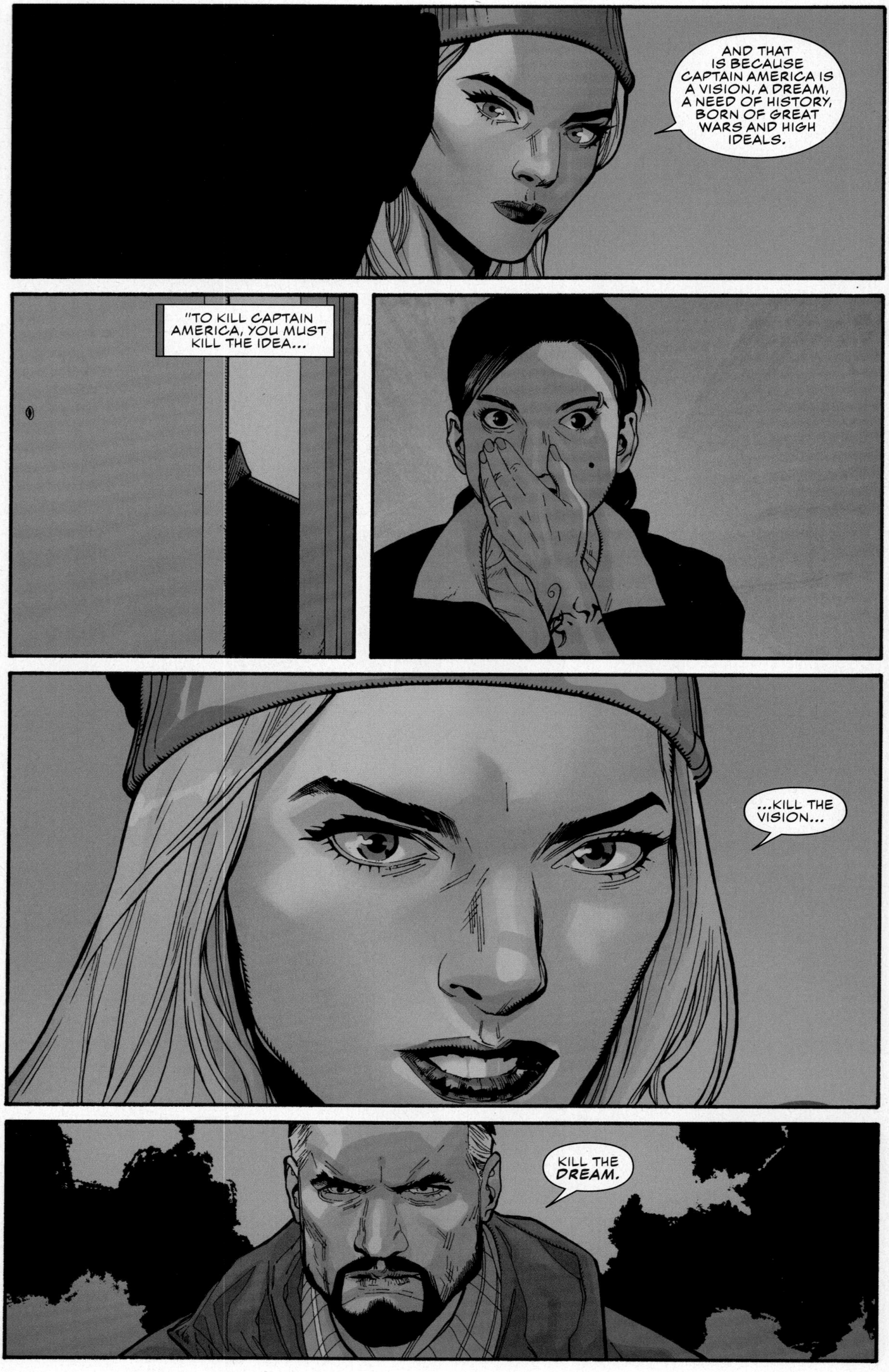
AND THAT IS BECAUSE CAPTAIN AMERICA IS A VISION, A DREAM, A NEED OF HISTORY, BORN OF GREAT WARS AND HIGH IDEALS.
"TO KILL CAPTAIN AMERICA, YOU MUST KILL THE IDEA...
...KILL THE VISION...
KILL THE DREAM.

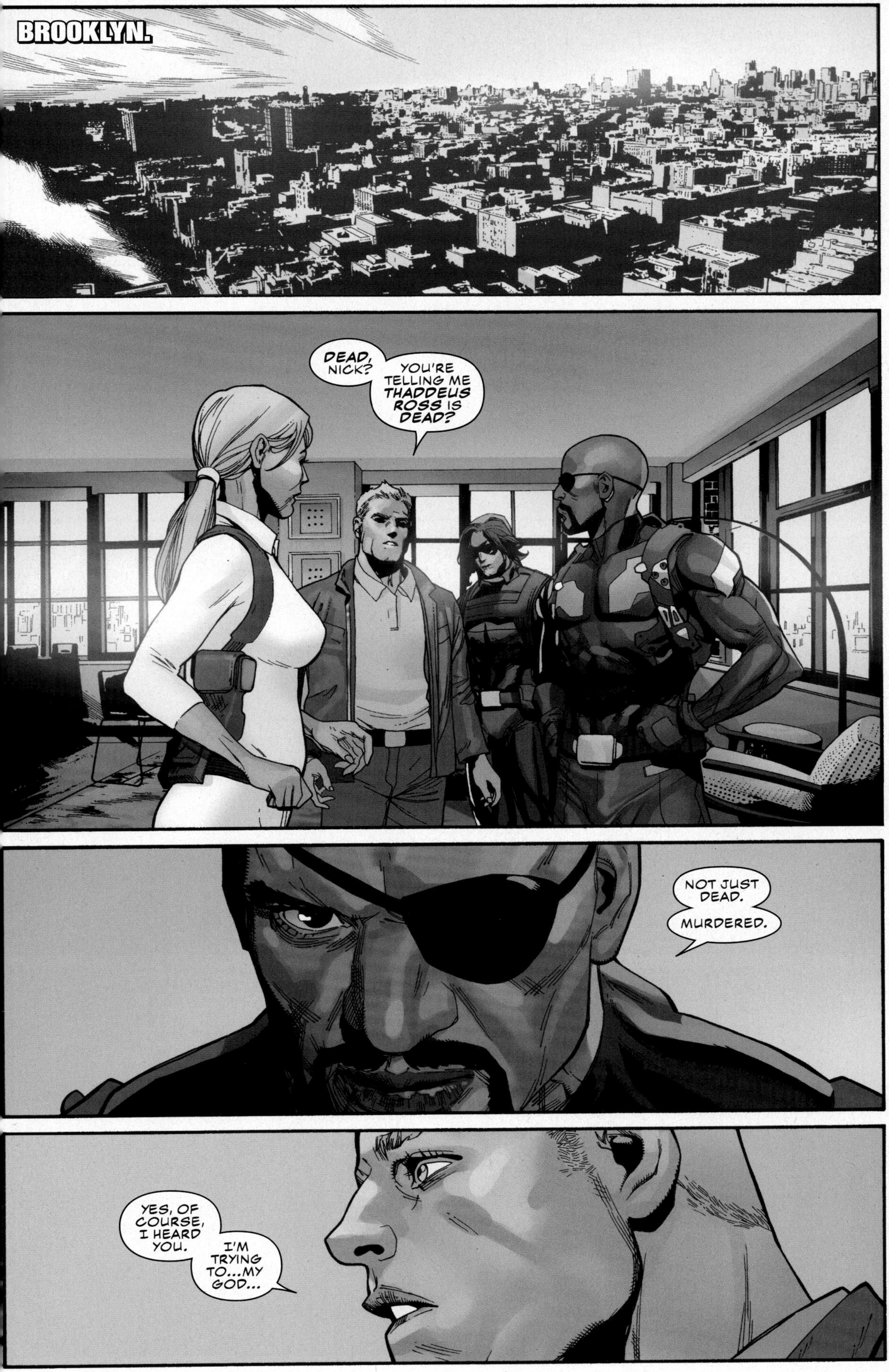
BROOKLYN.
DEAD, NICK?
YOU'RE TELLING ME THADDEUS ROSS IS DEAD?
NOT JUST DEAD.
MURDERED.
YES, OF COURSE, I HEARD YOU.
I'M TRYING TO...MY GOD...

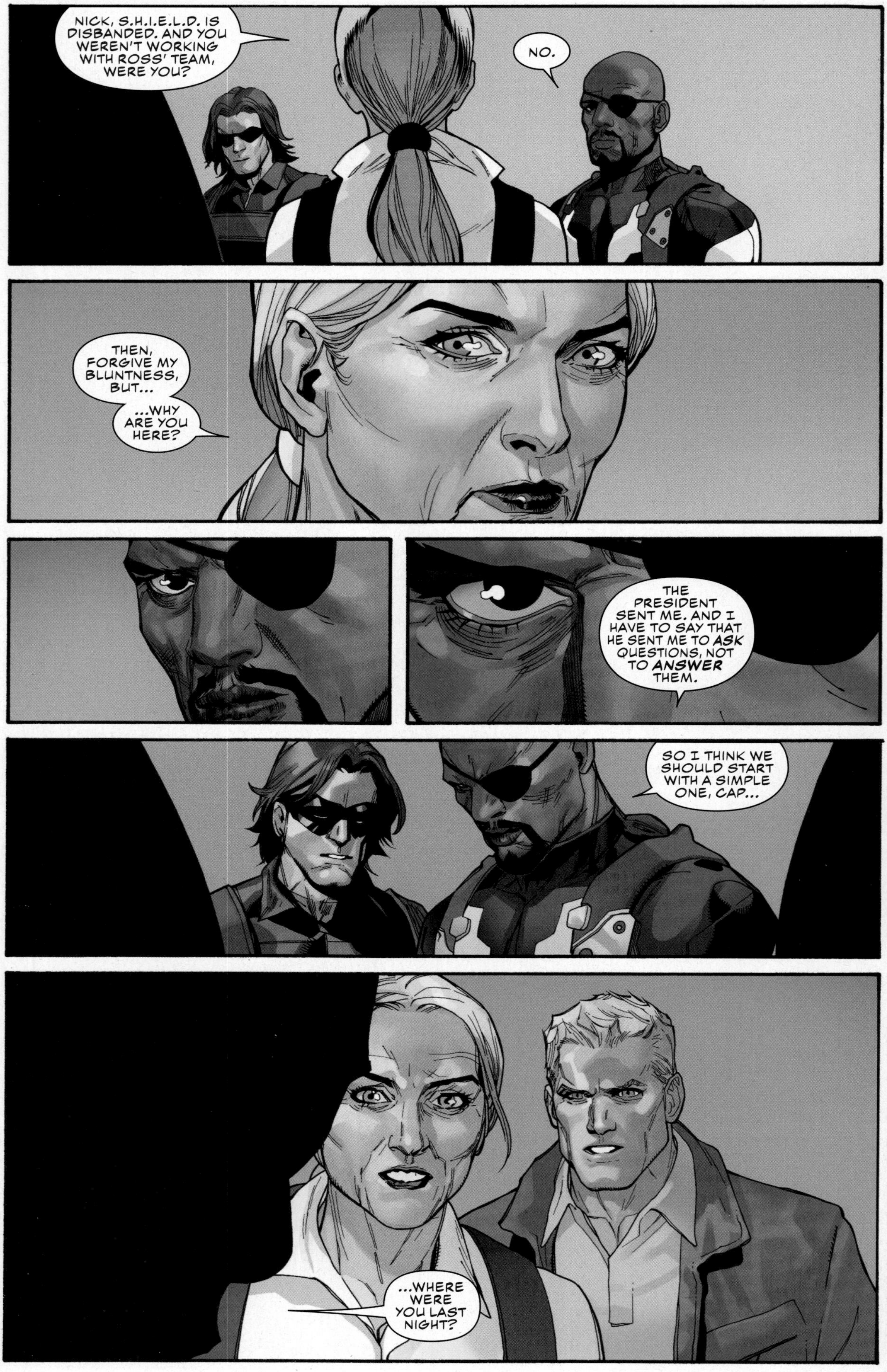
NICK, S.H.I.E.L.D. IS DISBANDED. AND YOU WEREN'T WORKING WITH ROSS' TEAM, WERE YOU?
NO.
THEN, FORGIVE MY BLUNTNESS, BUT...
...WHY ARE YOU HERE?
THE PRESIDENT SENT ME. AND I HAVE TO SAY THAT HE SENT ME TO ASK QUESTIONS, NOT TO ANSWER THEM.
SO I THINK WE SHOULD START WITH A SIMPLE ONE, CAP...
...WHERE WERE YOU LAST NIGHT?

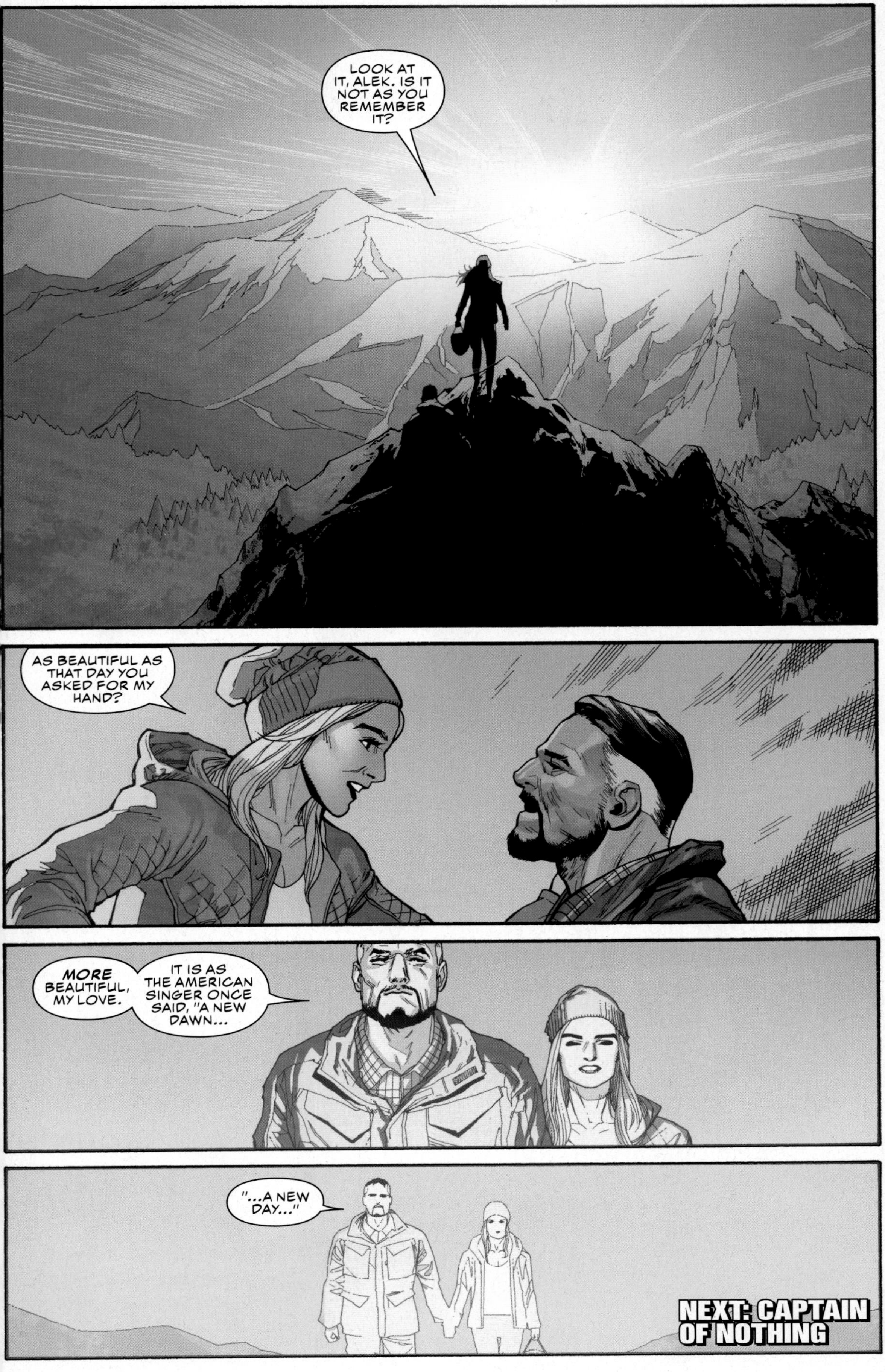
LOOK AT IT, ALEK. IS IT NOT AS YOU REMEMBER IT?
AS BEAUTIFUL AS THAT DAY YOU ASKED FOR MY HAND?
MORE BEAUTIFUL, MY LOVE.
IT IS AS THE AMERICAN SINGER ONCE SAID, "A NEW DAWN...
"...A NEW DAY..."
NEXT: CAPTAIN OF NOTHING

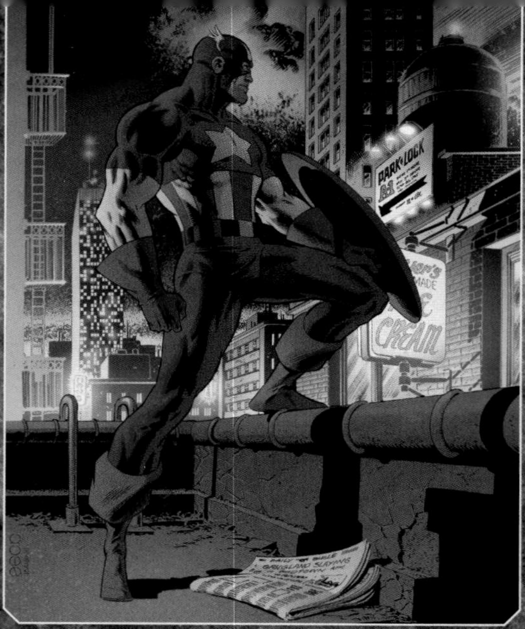
PARK & LOCK
CREAM

MIKE ZECK & RICHARD ISANOVE
1 VARIANT

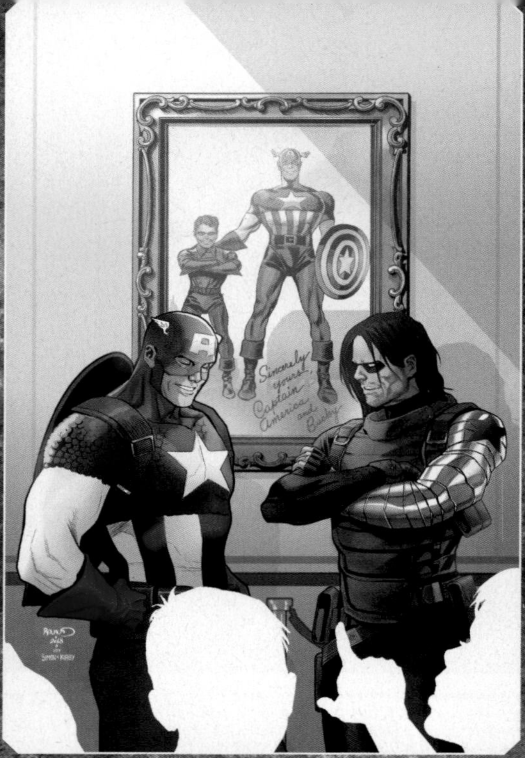
Sincerely yours, Captain America and Bucky

PAUL RENAUD, JOE SIMON & JACK KIRBY
1 VARIANT

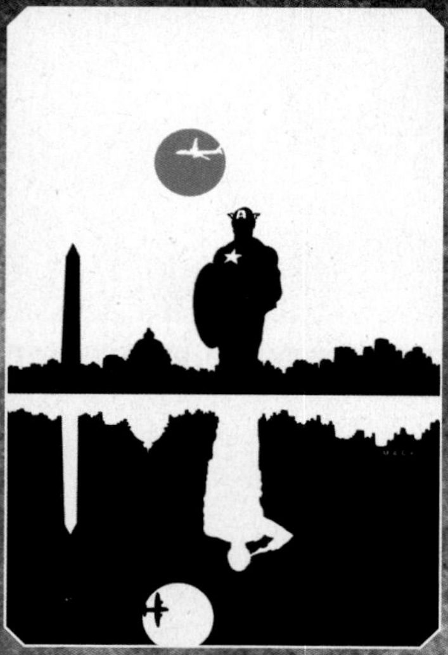

DAVID MACK
1 VARIANT

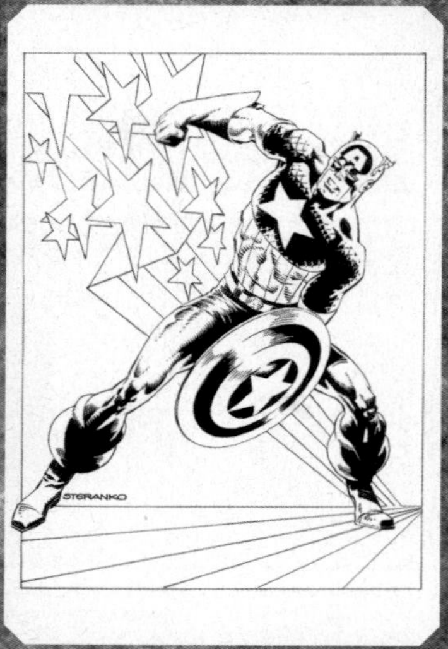
STERANKO

JIM STERANKO
1 VARIANT

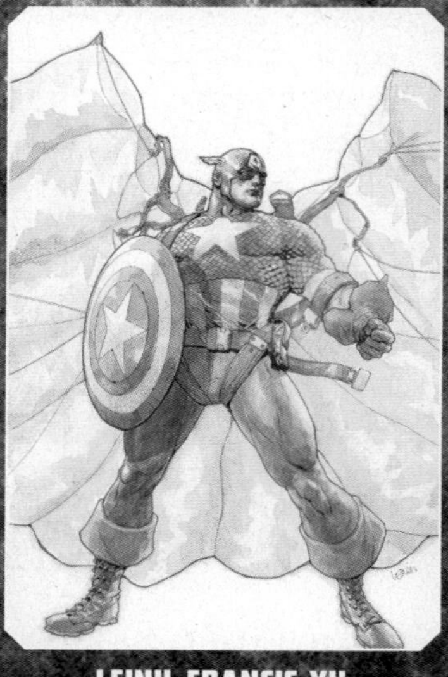

LEINIL FRANCIS YU
1 VARIANT